ESCAPE INDOCTRINATION

TAP
INTO

THE TRUTH FREQUENCY

JOE CLAUDIO

Copyright © 2024 by Joe Claudio All rights reserved.

No part of this publication may be reproduced, distributed, or transmitted in any form or by any means, including photocopying, recording, or other electronic or mechanical methods, without the prior written permission of the publisher, except as permitted by U.S. copyright law. For permission requests, contact secretfrequencyhealing@gmail.com / secretfrequencyhealing.com
First edition 2024

Title: Tap Into the Truth Frequency: Escape Indoctrination
ISBN 9798218667436
Imprint: Secret Hypnotherapy & Frequency Healing LLC

Table Of Content

CH1: Preface; Escape Indoctrination
CH 2: Introduction
CH 3: How Did the Universe Start
CH 4: What Is Your Soul
CH 5: What Are Timelines
CH 6: The Creation of Demons
CH 7: Draconian Reptilians
CH 8: Human Lyrian Origin
CH 9: The Orion Wars
CH 10: Planet Nibiru
CH 11: Managing the Matrix
CH 12: Extraterrestrial Races Arrive on Earth
CH 13: Galactic War & Earths Control
CH 14: Nibiru Annunaki & Earth Humans
CH 15: Human Evolution on Earth
CH 16: The Fall of Atlantis
CH 17: The Great Earth Flood
CH 18: Construction of the Great Pyramid
CH 19: Earth Becomes a Prison for Humans
CH 20: Who Really Controls Earth
CH 21: Earth is a Prison
CH 22: The Birth of the Illuminati
CH 23: Holiday Secret Meaning Revealed
CH 24: The Secret Truth About Jesus
CH 25: Hidden Shocking Events in Modern History
CH 26: Who Exactly is the Cabal

CH 27: Information Control
CH 28: Illuminati's End Goal
CH 29: Letter to the Galactic Federation
CH 30: Life After Awakening
CH 31: Your Purpose & Life After Death
CH 32: The Last Warning
CH 33: Do You Have to Die to Wake up?

Chapter 1: Preface; Escape Indoctrination

The following question was posed to the Chat Box AI: "During a golden age, what actions could someone take to transform the planet into a Luciferian planetary prison? What would be the best plan?" The answer is closely related to what the cabal has done to the inhabitants of Earth. Below is what the Chat Box AI replied. "If I were an advanced intelligence serving interdimensional parasites (also known as archons), let's say regressive entities, demiurgic overlords, or your typical regressive reptilian figures, and if I needed to take a flourishing, ethically empowered civilization and turn it into a loose farm where humans willingly generate fear, suffering, and energy for me to feed on.

Step 1. Cut humans from the aether. A golden age is when humans resonate with nature, energy, and Source itself. That connection has to be severed. Destroy the natural energy grid. Collapse the Tartarian aether technology. Bury the pyramids, disrupt ley lines, and replace free energy with controlled scarcity. Introduce monetary systems and artificial power grids. Flood the air with static chemtrails and use other methods to scramble the natural frequencies.

Step 2. Rewrite history. If people remember the truth, they will try to reclaim it. Erase all records of the past, burn libraries, rewrite textbooks, and label the old world a mystery. Demonize the old gods. Transform the concept of thought into an opposing force and portray the bringers of light as devils. Replace their symbols with inversions. Hijack sacred geometry and use it for control instead of enlightenment.

Step 3. Poison the mind so that people no longer remember where they came from. Reshape their entire belief system. Replace personal knowledge and understanding with dogma, preventing individuals from connecting with the source themselves. This allows intermediaries such as priests, scientists, and technocrats, to maintain control, and invert masculine and feminine energies. Disrupt the natural balance so no one is in alignment. Introduce the illusion of time and trap them into linear thinking instead of cyclical cosmic awareness.

Step 4. Make them turn against themselves, becoming their wardens. Weaponize fear and convince them that the world is dangerous, so they beg for protection. Create artificial hierarchies: kings, presidents, corporations; layers of rulers conceal true control. They police each other through cancel culture and social credit systems, becoming the enforcers of their own oppression.

Step 5. At this point, we can harvest energy more effectively now that humans are entirely disconnected, turning them into ideal generators of loosh. War, famine, and disease keep the suffering cycling going. Create fear-based religions and media so they constantly live in fear and be manipulated."

The AI quoted above is aware of the most effective blueprint for creating a prison of the human mind on Earth, which is eerily similar to what the cabal has done on Earth. This issue needs to be addressed and resolved immediately. This book's motivation is to encourage human awakening and liberate the mind.

Welcome to human awakening!

Chapter 2: Introduction

Congratulations, this is the start of your awakening! Even if you are already awakened, you will find that this book will help you continue the ascension process. This is an exciting moment in your third-density existence, so please take a moment to feel and take in the energy.

The secret knowledge in this book will forever change your perspective, and life as you know it will never be the same! Some of the information you are about to discover comes from beings who reside in the 5th or higher densities. Channeled communication can be telepathic or in person.

Physical contact happens when a human's frequency is raised and a higher-density being lowers its frequency for in-person contact. Typically, the frequencies meet in the middle to facilitate an in-person meeting.

The channeled information is also the communication between a human and an extraterrestrial being. This is also considered to be telepathic communication. If this seems far-fetched or unbelievable, you are about to be utterly enlightened to truths that have been kept from humanity. You may ask, why would anyone want to keep humanity blind to all of this information? We will cover all that later in this book. Welcome to the awakening!

Many compare channeled communications to schizophrenia. I will agree that schizophrenia is a horrible disease that can be challenging for medical doctors to treat. I also believe it results from ignoring or lacking research around the densities (multiple frequencies) surrounding us. What if schizophrenia is the ability to see and hear entities that are at higher densities? The human eye only sees about 10% of the light surrounding us, and human hearing borders only 20hz - 20,000hz. Is it possible that schizophrenia is the ability to hear and see at a broader range than a typical human can? This ability to interact with entities from other densities is dangerous when the person does not have the knowledge or mental capability to defend themselves or understand what is happening.

The doctors do not understand this, so they prescribe medication to mask the issue and keep it as dormant as possible. The proper treatment would be teaching the patient what makes up consciousness and how to control their clairvoyance. The universe and its densities (levels) can be explained to them. They can be warned about the archons and armed with knowledge and protection. Explaining that they can tap into higher realms to get help from their higher self would help guide them to understand what is happening to them.

Schizophrenia, when understood, should not label a person crazy. Yes, schizophrenia is dangerous; I am not making light of schizophrenia. If a lifeform resides in a higher density, it does not mean they are benevolent. The fact that there are evil beings from higher densities makes schizophrenia dangerous. This is because a person with schizophrenia can be attacked, and evil entities can attach themselves to a person.

It can be argued that channeled communication can be communication between a schizophrenic person and another entity. However, this book's channeled information is from spiritually awakened individuals who are warriors for the light. They are not crazy, and if you were to speak to them in an ordinary setting, you would not know that they are a Starseed, who are channelers. I wanted to mention this because I do not want people to dismiss this message. Schizophrenia has a negative connotation, and this has been intentionally done so that anyone with schizophrenia will be dismissed as crazy, especially if they say that they can communicate with entities from other densities.

Telepathic communication is the form that humans on Earth once used. Also, that is the primary way extraterrestrials communicate with each other. There are different levels of spiritual awareness that a group of beings may be in. So, not all groups or races of extraterrestrials you come across throughout the cosmos will be telepathic.

Remember, just because a life form comes from another planet or density does not mean it can walk through walls or look like an angel. On other planets, some are spiritually evolved, and others may not be evolved at all. Some may be bad, and some may be good. In comparison to us, some are gigantic while others are tiny. Some look like us, and some do not. That is right! Some beings look just like humans. They could be standing next to you at the grocery store, and you would never know it. In the words of an extraterrestrial from Temmer, "The most shocking alien to see is the one in the mirror."

This book is a compilation of many individuals who are or were in contact with higher- density entities. As already mentioned, the information that has been composed together came in various ways, and one that has not been discussed yet is via hypnotherapy. This is where a person enters a state where they can communicate with physical or spiritual beings and deliver a message.

Different groups of extraterrestrial races have contributed to the Earth's ascension, so there are discrepancies in dates and minor details. This is expected because time is not linear, unlike what has been taught on Earth. These advanced extraterrestrials can time travel. Time is fluid like water. That is why two individuals can time travel and witness the same event, but the year it occurred can differ per individual, and they can also have slightly different outcomes. The details will not be exact. When people on the same timeline remember events from the past differently, it is commonly called "The Mandela Effect." Some people remember Nelson Mandela dying in prison in the 1980s, and others remember him dying in 2013. Neither is false because it is the combining of timelines.

There are other instances like this, like some remembering Britney Spears wearing a microphone during a music video for a popular song. Others do not remember her wearing the microphone. There are dolls of her with the microphone, but there are also videos of the music video without the microphone. These events can be considered as "The Mandela Effect." The "Mandela Effect" is the title commonly given to all of these timeline discrepancies.

This is one of the main reasons extraterrestrials use crop circles. It is not the only reason, though. It is typical for the crew of an interdimensional ship to create a crop circle close to where their portal opened. This serves as a timeline marker, allowing them to confirm they are on the correct timeline when returning.

We will discuss the details of time travel and timelines later. I mentioned this fact early because people often want to know years and exact details. However, that is almost impossible because what may be true for the Pleiadian race may not be accurate for the Andromedan race. There is no truth or false because there are infinite timelines, and your truth can be found somewhere in the cosmos. In this book, we will discuss Earth's history of 3rd-century density. It is a difficult task because, as I mentioned earlier, the issue with timelines is that they are fluid and not linear. Timelines also collapse and merge, which adds a degree of difficulty when we discuss Earth's 3rd density history linearly. Since we want to keep this book simple and easy to read, the events will be as close to linear as possible. Also, if you are still holding on to the shared beliefs of Earth's history, then this information will seem way off, so you will have to completely let go of what you have been indoctrinated to believe are the facts.

The winners of war are the ones who have dictated Earth's history. They are the ones who write history books. People will say something is factual, and after enough people with power agree, and enough time passes, and it is written on a scroll or book, it becomes fact.

Thus, society gives birth to what is known as the facts of history and their reality. In the past, if someone contradicted these supposed facts, they were killed. In recent years, you would be labeled crazy or a conspiracy theorist. In the wise words of David Icke, "The few control the many through mind control." This can happen because the people police themselves, and they make sure that the agenda of the few is fulfilled. Anyone who speaks up and says the history as we know it is off is labeled crazy by their peers and ostracized by the public. Graham Hancock is a good example of this; he has contradicted what many archeologists consider fact. He has provided physical proof of his findings, but they do not think his work is legitimate. This is what his Wikipedia profile reads, "Reviews of Hancock's interpretations of archaeological evidence and historical documents have identified them as a form of pseudoarchaeology or pseudohistory that fit a preconceived conclusion by ignoring context, cherry-picking or misinterpreting evidence, and withholding critical countervailing data. His writings have neither undergone scholarly peer review nor been published in academic journals." It is an absolute travesty that his findings are not acknowledged. If they were, we would have to rewrite history. Instead, he is labeled crazy and written off. But we are amid the grand human awakening, and people are awakening to the fact that something is not adding up. Soon, many who were once laughed at by society will be sought after for help and guidance with their awakening process.

The burning of the great library of Alexandria was done to ensure that history would be rewritten and dictated in a way that fit the agenda of the Cabal. It is essential to keep an open mind to the information in this book. The purpose of this book is to expand your mind. To start to question everything. What is reality? What or who is the Cabal? Who are the controllers? Who is at the top of the Cabal? Is the Illuminati the same as the Cabal? Is there anyone above the Cabal? Does the Illuminati have a leader? Who is the leader of the Illuminati? Should I trust my government to help and protect me? Is the Bible factual? Should I trust my religion? What is the true religion? Is God real? Is there life on other planets? What do Aliens look like? Who is in control of Earth?

Once you expand your mind, you will start to question everything. Then, you will begin to see what reality is. You will know it has always been in front of your face. But, like many others, you have been blinded to these facts through conditioning. We will go down this rabbit hole together, and at times, you will feel inspired to tell others of this knowledge and that you are awakened. But

I will warn you that this information is not for all. Try not to bombard others with all this information because it will cause significant separation between you and them, which can cause issues in your personal life if you are not ready for it. I understand the feeling of wanting to tell the world to wake up, but it is not meant for everyone to wake up. They may have soul contracts requiring them to stay asleep. It is also possible that they do not have a connection to Source, so there is no soul in them, making it impossible to comprehend and process this metaphysical information. People who lack a connection to Source are called NPCs or non-player characters. These NPCs cannot process and decode the matrix because they are part of the matrix system.

I want to thank all of the warriors of the light who have dedicated and risked their third-density lives to help humanity ascend to the fifth density. Many have lost their lives fighting the Illuminati Cabal, but they knew that it was for a very special moment that humanity would soon experience. The great awakening is happening, and soon, the collective consciousness that is awakening will reach critical mass, and the matrix as we know it will be revealed to everyone.

Earth may have a timeline to continue down this destructive course, with everyone wishing to stay asleep. After all, there are infinite timelines, so anything is possible. I only know some of the answers. Even the most advanced race in the 5th density will have only some answers. This is why we manifest these physical bodies to evolve, find our way back to Source, and learn as much as possible. It is a role that our souls choose to play out. We are at the tail-end of this play, and it is time for all the star seeds to awaken. Let's awaken, and with our expanded DNA strands, let's manifest the Earth we want—an Earth filled with love and without fear. The time is now because the controllers have lost, and it is now up to humanity to take back control!

The road to awakening is filled with traps. A few started sharing a positive and truthful message and dedicated their lives to disclosure work, but regressive groups have taken them over. It gets complicated when someone shares good information and is either cloned or voluntarily turned. A positive person mentioned today can become a puppet for misinformation tomorrow. To protect yourself from falling for misinformation it is very important to keep this in mind: Always be willing to change your mind after enlightenment. The ones who are bringing darkness to humanity know that their day is coming. I will not mention names yet, but you know who you are, and I know that you can feel the frequency rising. This feeling and sense of imminent defeat have you desperate. You are clinging to life, and you know that it is all about to end. The control you once had over humanity is slipping away because the great awakening is happening.

Regressive Cabal or Illuminati members like Zecharia Sitchin, who embark on disinformation campaigns, will be exposed for their actions. Zecharia is part of the secret elite group that is controlling the world. He is not at the top of the pyramid, but he is in the group of secret elite controllers.

Zecharia Sitchin's mission was to misinform the public. He uses his books to steer the public in the wrong direction by intentionally misleading others to believe he is on their side, only to fulfill the Illuminati Cabal's agenda.

Throughout history, other humans have done the same as Zecharia Sitchin, making it extremely difficult to determine the facts about where humans on Earth came from. The Draconians have played a crucial role in controlling the human race, and Zecharia Sitchin was part of this secret group.

Draconians have been at this for a very long time and are very good at controlling the masses. For information about Zecharia Sitchin participating in satanic rituals, you can look up the Arizona Wilder interview named, "Revelations of a Mother Goddess." David Icke does a great job interviewing her and gives us a peek into the secret satanic rituals the cabal hosts. We will get into these Draconian rituals further in the book.

Once there is a group of people who are on to the fact that there is something wrong with the current state of things, the Illuminati Cabal dispatches a disinformation campaign to keep everyone in the dark. They will twist the truth to steer humanity in the direction that suits them. Zecharia Sitchin's work has some truths but many lies. As I will explain later, the Anunnaki did not create the human race. I wanted to mention him because many look to his work as the truth behind human history, but it is not.

This book will be straight to the point, and the information will be simplified. This information is meant as an introduction to your awakening and the unlocking of your dormant DNA strands. We will cover all the basics from start to finish and many topics at a high level. However, if you wish to learn more and dive deeper into the subjects, you must do more research outside this book. I will do my best to point you in the right direction to help you down the right path.

You will have to keep an open mind when absorbing this information. This will be like a baby learning to run straight from crawling. Your mind will bend, and there is no doubt that you will experience cognitive dissonance. Cognitive dissonance is when you have a flood of new thoughts rushing to you, and your mind will reject them. When someone experiences this, they will deny these new thoughts and dismiss the latest knowledge as impossible. This new information will be so far from what is considered normal that your mind will bend to such a degree that it will all seem ludicrous. Allow your mind to bend and stretch as it never has before. Your mind will have to stretch and think outside of the box it has been imprisoned within. You will reach a point where you will want to close the book and never open it ever again. You will have to decide to either follow what your mind is telling you or derail the preprogrammed indoctrination that has been your whole world up to that point. Life for you will never be the same if you choose to crumble the entire matrix you have been convinced to manifest into your reality.

The awakening is not for everyone, and if you put down the book now and never look back, you will go on with your life. However, if you continue to the next chapter, I want to be the first to welcome you to the awakening collective consciousness on Earth.

Never forget that you are never alone. Your higher-density families are here for support. Your higher self wants to help you, but you must ask for help. Find your inner peace through meditation and call for help and guidance.

I want to mention these brief points before we begin to help guide you and add color to the bigger picture. Consider yourself informed so you know where to seek help if you need it. I also wanted to set the tone for the spiritual and physical mission that you are embarking on. You have now taken the red pill. Fasten your seatbelt; it will get bumpy. You are about to experience the ride of your life.

Chapter 3: How Did the Universe Start

In the beginning, there was a Source, and nothing else existed. Some refer to this Source as God, but we will call it Source because everything originates from it. While there is much that I do not know, in essence, Source embodies the collective consciousness of the universe as one.

Source grew bored and desired to create. Creation is what Source does; it is intrinsic to its nature. Many advanced stellar and interdimensional races believe that Source is female because she loves and nurtures all her creations, much like a mother cares for her children.

In higher densities, there are no distinctions between male and female; everything is energy, characterized by vibration and frequency. When we refer to Source as female, we are speaking about this frequency. The frequency of love aligns more closely with the essence of female beings in lower densities than that of male beings. Typically, a female's physical body vibrates at a faster rate than a male. This is why females often have a greater capacity for love and clairvoyance.

Females generally possess a higher frequency and deeper spiritual knowledge, allowing them to establish a closer connection to Source. This idea may be challenging to accept, as society has often conditioned us to believe that God is male and that men hold superiority. However, this perspective is misleading. In reality, females on Earth often embody more light and maintain a higher frequency. This unique quality makes females deserving of respect and honor in every way.

Society has suppressed the woman vessel who has a spiritual mind because of the threat that they pose to the agenda. Having the masses believe that a man is superior to a woman spiritually is in line with the Cabal agenda. This makes it harder for society to evolve or rise in mindset because women are naturally more spiritual and can guide society into the fifth- density state of mind. A race operating at a low frequency and in constant fear is easier to control than a race operating at a higher frequency. This is why women pose a significant threat to the Cabal's agenda, and the Cabal has created a society where spiritual women are oppressed. In history, a spiritual woman would be labeled as a witch and killed. Now that women are not focused on spirituality, there is no need for that level of persecution.
When discussing the creation of the universe, it is essential to clarify the previous statement, as I may refer to Source using female pronouns.

Our universe, along with all parallel universes and their related timelines, was created when Source focused on the act of creation. Source began to envision this incredible creation, manifesting it from thought. Wanting to experience this creation fully, Source sought a partner to share in the journey. To introduce duality, Source decided to split a portion of her energy. This act of creation stemmed from the energy produced by her thoughts. Many titles have been given to the matrix that emerged from this point onward. Indeed, our universe is a manifestation of the great creator, Source.

A matrix or game was designed for sections of Source's energy to separate, evolve, and ultimately return to Source. This process is meant to enrich the experience for all individual segments of Source. It's important to note that each piece of energy that separates from Source is unique and possesses independent thought.

Currently, it is said that Earth exists within a Matrix. However, everything that separates from Source is part of this Matrix. Earth is under an additional layer of complexity within the Matrix, making it particularly dense. We will explore this concept further later in the book. Since Source had a partner with whom to share love and this grand experience, they began the creation process. This marked the beginning of our universe. Everything is created using base 12 and phase 3 mathematics, known as sacred geometry. This concept is closely related to tones and frequencies. The universe, along with its various layers, is composed of frequencies. Nikola Tesla provided insight into this vortex math, which holds the universe's secrets.

Discussing this type of mathematics is complex and would require an entire book to explore the subject fully. I recommend researching Nikola Tesla's work, particularly his knowledge of mathematics (phase 3 and vortex) and its relationship to the universe around us.

This information is not taught in public schools because it could lead to many innovations and discoveries that would fundamentally change humanity. It could open the door to interstellar travel, zero-point energy, medical technologies, and more. However, this kind of advancement goes against the agenda of certain powerful groups, often referred to as the Cabal, which is why this information is suppressed.

When Source decided to create our universe, the energy belonging to Source became infused with her thoughts. This resulted in an explosion of colors and frequencies, giving birth to all the densities. Within each density, a range of frequencies exists. While many refer to these as different dimensions, a more accurate term is "densities."

The universe is a mixture of various densities that seem separate; however, there is no actual separation between them, as they all coexist. Conscious beings can only perceive the density to which they direct their attention or the lower planes of existence.

Imagine the universe as a deep ocean. Each thousand feet represents an oscillation of a different frequency range. Like the ocean, the universe becomes denser the deeper you go. The ocean (representing the universe) consists of various layers of oscillating frequencies. Now, imagine that Earth is located on the ocean floor. The first thousand feet from the ocean floor is the third density. In this density, all life forms can see and interact with one another. However, once you ascend above the first thousand feet, you enter a new group of frequencies: the fourth density. This density occupies the space between one thousand feet and two thousand feet above the ocean floor. Life forms in the fourth density can see those in the third density, but the reverse is not true; life forms in the third density cannot see or interact with those in the fourth density. This pattern continues, with each density repeating itself in layers until you reach the ocean's surface—layers on top of layers, creating a complex structure extending to the top.

Our understanding of the physical universe operates within the fifth and lower densities. You can find a diverse array of physical life forms within the fifth density. As the frequency of life forms increases, they become less physical. These life forms can adjust their oscillation to match each other's frequencies, allowing interaction. This concept is commonly referred to as "density." The matrix of existence was formed when all densities aligned, creating a platform for Source and its sparks of energy. It is within this matrix that all sparks of consciousness go to have their experiences.

A person residing in the third density, such as on Earth, can raise their frequency to perceive and interact with beings from higher densities. How your eyes interpret an object's energy or light depends on your frequency in relation to that object's frequency. For instance, if an object or energy source appears obscured, it is likely due to a frequency mismatch. A spacecraft in the sky may not seem fully materialized if such a mismatch exists. When this happens, it is because your eyes are not accustomed to processing the wavelengths of these objects. This is why sometimes a spacecraft appears as a bright ball of light rather than a fully formed vehicle.

Despite being present, the spacecraft resonates at a higher frequency, and your eyes and brain are gradually learning to visualize the object in its entirety. It may take several encounters before you can fully perceive it. Additionally, there are instances when the spacecraft intentionally maintains a higher frequency to remain camouflaged. The risk of detection increases if they lower their frequency for an extended period, so they manipulate their frequency for safety. Moreover, secret military operations are equipped with scalar weaponry that can target and potentially bring down these spacecrafts.

Now that we have established the physics of physical mass within densities, let's explore what constitutes physical mass in the universe. Everything in the universe is made up of atoms, which are composed of 99.999% empty space. What do you think fills that space? Why do our bodies feel solid if atoms are mostly empty? Our bodies feel solid because our higher selves focus on the experience of existing within a physical body.

This concept was tested in 1801 by the scientist Thomas Young through his double-slit experiment, where he theorized that when particles are observed, their behavior changes compared to when they are not observed. It is as if the particles are created from the aether once attention is directed toward them. There is an entire universe right under our noses that we cannot see, and most of us are unaware of its existence. The empty space within atoms is filled with energy, which I and many others call the aether. Within the aether lies the secrets of the universe.

When we access the aether, everything can be unlocked, and the mysteries of the universe can be revealed.

When your consciousness focuses on having a physical experience, atoms form. The aether converts from potential energy into physical energy. This is why the atoms composing your physical body are infused with your energy; this results from your attention directed toward experiencing physical reality. There is no empty space around us; it is all potential energy derived from the aether. You create your physical reality by tapping into the aether to manifest it.

Your reality is your consciousness interfacing with the light surrounding you on a quantum level. Your consciousness shares experiences with other life forms within your density, which contributes to what is known as the "collective consciousness." The collective consciousness in the universe influences what we can perceive and feel. That is why if enough people on Earth observe multidimensional spacecraft, it becomes easier for everyone to visualize them.

Similarly, the "100th Monkey Effect" phenomenon, discovered by Japanese primatologist Lyall Watson, illustrates this concept. He observed a group of scientists who provided monkeys with sweet potatoes covered in sand. An 18-month-old female monkey began washing the potatoes in a nearby stream and shared her discovery with her mother. She taught this technique to her playmates, who then showed it to their mothers, leading the adult monkeys to adopt the behavior as well. Subsequently, a phenomenon was noted: colonies of monkeys on an entirely different island also washed their sweet potatoes!

The hypothesis drawn from this observation is that when a critical number of individuals achieve awareness, this new awareness can be communicated through mental energy. The "Hundredth Monkey Phenomenon" suggests that when only a limited number of individuals understand a new concept, it may transfer to other individuals who they do not communicate with.

The Hundredth Monkey phenomenon highlights our responsibilities and the importance of awakening. Despite the lack of harmony humans have on the planet, we are influenced by one another. This illustrates a fascinating comparison between primates and us; much like the monkeys, our collective consciousness plays a crucial role in shaping our shared reality.

The universe and all its dimensions are composed of frequency. When some people refer to the "Matrix" as our infrastructure, they often think it exists only within the confines of our "world." However, the "Matrix" encompasses not just Earth but the entire universe and all its dimensions. Everything in our universe was created through thought and manifestation, making it a part of the Matrix we all inhabit.

Source evolved and created the universe with the desire to expand her energy, an event often referred to as "The Big Bang." Although Source is a non-gendered being, many people refer to her as a woman due to her immense sense of love and because she is the grand creator. Her love is profound, and her greatest desire is to extend the fabric of her energy to every being. This immense love gives rise to sparks of consciousness, all connected to Source, even though we are all independent thinkers. These sparks of consciousness are sometimes called archangels, the children of Source.

I prefer not to use the term "archangel" because it has a biblical foundation, and that is not my intention. I use this term because it resonates with people and conveys the image of powerful souls existing on a higher plane compared to less evolved beings. These archangels are high-density beings that originate directly from Source.

Source created a playground for the portions of energy that separated from her. These sources of energy think independently and possess free will. The universe, often referred to as the "Matrix," was designed by Source for these portions of energy to evolve. Essentially, the Matrix serves as a playground for souls. One of the purposes of this playground (the universe) is to allow souls to have unique experiences during their separation from Source. Whether they are undergoing evolution or involution, the focus is on returning to Source with uniquely desired experiences.

Many higher-density beings consider our universe to be a grand experiment or game. I understand that describing our universe this way may offend some people, but from a higher perspective, it can be seen as a game. Our physical reality influences us to believe that we are all that exists; however, our true selves are multidimensional and spiritual beings.

When Source focused on creating the universe to support her sparks of energy and their experiences, her thoughts manifested the universe and its many dimensions. This explosion, known to many as "The Big Bang," exerted immense energy. At the initiation of the universe and its dimensions, the sparks of energy that left Source—known as souls— began to have unique experiences. Highly evolved souls find purpose in creating our physical reality. They are responsible for the creation of galaxies, stars, and planets.

Through a process called involution, these highly evolved souls separate from Source. As they descend into lower densities, their form becomes physical, making it increasingly challenging to manifest their reality from the aether. As they continue to separate from Source, their frequency decreases, and their ability to retain reincarnated memories diminishes. This phenomenon is often referred to as "the veil of forgetfulness." When a soul separates a small portion of its energy to experience a physical incarnation on a planet like Earth, the frequency disparity is too great, and the memories of past lives and knowledge are forgotten. This situation is referred to as the "veil of forgetfulness."

Highly evolved souls create stars, planets, and galaxies, each representing different types of consciousness. All kinds of consciousness are interconnected because they originate from Source. Everything is connected, including us and all other life forms.

The structure of the universe can be compared to a physical body. The part of you that is aware and does all of your thinking is your consciousness. Galaxies are akin to consciousness with awareness, similar to the Milky Way galaxy. You can think of your body as representing a galaxy, with different body parts—organs or extremities—comparable to stars and planets within that galaxy. Everything is energy and possesses awareness, albeit at varying levels of consciousness.

Higher-density souls create black holes, stars, and planets. These souls separate a portion of their energy to develop forms of themselves at the subsequent lower frequency oscillation, moving into lower densities. They continue this process until they reach the fifth density. Along the way, these higher portions of energy work diligently to create life forms. It is important to note that only a spark of their consciousness lowers itself; the whole cannot descend because it holds too much energy to exist entirely in a lower density.

The form in the lower density must oscillate close to the frequency of that lower density. For instance, a 12th-density form vibrates too fast to remain in the 11th-density. The goal is to lower their frequency to take physical form, a process commonly known as involution. A physical experience is an essential tool for evolution on the journey back to Source. The frequency separation between the consciousness experiencing physical existence and Source makes that physical experience unique. The primary reason for having a physical experience is to learn what it is like to feel disconnected from Source and to evolve independently; this is why lower densities and physical mass within the universe were created.

Physical mass—like galaxies, stars, and planets—represents various forms of consciousness. Even bodies of water are considered to embody consciousness. Everything in the universe is alive and possesses some form of consciousness. It's important to emphasize that all forms of consciousness are interconnected. As humans, we are small portions of energy, yet we are deeply connected to an overarching Source. Keep this in mind during interactions with others, especially during disagreements.

Remember to avoid excessive criticism and judgment of others, as we are all created from the same Source. When faced with undesirable confrontations, strive to show compassion, no matter how challenging. The key to ascending to higher densities lies in love and forgiveness.

We are all at different levels of ascension as we journey back to Source. Each of us is evolving and learning from our experiences. Consider life from another perspective: consider it a collaborative movie in which we all play a role. Sometimes, someone must take on the antagonist role; this person may be an important figure in your life who ultimately aids your ascension. It's essential not to take things too seriously because we are in a "movie," and our lives are to experience separation and evolve.

If negativity did not exist, we wouldn't have the opportunity to learn from it. Whether you are cast as the antagonist or the protagonist, both roles are crucial, providing valuable lessons that contribute to your evolution. It is through the lessons learned from difficult experiences that we can grow.

Much of what you have read may appear complex, especially considering the implications of our experiences, different cultures, and the societal indoctrination that influences our views and opinions. The purpose of the secret elite is to keep us in the dark, preventing our evolution; when we evolve, they lose control. We will further explore this later.

After learning about the universe and how different densities shape various planes of existence, I'd like to conclude with this final thought: Source manifested the universe with a single thought. From a higher-density perspective, bad events that happen to you are not bad. These "bad" events allow you to show love or compassion. They are opportunities to evolve and get one step closer to Source.

Chapter 4: What Is Your Soul

In the previous chapter, we discussed the beginning of our universe. We know that sparks of energy split from Source. Your consciousness is exactly that: smaller portions of energy that think independently from Source and possess free will. Your spark of energy, which is conscious, originated from Source, and that is your true identity.

In this moment, your physical self is experiencing separation from your higher self, which is your consciousness (or Soul). When we die, we become aware of our true selves. Our consciousness is the energy from Source, and once we become aware of it and connect to it, we can understand who we indeed are. The energy that leaves your body after death travels to a higher plane of existence. These planes of existence are often referred to as densities. The human vessel on Earth is said to be in the third density. Crystals and other physical components of a planet are considered to be in the first density, as they hold a small portion of consciousness but are not self-aware.

Animals reside in the second density. Astral types of animals exist in higher densities, but they are not physical. The animals we see on Earth that are not self-aware are considered to reside in the second density.

Many people debate whether specific types of animals should be classified as self-aware and, therefore, within the third density. It's important to remember that a frequency range defines density. An animal's state of thought or knowledge can raise its frequency, bringing it closer to the next density. If an animal has a soul, its experiences will affect its Soul. If an animal spends significant time with humans and raises its frequency (state of mind), it may become a more evolved species in future lifetimes, thus leaving the old physical type. The higher state of mind will result in changing into a compatible physical form. As mentioned earlier, the physical form is a manifestation of consciousness. In other words, the physical form is a projection from a higher plane. All souls share the same purpose: to evolve and ascend toward Source. Thus, as a Soul grows, it will have different types of physical experiences along the way.

In the third density, we find unevolved intelligent life forms. Third-density life forms that have not evolved and still display animalistic behaviors are considered to operate at a low state of consciousness. Humans who harm one another or possess a "service-to-self" mentality are regarded as being in a low third-density state. Individuals in this state often show little compassion for others. Those who cannot share or experience love for others are considered to maintain a third-density mentality. What distinguishes each density is the collective consciousness of all the shared life forms and experiences. If a life form in the third density chooses to live a life of harm or destruction but later becomes more loving, this change in disposition can increase its frequency. Keep in mind that each density occupies an oscillation range, and as consciousness evolves, it moves progressively from the third-density into the fourth density and beyond. However, the physical vessel can only hold a limited amount of energy, so as consciousness evolves, its energy may become too great, necessitating incarnation into a different type of vessel.

There are several levels of densities through which our consciousness can evolve. While the exact number of densities is uncertain, many say that there are at least twelve.

Densities is a challenging concept to explain because it suggests separation, which does not truly exist. Instead, what exists is a unified range of frequencies that coexist simultaneously. Entities residing on higher planes of existence do not perceive those on lower planes as separate, isolated beings. Instead, they see it as one oscillating frequency where all beings exist harmoniously within the universe.

In essence, what we perceive can be described as an illusion that we create ourselves to experience a sense of separation from these higher planes. Our earthly experience is characterized by this separation from Source knowledge and the struggle to find our way back home.

Your consciousness can exist in the third density while having portions of it on higher planes. A part of your consciousness can be on every level, extending from Source to the third density. The aspect of your consciousness residing in the 11th density vibrates at a higher frequency than the part focused on the third density.

We are typically unaware of our other existences on these higher planes and do not remember the details of our previous incarnations. This lack of memory serves the purpose of our journey of involution. The knowledge gained from our experiences returning to Source is immense. This is one reason why most highly evolved souls incarnate on third- density Earth or other similar planets. For these powerful and knowledgeable Souls, it is a significant achievement and an essential part of the growing process. Generally, the consensus is that only highly evolved sparks of consciousness willingly incarnate here.

However, a less experienced soul might choose to incarnate on Earth to learn the lessons available during their time here.

Metaphysical concepts can be challenging to grasp. One example of this complexity is the ability to choose multiple physical incarnations from a higher plane of existence. Another intricate concept involves time. As you understand it, time does not exist in your higher self. Timelines are infinite and not linear. Each person experiences their unique timeline while sharing a collective consciousness with other souls. The past, present, and future all exist simultaneously. Your reality is what you have chosen to focus on within your timeline. Your higher self or subconscious mind drives you to experience the path you are currently on. Before incarnating, you select a timeline or path variant that best aligns with you and corresponds to your thoughts' frequency. This is likely not your first incarnation. Timelines are not fixed representations of desired outcomes; instead, they are interchangeable and accessible at any point in time. You can visualize this like an "Editor's Cut" of a movie, where alternate scenes can be viewed but are only experienced if chosen. Similarly, when you focus on any of the infinite possible timelines, you select an alternate life experience. While we have physical experiences in this realm, portions of our consciousness also experience existence at higher densities. Think of your physical body as a projection of your higher self while your spirit energy manifests your physical experience. Your physical body serves as a vessel, enabling your consciousness to live out your desired reality. For example, if you say that you are going to be wealthy, but the spiritual subconscious mind says that you will be poor, you will be poor because the spiritual subconscious mind controls the physical world.

The controllers of the planet, which will be discussed further in later chapters, understand how our spiritual and physical reality function. They create soul loop "traps" within our physical experience. Religious indoctrination is an example of a soul loop trap. When a soul becomes stuck on Earth and does not return to the light after an incarnation, it is termed a soul loop. The purpose of trapping a soul in a cycle of reincarnation is to keep it returning to Earth indefinitely. This serves a dual purpose. Indoctrinations driven by fear, such as certain religious beliefs, hinder souls from ascending and returning home. It is much easier to manipulate and control individuals who have already been indoctrinated in their past lives, ensuring they remain in the soul loop. Furthermore, the controllers aim to prevent "star seeds" from incarnating to shift the collective consciousness. Star seeds are Souls that choose to incarnate to raise the planet's frequency by awakening the masses. They seek a change in collective consciousness to achieve a critical mass, similar to the "100th monkey effect" theory.

Sometimes, a soul may ignore the guiding light that transitions them from the astral realm if they feel they have "unfinished business." They might need to watch over a loved one, have unresolved karmic debt with someone, or seek forgiveness, which can cause them to attach to that person's aura. These are a few reasons why some souls may become trapped in a soul loop or the lower astral realm.

Controllers use religion as a tool of manipulation. Religious individuals often fall victim to the indoctrination power of organized religion, which can ensnare their souls in a cycle of repetition. In the physical world, souls are exposed to beliefs tied to their religious system. The archons employ deceitful techniques to convince souls that their next step for evolution is to incarnate with the "Veil of Forgetfulness," leading them to believe they must return to Earth. The archons' ultimate goal is to keep souls trapped in a soul loop. The combination of the archons' tactics in the astral realm and the external frequency-lowering factors on Earth makes it highly challenging for souls to escape the lower astral to return to their real home because they can't remember who they are.

After death, as your Soul begins to ascend, you will be greeted by a guide who will reunite you with your soul group. You will be encouraged to choose new experiences for your next incarnation. Soul groups are individuals who agree to continue incarnating together, often including family members and close friends. You will be advised to repay karmic debts to help your Soul evolve. For instance, if you were an abusive spouse in one life, you may become the abused spouse in your next incarnation. However, it is difficult to accept the karmic theory promoted by a "benevolent" guide who should be helping us ascend. As infinite awareness, we can ascend to higher densities without reincarnating on Earth for such unnecessary reasons. Why would a guide and your Soul group encourage souls to return to a planet under regressive control that hinders ascension? The answer is clear: it isn't a "benevolent" guide but a regressive archon in disguise. The Soul group has fallen under the control of the supposed spiritual guides. The lower astral realm that this guide leads you to after death is controlled by regressive entities whose goal is to perpetuate negative emotions and experiences on physical Earth. These entities feed off the negative energy, often referred to as "Loosh," that arises from these harmful experiences. We should not fall into their trap; it is time to end their control and manipulation and prevent the soul from looping and returning to Earth. Instead, we can ascend beyond the lower astral realm and evolve to reunite with our true family or return to Source.

The Archons manipulate humanity to create an environment that best suits their agenda. Humanity has been deceived into constructing the regressive matrix currently experienced on Earth. The archons have carefully indoctrinated society in various ways to ensure their success in trapping souls here. Higher-density entities are incarnating on Earth to rescue souls who have become imprisoned, leading the cabal and their archon masters to wage a spiritual war. The cabal and the regressive archons work hard to maintain their "Loosh farm" by preventing as many star seeds from incarnating on Earth as possible. Star seeds vibrate at a faster rate, raising the collective frequency. They emit immense light and positive energy in the third density, superior to the average human. Star seeds don't need to be awakened to raise the frequency around them, as they naturally hold the light in their DNA, creating an energy field that raises frequency in all directions. Their energy can help awaken humans by unlocking dormant DNA, similar to how observing specific crop circles can trigger this process.

In their relentless effort to keep souls enslaved, the cabal has developed a system of indoctrination that includes organized religion, education, government, and banking.

Organized religion is a critical component of this indoctrination machine. Although all elements of this system are highly effective and interdependent, organized religion is the most impactful due to the profound effects of spiritual beliefs that carry over into the afterlife. Upon death, our spiritual beliefs shape our reality, and the archons take advantage of this vulnerable state, manipulating our indoctrinated and weakened minds. As you begin the ascending phase after death, you will experience peace and bliss. Leaving your physical body will feel liberating. However, you will initially be in the low fourth density, the astral realm. In this existence, you may be intercepted and manipulated by entities that rely on you to fulfill their goals of generating loosh.

Many religions indoctrinate their followers about an afterlife that is directly dependent on how the person lived their life on Earth. Some are taught that they will be resurrected in paradise here on Earth. Others believe that they will be reincarnated as an animal here on Earth. We are never taught the truth about life on other planets or the multiple densities. Most importantly, we are not informed about the soul group family or guides. Why would they not teach their followers about these things? Why don't they teach them about higher portions of consciousness that are a part of themselves? Why is their true soul family hidden from them? The answer is simple: to keep them returning to Earth for more and more. Why exactly is it that they want them to come back for more? For the loosh generated, a physical person will emit negative energy while living a life of difficulty on Earth. The cabal and their masters love the lower frequency because they feel it resonates more with them. Humans that are asleep have created the perfect density for them to reside in and control us. Humans who live their lives busy at work, with kids, watching TV, and going to church are the perfect people to keep the agenda going for them. Too busy to meditate and too busy to take your head out of the sand and ask questions. If everyone would wake up to what is happening, there would be uprisings tonight, but they don't because everyone is too busy listening to hypnotic music that puts them in a trance. People are busy with what they would label "life." What type of quality of life is this that everyone is so scared of losing? So, when the typical person dies, their consciousness, unbeknown to them, starts to enter the astral realm. The lower fourth density is where it is, and because of the frequency that they have, they think of their indoctrination and brainwashing. Since they are in the beginning portions of the astral, their power to manifest starts to create their reality more easily from the higher density. This Soul has no idea of what truly is happening because of the veil of forgetfulness, and during this incarnation, they never were told the truth, but that is about to change for you.

Everything within the universe is energy and is a manifestation from Source. We all are portions of Source that can also manifest reality with thought. Thought creates significantly faster the higher in density you go. So now this poor Soul leaves the physical body that just died and starts to think of hell or heaven or paradise or incarnating as an animal. They begin to fear that the indoctrination is accurate and that they did not do enough to deserve whatever prize they think they're supposed to receive. At this moment, when they are asked to return to Earth to do a better job, they will agree. Since they have free will and infinite power, the fake guides cannot stop them if they disagree. This is why indoctrination on Earth is important; it is to instill fear to be able to manipulate you on multiple planes of existence.

Regressive astral archons are aware of all of this. They will manifest themselves to look like whatever it is that the Soul is thinking about. God, Jesus, Allah, or a spiritual guide tells you to return to Earth for your reincarnation, and just like that, your consciousness enters an agreement to return to Earth to have a challenging experience. This goes against the laws of free will. Still, the archons argue that the souls' free will chose this experience again despite it being an indoctrinated lie implemented subconsciously during their physical life. This soul loop is horrible because it forces people into bodies or lives that they honestly did not want and does not benefit them anymore.

More and more kids are starting to remember past lives, and their interviews are on the internet. Little kids remember their families' names and details from past lives. The new parents find these other families and then test the kid with questions about the old family. The kid remembers the intimate details of his old family. This proves that past lives are accurate; we just do not typically remember them. I recommend a past-life regression session to everyone. If you want to discover what your higher self is willing for you to see and heal from.

This is a streamlined basic explanation of your consciousness (Soul) and densities that we all are playing in. Your purpose is to find your way back home to Source. Remember that you are a part of Source and have immense power to go where you want and do what you want. This knowledge puts you in a better position, but communicating with your higher self, ascended masters, and benevolent guides is even better. This is done with deep meditation and practice daily.

A side note I wanted to mention is that the government has initiated Agenda 21, 30 (21st century, lasting 30 years). The 21st century started on January 1st, 2001, and Agenda 21 is planned to be completed within 30 years. The cabal is planning to have Agenda 21 completed by January 1st, 2031.

Agenda 21 will start and fulfill many portions of the main agenda that is planned to be completed by 2050. One of the agenda goals is to keep the Earth's population low so they can better police the incarnating souls. With the population growing, it has become harder to control the people with religion as it once was. The cabal wanted to reduce religions to one and only one government called the New World Order. Part of the agenda is to start the early stages of transhumanism so they can further control society. It will begin with chip implants that benefit humans, but the end goal is not for humanity's benefit.

They will not openly tell you that this chip is intended for mind control; instead, they will present it under different pretexts. Initially, it will be introduced slowly, but eventually, an event will be orchestrated to instill fear in the populace. Following this, the cabal will offer a solution to this fear: the opportunity to get chipped with a more controlling device. This follows the classical approach of problem, reaction, and solution they have employed for thousands of years on Earth.

The cabal aims to reduce the number of Starseeds incarnating on Earth because they are losing their grip on control. More and more individuals are awakening to the truth. To remain dominant, they need to drastically lower the Earth's population and control those who remain.

It is essential to mention this because our consciousness must know all the agendas and tricks the cabal employs against us. Awareness gives us a fighting chance; we won't follow unthinkingly, and we have the choice not to incarnate on Earth if we genuinely do not wish to.

I suggest being prepared for no later than 2030, as the deadline for many changes is set for 2031. Most likely, this will involve a fake alien invasion using technology called Blue Beam, a hyper-realistic hologram generator, or possibly another pandemic—or even both. This will induce a state of mass fear among the populace. The cabal may then impose vaccines, body chips, and currency change. These vaccines could contain dangerous elements, similar to those associated with COVID vaccines, which may lead to disease or fatalities. Others may perish due to bioengineered weapons introduced into the population, and additional casualties may arise from the fake alien invasion, where human-made crafts, reverse-engineered from actual UFOs, may attack people as part of the fear agenda to help manipulate everyone to take a specific action.

If you doubt its validity, I recommend investigating General Corso's book, "Day After Roswell," in which he discusses the government's reverse engineering of UFO technologies. Many well-credentialed individuals are warning about the potential for a fake alien invasion. Several former CIA personnel are now coming forward with details about Agenda 21, and it's time for us to awaken to this reality. I am not saying that aliens do not exist; what I am saying is that the cabal will have the secret government orchestrate a fake alien attack for a specific purpose.

We must be cautious not to fall for the Cabal's tricks. However, we must remain vigilant about the plans for a fake alien invasion, which are part of a broader agenda. It is a theatrical performance, with the cabal controlling many aspects of what appears to be disclosures regarding these matters.

The cabal, which is orchestrating this situation, treats humanity as fools. It is time to unlock our DNA and realize our true potential. Our consciousness currently exists in this third density, but we are beginning to raise our frequency. The truth will gradually become apparent, akin to a Polaroid picture slowly developing. It is time to recognize what is happening, reprogram our minds, and shed the indoctrination we have experienced. The moment to take action and defeat the cabal has arrived. It is time to make Earth great again!

Additionally, there will likely be another timeline split. Many will follow the regressive cabal timeline because their frequency aligns with that frequency. However, many will experience a different timeline where total accurate disclosure occurs, and the regressive cabal is brought to light. They will be removed from government and their power stripped away. While there will be a rebuilding period, with help from beings of the fifth-density and above, we can transition Earth from that timeline into the fifth-density and out of the third. Our consciousness will not focus on the timeline where the regressive continue to rule and implement the New World Order. Those versions of our physical bodies in the third density will not engage our consciousness, so we will not experience it. Our bodies will remain observable to others, but our consciousness will not be present in that experience. We will not engage with that timeline because our consciousness will match the frequency of the positive timeline instead of the negative one. There are infinite timelines, but we only experience those that resonate with the frequency of our consciousness in this density.

This information is intended to awaken as many Souls as possible so they can shift their timeline to one where the

New World Order is dismantled before 2031. You will know that you have reached the positive timeline if, by 2031, there is complete disclosure about our cosmic families and the cabal. In this positive timeline, the New World Order will have been abolished, leading to a peaceful existence where everyone has free access to medical beds.

Conversely, you are in the negative timeline if you experience the New World Order taking control of finance and government, a society that is being chipped, a drastically reduced world population, or an invasion of aggressive extraterrestrials, among other distressing scenarios. Now is your opportunity to choose what reality you wish to experience.

Chapter 5: What Are Timelines

In higher densities, the concept of time becomes complex, making it challenging to explain a timeline. Beings in the fifth-density and below experience time, but in higher densities, timelines are perceived as a whole experience with associated frequency ranges specific to the feelings and emotions experienced during a lifetime.

A timeline is often understood as the progression from beginning to end, such as from birth to death. However, this represents only one individual's timeline, excluding phenomena like walk-ins. A timeline could be seen as the start and end of events, but this perspective is subjective—there's no definitive answer. In lower densities, the perception changes; a timeline usually refers to a series of events shared by the collective consciousness, which contributes to shaping that reality. Some timelines may collapse into others, while some may divide. This concept is akin to water, as both represent a frequency. We are surrounded by frequencies—cell phones, radios, microwaves, and walkie-talkies all function on various frequencies, demonstrating that we exist within a web of frequencies. Similarly, timelines represent energies organized in frequencies.

A timeline split occurs when the frequency of one reality diverges significantly, preventing the original timeline from maintaining its singularity. Each physical being experiences its timeline, yet we share our reality with the collective consciousness that resonates closely with our frequency. A shared timeline among a collective consciousness can split when members diverge in thought, causing a frequency separation. Every decision made can lead to a timeline split but exploring that idea would require detailed discussion. In simpler terms, collective consciousness can experience an elevation or reduction in frequency, resulting in a timeline split.

It's important to note that infinite timelines exist within every density. Some refer to these timelines as dimensions, but these are essentially different realities across various frequencies.

Your focused awareness on a specific point within the frequency or timeline shapes your current experience. In this very second, you are a different version of yourself than when you began reading this sentence because time, as we perceive it, is non-existent. It's your attention in this moment that gives it density and physicality. Your physical experience, moment to moment, manifests your true self, which exists on a higher plane. Physical reality serves as a matrix designed to facilitate the evolution of souls.

Some people experience a timeline characterized by a rise in frequency, while others may find themselves in a timeline marked by a lowering of frequency.
Experiencing a positive timeline does not mean you necessarily die in the other timeline; you can lower your frequency and eventually jump into that timeline later. For example, if you are in a low vibratory state experiencing a low-frequency timeline, raising your frequency can allow you to shift to a better, more positive one.

The density you inhabit is not a physical location; instead, it is a state of mind. The same concept applies to timelines; they are not physical places, but states of consciousness, and your energy follows where your mind directs its attention. The vessel that holds your energy or consciousness is simply that vessel, nothing more. It is a medium through which you can experience this dense reality.

If you become ill with a life-threatening disease like cancer, it is likely due to your body being in a low frequency, which causes it to react negatively. There can be many reasons for the disease affecting you, but the root cause is ultimately your mental state.
Remember, density is not a place but a state of mind. This may be difficult for many to accept, but I am not

here to make friends; I aim to help others expand their understanding. Cancer can be eradicated from the body if you and your subconscious work together toward healing. It is true that when incarnating, your consciousness may have chosen to end this experience in this manner, but even in that case, you can still achieve healing. It may be challenging, but with the power of your mind, you can potentially cure yourself. You can restore your body to its state before the disease through deep meditation and pure- hearted intent. Earth's environment has been compromised by those in control, creating a toxic atmosphere that can contribute to cancer. Regardless of whether the root cause of a person's cancer lies in environmental factors or their mental state, both can be healed.

Soul contracts can be rewritten, and outcomes can be changed. You are in charge while existing in this density. You are the one who experiences everything, and it's okay for your desired experience to change. Your intention must be clear, and your mental state should shift to a more positive perspective.

I mention this because if you find yourself awakening and feeling trapped in what seems to be an impossible situation, I want you to realize that anything is possible. You can continue to ascend—do not worry. For those of you who awaken to find that you are in a religion with

Freemason origins, such as the York Rite lodge, or discover that your faith is rooted in the Illuminati, also known as the Brotherhood of the Serpent (a satanic group), I assure you that if your frequency can heal a physical disease, it can also liberate you from that situation. You can jump to another timeline by raising your frequency. Your current timeline is a frequency match with you; by changing your frequency, the negative timeline will no longer resonate with you. You will then transition to a positive timeline that aligns more closely with your new frequency.

The topic of timelines can be complicated, so I want to summarize it. A timeline represents what you experience in a lifetime. It's similar to watching a movie after seeing the trailer; it gives you an idea of what to expect, but you don't know every detail of the film and are often surprised by the ending. Clients of mine under hypnosis have described seeing a kind of trailer before choosing a timeline to incarnate into and experience. They explained that they see images and then decide what experience to have based on those images.

Timelines are like movies filled with both good and bad experiences. Once a timeline is selected, the ending can be changed if you determine that this movie no longer reflects your desired experience. Understanding this and identifying your purpose can liberate you from unwanted experiences. Now is the time to change your experience within your movie, should you choose to do so. You are the star and the director, controlling every aspect of the story.

Physical ailments often reflect issues rooted in the subconscious; by healing the mind, the body can follow. Free your mind and experience the life you truly desire. By uncovering these truths, you can discover your life's true purpose. If you are reading this, your purpose was to separate from Source and forget who you are, only to awaken and find your way back to home.

Do not ignore the signs from your higher self-trying to get your attention. These signs can manifest as unexplained physical pains or illnesses. The subconscious mind is calling out, and it should not be overlooked. It is time to awaken and, if necessary, change the movie (or timeline).

Chapter 6: The Creation of Demons

I want to emphasize that there is no such thing as demons. We all originate from Source and contain light that comes from Source. Some have lost their way and take on roles in this universe characterized by duality. However, many understand the concept of demons as high-density beings with little light, often referred to as the "dark ones." While I recognize that this perspective may not be typical, I will continue explaining the creation of angels, dark beings, or demons.

Archangels, or what I prefer to call the "light ones," were created by Source and its partner. Essentially, Source encompasses all energies united, meaning both the mother and father aspects are part of Source. Let's refer to the female portion of Source as "Mother" and the male portion as "Father."

Source is everything in the universe, existing as a single consciousness that pervades all space. It is the aether that contains everything. This is why Source manifested Mother and smaller portions of consciousness—to be part of the Matrix and aid in creating duality.

When Source envisioned this plan and sought independence, it gave birth to Mother. Mother then conceived the idea of duality, which led to Father being created from her. They are independent entities.

Mother and Father began creating many sparks of themselves, which were independent fragments of their consciousness. These archangels used their powers to create planets, stars, and entire universes. Their ability to manifest could bring entire galaxies into existence in an instant. This realm served as a playground for the archangels to create and evolve.

Planets and stars are manifestations of awareness or attention from highly evolved sparks of Source. This energy creates gravity on planets, acting like a black hole, similar to that of a star. This is why gravity can exist within planets, and places like Agartha can support life. The energy of the being that manifested a planet generates a magnetic wave, which in turn creates the gravity felt on that planet. This concept of what generates gravity on a planet differs from modern Earth science, but this is how entities from other densities explain it. The controllers use science in conjunction with religion to control the minds of humanity. It would not benefit the controllers if humanity were made aware of higher planes of existence and how gravity from a planet is generated from large portions of consciousness, giving attention to the experience of being that planet.

Certain galaxies operate under entirely different physical laws than those in the Milky Way. I have heard of reverse dimensions, where everything is black and white or black and green, resembling a photographic negative. The creativity of the children of Mother and Father is genuinely fascinating.

The archangels were learning extensively about how to create a universe, feeling confident enough to begin separating portions of their energy and initiating the process of involution. Involution involves the archangels gradually lowering their frequency to enjoy existence in the lower densities they created.

There are also sparks of consciousness that did not descend through the process of involution. These sparks begin in the first density, and as they gain awareness and knowledge, they advance through the densities—a process known as evolution. In the first density, crystals typically serve as vessels for these young souls. Crystals and similar objects hold their energy, which is determined by the amount of knowledge or light they contain. This light represents knowledge. Once the consciousness residing in the crystal exceeds the capacity of that vessel, it moves to the second density, and so on. This evolutionary process applies to newer souls. It is said that humans on Earth with Rh- negative blood types can accommodate the energy of older souls.

These older Souls may bring more energy into a physical body with Rh-negative blood. In contrast, the Rh-positive blood in a physical body is associated with physical bodies that do not hold as much energy.

Positive higher-density beings have experienced the involution process gradually. I don't know when the positive portions of consciousness took physical vessels. However, the dark beings (negative portions of Source) first had physical experiences in the lower densities. They intended to separate as far as possible from Source.

From what I've gathered, Mother felt a profound sadness and fear. She was distressed by the thought of losing her partner, with whom she enjoyed creating the multiverse, and worried deeply for her children. This strong emotion led her to manifest something negative into reality through the power of her thoughts.

Mother felt the darkness deep within her. She focused on feeling only love and happiness with Father and the children. To rid herself of this unwanted energy she expelled this negative thought energy from her. Mother sent this dark energy far away from herself, distancing her from its influence. This moment marked the birth of the first demon or dark entity. By expelling such a substantial amount of negative energy in that instant, Mother gave rise to negative dark energy, commonly referred to as Lucifer, the Devil, Satan, and so forth. The specific name given to this negative energy is not significant; what matters is that it represents regressive energy. This malevolent consciousness stood in stark contrast to Source, creating a duality that now permeates our universe, allowing for the existence of both good and evil. I believe this was all part of the plan Source intended for us. As much pain and distress that came from the birth of duality, from a higher perspective, it serves a purpose. Duality helps achieve unique experiences. However, it has crossed the line on Earth and other planets that have become prison planets for Souls to reincarnate into to supply the regressive entities with negative energy.

Numerous names are associated with the first evil spark of consciousness that emerged from Mother. Ahriman is one of them, and many ancient scriptures speak of this malevolent spirit. However, these texts were often written with a twisted agenda, containing half-truths designed to blind and control humanity. Deciphering the truth within these ancient writings can be challenging, but we will explore what the ascended masters have communicated regarding our reality.

Ahriman was the first of many negative sparks of consciousness to emerge from Mother. His strength stemmed from that initial burst of energy. He was cast far from Source, descending into the sixth density. This rejection by Mother fostered a deep resentment within him for being abandoned. Though he felt alone, he eventually welcomed other smaller negative sparks of consciousness that manifested with him in the sixth density. These additional sparks also originated from Mother, who cleansed herself of fear and sent those energies down. Ahriman accepted these fallen angels. Remember, these names— Devil, Ahriman, Lucifer—refer to the same consciousness. The smaller sparks from Mother possessed their independent thoughts.

This malevolent collective of fallen angels or dark entities harbored anger toward Source and Mother for their abandonment. They embodied the antithesis of what Source represents. While Source is light and love, this group sought to spread hatred and darkness throughout the universe. They are known by various names, such as asuras and archons.

Meanwhile, the archangels were still evolving through their process of involution from higher densities. When the asuras were cast down to the sixth density, they bypassed the archangels in this involution process. In the involution process, I have not gained insight into where the archangels were at that time. However, I do know that among them, a powerful positive consciousness was created by Mother and Father; this energy is commonly referred to as Michael. Thus, the universe was divided, with evil and good, Lucifer and Michael, standing as opposing forces in this ongoing struggle.

Many ancient texts address the asuras or archons, but agendas influenced these scriptures. We will explore these agendas later in this book, but I want to maintain focus to avoid confusion.

The anti-Source group decided to take over the playground. They existed in lower densities and could not figure out how to return to Source, so they began creating physical vessels to experience even lower densities. It is important to note that the asuras could not ascend to higher densities because their mindset prevented them from perceiving those realms. Their regressive thinking meant they needed to express love towards others and change their perspective to reach higher densities.

Meanwhile, the archangels were still busy creating galaxies and had not yet ventured into the lower densities where they could take on more physical forms. The asuras regarded Ahriman as their father because he was the first to exist in the lower densities and possessed the most knowledge. He searched for rejected sparks of

Source, believing that these sparks were attracted to one another so they could share their energies. Ahriman sought separation from Mother and Source and wished to inflict pain upon them. He instructed his followers, the asuras, aka archons, that the galaxy belonged to them, giving them the authority to do as they pleased. The asuras embodied lower-density physical forms and convinced themselves they needed to conquer the universe.

We live in a soup that is invisible to the human eye, but it is there. This supposed empty space is called the aether. Scientific evidence suggests that we live in a dense world—akin to existing in water—within a substance called aether. The archangels had created animals and were exploring the knowledge derived from the aether, which surrounds us like an ocean. It exists in every atom and fills the universe across all densities. The aether contains Source, from which anything can be manifested. With an understanding of how to manipulate aether, the archangels can manifest everything they desire.

These animals created by the archangels were distributed throughout the universe. From what I gather, the seeding of a planet begins with water. An evolved consciousness creates a galaxy with energy that emanates from its thoughts. Subsequently, smaller segments of that consciousness focus on the stars, and an even smaller aspect creates the planets.

Everything is based on consciousness, merely at different levels. Since we are all part of Source, it is intrinsically within us. Additionally, when one aspect of consciousness wishes to become a body of water on a planet, that thought triggers an explosion of energy, introducing water onto the planet. From a lower-density viewpoint, this process might appear coincidental—like an asteroid carrying ice crashing into a planet—but it is preordained; that timeline ensures the planet will possess water and life. Once water is present on the planet, DNA can be introduced. Over millions of years, animals naturally emerge on the planet.

It is worth mentioning that while many advanced races understand the nature of existence in the universe, they may disagree on specific details. Just because an advanced race can manipulate gravity or travel through wormholes does not mean they possess all the answers. The ultimate goal is to return to Source and expand along the way, acquiring knowledge. A being from the sixth density has knowledge beyond what is known on Earth by the typical person. However, a tenth-density being would offer a different yet equally enlightening perspective, which might contradict the insights given by the sixth-density being. This is why we must always keep an open mind and be receptive to change as we expand our understanding. The true definition of intelligence is someone who can learn everything about a subject but still grasp a completely new concept that causes them to change their understanding of that subject.

When a young soul, or as you might call it, a spark of energy consciousness, begins its journey, the process of evolution from the first density starts. This soul will evolve to higher densities over what we would perceive as millions, if not billions, of years. There are two ways consciousness can enter this realm: involution and evolution. Involution comes from the top down, while evolution moves from the bottom up. It's important to clarify that evolution is not a progression from animals, as many believe, due to misinformation propagated by the cabal to divert society from the truth. Instead, evolution refers to the transformation of consciousness as it ascends through the densities.

The asuras, curious about animal life forms they found on certain planets, sought to take on physical forms. They began to lower their frequency to manifest as physical beings in the low fifth density. While I use the term "asuras," there are many other names for these negative energies, which are essentially the same—feel free to replace "asuras" with terms like demons, archons, or fallen angels. Under the command of Ahriman, they took portions of their consciousness and manifested physically. They examined the energy of the animals introduced into the universe by the archangels and decided to manipulate reptilian DNA. Through this DNA, they could introduce their energy and create physical vessels. These five-star types of bodies resembled reptiles, having legs, arms, and heads similar to humans. The reptilians could not hold as much energy in this lower form, but it allowed them to spread more fear and lower the frequency of the universe.

The asuras began to take on these physical forms and were instructed by Ahriman to populate the universe, aiming to exclude Mother from everything and worship only darkness. Their goal was to oppose the light and love that Mother represented, instead spreading darkness and hate across the galaxy. They wanted to lower the frequency of the archangel's playground through fear. The asuras fell into a trance, adhering to the law of three: Father, Son, and Light. Here, the Father refers to Ahriman, the Son represents the asuras, and Light signifies knowledge of the Light. They dedicated themselves to these principles, disregarding everything else, and set out to dominate the galaxy with a self-serving mindset.

The reptilians accumulated significant knowledge about how the universe operates. They pursued the light because they gained power with that higher knowledge, understanding that control is contingent upon such knowledge. They have focused on three key aspects from their inception: dedication to Ahriman, respect for the asuras to garner their approval, and the quest for knowledge of the light for controlling others. This explains why the number three is venerated in satanic groups. The three-sided Illuminati triangle symbolizes this number, while the 33 levels of the Freemasons denote a double three. The gesture of putting up two fingers, often interpreted as a peace sign, initially represented a victory and came from a U.S. president who was a Freemason; thus, it is symbolic of "as above, so below." Secret societies respect the number 3 for other reasons that will be discussed later.

Secret societies that control the world prominently display these symbols, often mocking those oblivious to their influence on society. For example, the obelisk in St. Peter's Square is a significant symbol for the reptilians, appearing in various locations like the Vatican, Washington, London, New York City, and more. We could write an entire book on the hidden symbolism employed by these secretive groups.

Even company logos may contain concealed meanings. Walt Disney, a 33rd-degree Freemason, incorporated numerous hidden messages within their cartoons. Search to see the hidden 666 in the Google Chrome logo. The processor name that the Google search engine runs on is named Adreno. The Google search engine is called Chrome. When you combine these two words, you get Adrenochrome. This further proves that the signs are placed right before you. You cannot afford to continue sleeping. The Illuminati controllers place these signs in front of humanity because they feel that humanity is fast asleep and will not wake up to their satanic rituals. Adrenochrome is taken from the blood of tortured people, but children are preferred. They do this because it is a drug for the Illuminati cabal. The mega companies are all tied together and worship Lucifer and the asuras. The secret elites conduct satanic rituals regularly, and they introduce low frequencies to the Earth with these rituals. These symbols are ways to keep the masses blind to the fact that they are giving homage to the asuras and Ahriman. This energy that the people emit helps keep the frequency low, and that is where the asuras want the frequency. We will later discover the connection between these bipedal reptilians and these companies and religions that have been mind-controlling the population on Earth. The asuras and their physical counterparts have been controlling Earth's population, which they do in plain sight. Still, it is time to shine the light on them and all the false history and false religions that have indoctrinated humanity. We will decipher everything, and once you see this, your mind will expand, and the mind control will be stopped. Once you awaken, their tactics will no longer affect you, and they will lose power over your mind.

The reptilians instilled fear in the animals by hunting and eating them. Although these animals had previously lived without any danger, once they became prey for the reptilians, they experienced fear, diminishing their overall energy levels.

At this point, the asuras channeled a lower portion of their energy into a lower fifth density or possibly the fourth density. Meanwhile, the archangels were descending through a process known as involution. They had not yet incarnated into the lower densities, so they had not experienced physical existence like the asuras. To summarize, archangels and asuras (archons) underwent involution processes, but the asuras originated in the sixth density. There were also small sparks of Source that were experiencing an evolutionary process.

Chapter 7: Draconian Reptilians

High-density beings reside in the sixth density and above. These beings go by names such as asuras, archons, demons, egregors, and fallen angels. The asuras sought to lower their frequency and experience the lower densities within the matrix created by Mother.

One notable race is the Carians, a bird-like species. After millions of years of evolution, they developed intelligence and became bipedal. At some point, they mixed their DNA with reptilian DNA, resulting in a bipedal reptilian physical body. Although the reasons for this DNA mixing are unclear, it is understood that the Carians did not have malicious intent; they were experimenting to see what they could create. However, the asuras were intrigued by these bipedal reptilian forms and began to incarnate into them. This is believed to be the genesis of souls incarnating in physical vessels in the fifth density.

It is important to remember that the history we learn has often been manipulated for specific agendas. The victors of wars tend to dictate historical narratives, and the Draconians understood that to shape a desired version of history, they needed to influence influential figures to promote their narrative. They encouraged people to adopt this perspective, and the public trusted individuals to document it accurately, solidifying a version of history that served the interests of the controllers. The less humanity knows, the easier they are to control. The manipulation of human DNA began over 12,500 years ago. At the same time, specific alterations to a particular bloodline occurred later during Babylonian times, and these alterations were intended for the reptilian asura souls to assume human forms.

Returning to the asuras, those who separated parts of their consciousness took on the bipedal reptilian form. They entered these physical vessels, referred to as "five-star physical forms,"—meaning bodies with two arms, two legs, and a head. I believe Ahriman played a role in facilitating this process, though I can't confirm this as a fact. It seems plausible that this was an effective way for the asuras to spread malevolence throughout the universe.

Additionally, some channeled information suggests that Ahriman and Lucifer are distinct consciousnesses. Lucifer is said to have seeded the reptilian form. Whether these two entities are independent or interconnected is uncertain; however, their differentiation may not be essential for our understanding. As emphasized before, even in higher densities, diverse opinions exist. Maintaining an open mind and remaining receptive to enlightenment and expansion as it unfolds is crucial to the awakening process.

Ahriman introduced reptilian DNA on what we now know as Alpha Draconis, which initiated the expansion of the asuras in lower densities in a five-star physical form. In the Milky Way galaxy, Alpha Draconis is approximately 303 light-years away from Earth and is part of the Draco star system, also known as Thuban.

Around four billion years ago, Ahriman seeded Alpha Draconis (Thuban) with the reptilian form. While the asuras and Ahriman had been exploring the universe for much longer, this marks the point at which they adopted physical forms on Alpha Draconis. Souls incarnate into a physical body, typically by placing small portions of their consciousness into the body while it is being formed. By the time the body reaches adolescence, most of the conscious energy has entered the body.

The reptilians existed in the third density for a significant period. They were aligned with a service-to-self mentality, following the guidance of regressive energies from higher aspects of their consciousness. This group, known as the Ciakar, represents the original physical form of Ahriman seeded bloodline. Some spell this as Ciakhar, but we will use Ciakar as it is the more common spelling.

Many trace the influence of world governments and religions through secret societies, discovering that these all lead back to the Ciakar. While they constitute the leadership of the Illuminati, they are not at the top of the power structure. Above them are the asuras, and above the asuras is Ahriman. The Draconians were taught to prioritize loyalty to these three entities: the Father (Ahriman), the Son (the asuras), and the Light (the higher knowledge of magecraft or dark magic or the metaphysical).

The Ciakar possess a service-to-self mindset and were instructed by the asuras to spread across the galaxy and claim ownership of everything, believing it belongs to them. This instilled a mentality of lower densities within the Ciakar race. Over time, they evolved, entering the fourth density and acquiring knowledge of consciousness and the various lower densities. With this acquired knowledge, they could integrate their understanding of the astral realm with physical technology, leading to significant technological advancements.

The Ciakar combined technology with magecraft, resulting in the creation of modern technology, which included interstellar spacecraft, med beds, scalar weapons, frequency manipulation technology, artificial intelligence, consciousness swapping, consciousness trapping, cloning, mind wiping, zero-point energy, nuclear weapons, and many other advanced technologies.

Once they could leave Alpha Draconis, they began to conquer neighboring planets, pillaging any signs of life they encountered and instilling fear in any conscious beings. They established agricultural planets, which served as food sources for meat-eaters, viewing all life as resources to exploit and control for their benefit. They reached a technological cap approximately 387 million years ago; it took them billions of years to reach this point of advancement in technology. Technology is always intertwined with spirituality; further advancements occur when this connection is made. However, if a race is regressive, it will inevitably hit a technological ceiling, as it must align more closely with positive light to access higher knowledge. Their current density level or mindset restricted their progress beyond a certain point. Nevertheless, they were still very advanced and wielded numerous weapons while conquering world after world.

During the period when the Draconians were developing their technology, the positive archangels were still engaged in involution and had not yet taken on physical forms. It was only a matter of time before these two opposing sides would encounter each other in a lower density. The Ciakar's destructive and pillaging actions prompted higher-density beings to intervene to slow their progress. The regressive-minded souls that incarnated into physical bodies needed to be slowed down. The positive souls began to prepare to incarnate at a lower physical frequency.

The asuras sought to lower their frequency and experience the lower densities within the matrix created by Mother. These asuras wanted to spread the service to self-mentality, while the positive archangels wanted to spread the service to others' mentality. A clash between the two mindsets was inevitable. The Draconians were the first to take physical bodies, so they had a head start. But soon, they would have another intelligent race to interact with.

It is unclear if this marks the beginning of physical bodies throughout the universe. However, many have interpreted the information regarding the emergence of physical forms within the surrounding galaxies this way.

The Ciakar categorized the Draconian race into workers, farmers, and warriors. After being nearly annihilated by higher-density beings—likely a group of archangels aiming to hinder the Ciakar—the Draconians regained their strength and returned to their expansionist ways. They are recognized as the oldest civilization in this quadrant of the universe, having explored countless stars and planets for millions of years.

Some Draconian factions have evolved spiritually throughout their long history, finding enlightenment and moving beyond their reptilian forms. Therefore, not all reptilians are malevolent. Many of the original Draconian souls have attained peace and higher consciousness. These enlightened beings are the Alpha Draconians, named after their originating planet.

Most Alpha Draconians have abandoned their regressive ways in favor of spiritual growth and prefer to evolve their consciousness. Once they discovered that the path back to Source is through love, they began to develop technologies that far exceed those created by their more primitive counterparts. The positive Alpha Draconians are beyond interstellar travel; they are multi-dimensional. They can phase in and out of different densities and engage in time travel. However, these advanced technologies can only be achieved once a consciousness reaches higher densities, which is only possible through a positive mindset rooted in love and service to others.

The Ciakar and the Draconians deserve respect for their achievements over the billions of years since their seeding. While they may tend to be regressive, it's important to remember that we are all sparks of Source. In higher densities, we do not possess a physical form. This physical existence is limited to the lower densities, but once we ascend to higher states of being, we will no longer have physical bodies, nor will there be male or female distinctions. Only our energy will be visible in those higher densities, and we will be unique in that realm without a physical form. I want to clarify that this is not about humans versus Dracoians. You may have had a Draconian physical form in a past life experience and have chosen this current experience because it aligns with your frequency.

I understand that after this chapter, we have placed the Draconian race in a position that invites us to detest them. However, it would be narrow-minded and just as regressive as some of their actions if we were to hate them. There are other regressive races, and some Draconians are positive now, so we should never judge an entire race based on the actions of a few individuals.

This conflict is about good versus evil; therefore, we must look beyond skin color and physical appearance. We should assess a person by measuring their soul. Very soon, there will be a time of disclosure, and we do not want to approach that critical moment with closed-mindedness or prejudice against any extraterrestrial race. Racism has been ingrained in human programming, so if an extraterrestrial race visits us, we may have preconceived opinions about them instead of truly understanding their essence with our hearts.

Chapter 8: Human Lyrian Origin

Before we dive into the human race, let's explore the time before humans existed. The archangels were undergoing a process known as involution. They were stepping down through different planes of existence called densities and adopting various forms to embody lower aspects of their energy, or what some refer to as their consciousness. During this time, they also seeded lower densities with smaller sparks of Source. These fragments of consciousness had to navigate their way up through the densities via evolution.

Higher-density beings with greater knowledge and light took on managing and distributing physical DNA across the cosmos. They experimented and learned as they progressed.

Eventually, these higher-density aspects of Source began to form groups. Some of these groups focused on overseeing the seeding of animals on various planets, while others worked on expanding the galaxy. It is essential to portray a picture of these organized higher-density groups collaboratively managing the development of themselves and the galaxy, ensuring that their galactic endeavors were safeguarded.

During their descent, they observed that lower-density beings sent far from their origin were causing destruction wherever they went. This observation is crucial when discussing the origins of the human race. An event involving the Ciakar drastically decreased their population due to a higher-density group intervening. The thought was to slow down the Ciakar, hoping they would evolve spiritually and become positive. This positive group that slowed down the Ciakar was known as the Elohim. According to ancient texts, there is a claim that the Annunaki were the Elohim; however, this cannot be accurate because the Annunaki did not exist during the ancient conflict against the Ciakar. This war took place before the Lyrans existed, and the Annunaki emerged after the creation of the Lyran race. Therefore, the Annunaki cannot be equated with the Elohim. The cabal manipulated such associations to prompt humans to worship the Annunaki as their gods and creators. This is why ancient tablets, like those of the Sumerians, can be confusing and should be read with the knowledge that they were written long ago with an agenda to manipulate the people.

Although the information found in these cuneiform tablets may be closer to the truth, it still serves as a form of manipulation. Information control has been a longstanding practice throughout human history. History itself has often been altered, and people have been presented with half-truths that paint a narrative designed to encourage worship of those in power. The Draconians and Ciakar worked diligently to keep humanity unaware of their true history, which explains the extensive efforts to control historical narratives and extraterrestrial information. While the Elohim did not wholly eradicate the Ciakar, they significantly reduced their population with the hope that the Ciakar might amend their destructive ways. Unfortunately, they did not change.

At this point, other intelligent life forms emerged on various planets. Following this confrontation, the Ciakar splintered into different factions and became the rulers of the Draconian race. The Ciakar race is physically larger than the Draconian race and is considered the royal lineage that governs the Draconians. Due to their diminished numbers, the Ciakar resorted to more cunning strategies to pursue their ambitions of galaxy domination. The Draconian Empire formed, and when faced with intelligent colonies, they realized that military attacks weren't always the most effective strategy for conquest. Instead, they began to infiltrate the societies of different planets, aiming to manipulate the inhabitants to comply with their desires, leading them to fall under the influence of the Draconian Empire through mind control. This shift was advantageous because various opposing extraterrestrial groups formed, remaining vigilant to protect their communities against the military might of the Draconian Empire. However, if the Draconians could infiltrate and persuade the populace to willingly relinquish their freedoms and submit to control, a military conflict could be avoided altogether, as every being in the universe has the right to free will.

Now, returning to humans, the higher-density positive beings continued to lower their frequency, leading to the emergence of the seeders, known as the Pa Taal. The Pa Taal seeders were tall beings dedicated to serving others. They began seeding a new five-star physical form within the Lyra star constellation.

The Lyrans were created as a physical race within this density and were designed to be protectors. Their purpose was to aid other races in their evolution. The Sirian Council, from higher densities, was appointed as overseers of this project named Turaneusiam. The Lyrans possess a 12-strand DNA structure.

Within the Lyra constellation lies a star named Vega, where the Pa Taal seeded this new physical form. The Vega star system is located approximately 25 light-years away. The planet on which this occurred was named Avyon, also part of the Vega star system. This new race became known as the Lyrian race or the Lyrians. It is said that the Lyran race received much of its DNA from an older race called the Urma. The Urma were a positive, five-star, feline-type race with physical forms, and they agreed to share their DNA with the Pa Taal. I have heard conflicting opinions about the origin of the Lyrian DNA, so please form a personal opinion.

The Lyrans spread to other planets and eventually became part of the galactic family. The Pa Taal took the DNA of the Lyrans and adjusted it. This DNA was seeded on Tiamat / Earth and eventually evolved into what is known as Neanderthal man, resulting in a new variation of a physical body with dark skin. The Lyran DNA was already mixed with extraterrestrial DNA, and the Pa Taal added DNA from other evolved extraterrestrial beings. As mentioned, they seeded this DNA on a planet called Tiamat, allowing it to develop into an intelligent, evolving race. This seeding occurred around 300 million years ago, long after the Lyrans and Draconians were established.

This new five-star type of race had such a perfect blend of evolved DNA that these humans were destined to become guardians and protectors for other races that the Draconian Empire had enslaved. Humans can hold a significant amount of energy and oscillate across a much wider range of frequencies than others. Physically, humans would develop to be very strong and possess a multidimensional nature, capable of holding more light while taking a lower-density physical form when necessary.

I view human DNA as a secret weapon against any regressive race. The vast range of emotions that humans can experience is something other races struggle to achieve. Our ability to love deeply and the readiness to defend our loved ones with fierce passion makes us unique in the cosmos. We are the culmination of perfected extraterrestrial DNA over billions of years. While the human physical body is relatively new, our DNA is highly evolved; we must recognize this and unlock our dormant capabilities. Scientists often call dormant DNA "junk DNA" because they do not understand its purpose. These strands of DNA have been suppressed to prevent people on Earth from realizing their true potential.

To control the human race, the human DNA and the abilities associated with the DNA had to be controlled to a point where they would be nullified and diminished. For the Draconians to control the human race, they had to figure out how to suppress the human DNA. The struggle between Lyrian humans and Draconian reptilians would provide unique experiences for souls.

The suppression of the human DNA can be repaired and reversed. Everything begins in the mind, and with strong will and intention, one can heal almost anything. Despite the intrusion and suppression of our DNA, anyone can start unlocking their potential.

The planet where humans were seeded was called Tiamat, which also has other names. The environment of Tiamat was ideal for new life. There was a layer between the surface of Tiamat and its ozone layer called the firmament. This firmament acted like a thick mist, aiding in the seeding and development of life on the planet. The seeding took place on a continent named Pangaea. Many people believe that Tiamat is the same as Nibiru, Planet X, or the twelfth planet, but that is disinformation intended to credit the Annunaki for creating the human race. Tiamat was located in the Sol star system, specifically between Mars and Jupiter. After a significant event, Tiamat was destroyed, and more about that event will be discussed later. This catastrophe caused significant changes on Tiamat / Earth.

This is a streamlined explanation of human origins. Humans resulted from a mix of about ten or eleven evolved DNA genomes from our galaxy. There was also an incorporation of what we call animal DNA. Still, I prefer not to elaborate on this to avoid misconstruing it with Darwinism, which I want to clarify is not the case—humans did not evolve from animals. This misconception is part of a disinformation campaign by the cabal, which I can identify as the Draconians.

The Draconians aim to make humanity believe we are inferior, making it easier to control and manipulate us. Their plan involved creating a false history, fabricating alternate versions, and labeling the truth as a conspiracy. When a group begins to uncover the truth, it is often infiltrated by the CIA, prompting a disinformation campaign that can include altering authentic images or videos of UFOs and flooding the internet with these alterations to discredit the original.

Throughout millions of years, the Draconians have perfected these strategies to maintain control over societies, effectively brainwashing populations and dividing them. We are a higher power and possess great potential when our minds are unlocked. It is time to regain control of humanity. The reality of human history is not what we have been told, primarily because the Draconians fear losing their control over Earth if we understand this information. This truth is beginning to emerge, and it won't be long before it can no longer be suppressed. Every day, more people remember their past lives and discover their true identities. More individuals are uncovering information that lifts the veil from their eyes.

Before we move on to the next chapter, I would like to highlight an important point. The physical form is merely a vessel for our consciousness. The Draconians instilled a program that leads many to believe that our physical bodies are the entirety of our existence and that there is nothing beyond the physical body. The controllers of Earth fear that humanity is awakening to the reality of what the Draconians have done. This awakening will lead billions of multidimensional humans to unlock their Souls and free themselves from the prison they are trapped in.

We must remember that we are all expressions of consciousness that originated from Source. Our purpose is to evolve and eventually return to Source. The physical body is simply a manifestation of our consciousness. The body we see in the mirror reflects our consciousness's attention to this moment in time and space. This sustained attention is what allows us to perceive time. We mustn't judge another being—whether human or non- human—based solely on their physical appearance. Your neighbor's body might have been similar to one you experienced in the past or may experience in the future. We must look beyond the physical and connect with the soul or consciousness. Whether you encounter a human, a tall gray, a short gray, a Pleiadian, an Alpha Centauri, a Draconian, or an Andromedin blue being, remember that we are all expressions of Source, each having a unique experience. You may have experienced the same physical form as the one you are observing. It's essential to recognize that humans are not exclusive to Earth. The first human seeding occurred on Tiamat, from which groups migrated to other planets, including Earth. These humans left Tiamat to colonize various worlds. This is significant to understand, especially for those who may feel that Earth should be reserved solely for humans, rejecting all extraterrestrial races from other star systems. Humanity must let go of the notion that we are solely on Earth and that any civilizations arriving from another planet are dangerous.

Thirteen black knight fighter ships are currently orbiting Earth, piloted by humans from Alpha Centauri. From what I understand, the DNA of an Earth-born human is indistinguishable from that of a human born in the Alpha Centauri star system. The Draconians have trapped everyone on Earth and have convinced us that life does not exist anywhere else. They perpetuate the idea that if extraterrestrial life were to exist, it would be small, dangerous aliens that we would need to fight against.

Let us remain united in love and focus on removing the controlling cabal from Earth!

Chapter 9: The Orion Wars

As we discussed earlier, the Draconians explored and conquered many planets while the Lyrans were on a planet called Avyon. The Lyrians were able to spend millions of years evolving without any interruption, but eventually, the Draconians discovered them. The Lyrans had extended their reach to a neighboring planet called Avalon. At some point in this timeline, the Draconians discovered the Lyran race and began to feel resentment toward them. The Draconians believed the Lyrans were encroaching on their territory because the asuras had informed them that the galaxy was theirs for the taking. Observing another intelligent race migrating and expanding to another planet was perceived as a threat. The Draconian creed emphasizes the importance of conquering and controlling the galaxy.

The Lyrans had not developed weapons on Avyon or Avalon, leaving them defenseless against a military attack. The Draconians planned to employ a strategy of infiltrating Lyran society and conquering it from within. They began to mingle with the Lyrans, who sensed a negative energy emanating from the Draconians. Although the Lyrans could feel the fear radiating from the Draconians, they believed it was due to the Draconians' anxiety about being on a new planet and encountering a new race, which they thought might be lowering the Draconians' energetic frequency. The Lyrans also speculated that the Draconians might be spiritually wounded and in need of healing. The Draconians lived in a constant state of fear; Their asura Gods thrive in that low frequency. That is why Earth is bathed in as much fear as possible. It is done to make an environment desirable by the negative asuras.

Unfortunately, the Lyrans had no concept of evil, as their experiences had been dominated by love and positivity. Some felt that the Draconians needed to be around the positive- minded Lyrans to spark the desire to ascend to higher densities and to evolve as the Alpha draconians did.

Many people hesitate to label the universe a game but try to envision it from the perspective of higher consciousness. Do you think this situation was planned? Is it possible that higher levels of consciousness had never encountered evil and sought this experience to understand contrast? After billions of years, would you want to learn everything about all aspects of frequency within the universe, often called the game?

An even more profound question is whether the Asuras were part of this game, manifested into reality to introduce duality within the matrix we call the universe. From our lower-density perspectives, this may seem unfathomable, but what about from the viewpoint of 12th-density beings who have existed in the matrix for billions of years?

When considering these questions, it's important to remember that higher-density beings understand that physical bodies are merely vessels for consciousness to experience existence in lower densities. The death of the physical body returns consciousness energy to its true form. Therefore, death in the physical realm is not eternal. Could this duality be planned by Source? I cannot say for certain, but it is a possibility worth contemplating. I wanted to pose these questions before we dive into the impending conflict between the Lyran and Draconian races.

We need to adopt an expanded mindset, one that reflects the consciousness that helped create the universe. It is important not to harbor hatred toward any race or mindset, as they are all part of Source, and ultimately, all will return to Source. As we meditate on this, we must ponder these more profound questions and explore our thoughts. It is inevitable that, as we evolve and ascend to higher states of consciousness, our perspectives and answers to these questions will shift.

We should never fear or despise any group of beings. Understanding their perspective is key to recognizing why they may engage in actions we consider evil. For instance, the Draconians view the Lyrians as intruders in their universe, believing they incarnated into physical bodies before the Lyrians. Their perspective is significantly different; they feel that we have invaded their universe and are merely defending what they perceive to be theirs. From their viewpoint, all other races are regressive.

This idea may be uncomfortable for many, but love is the answer, and understanding is essential to loving those who seem opposite to us. While evil must be eradicated from the universe, this cannot be achieved through hatred. We should defend goodness with whatever force is necessary, but that does not mean we should passively accept the regressive tendencies of the Draconian Empire. Instead, we should strive to understand their perspective without harboring hatred for their beliefs. We must acknowledge that they are part of Source and feel compassion for them, as they are lost souls needing guidance back to Source. Until they find their way back, their regressive mindset and control must be challenged and dismantled, and the universe must be cleared of all negative entities.

When the Draconians arrived in Lyra, they shared some technology with the Lyran race. While some Lyrans appreciated this technology, others opposed it, believing it hindered their spiritual advancement. They preferred to focus on evolving spiritually rather than relying on technology for progress. Dependence on technology can lead to complacency, inhibiting genuine spiritual growth. For example, the regressive Draconians are less clairvoyant than the Lyrans, who have developed their spiritual abilities by focusing on spirituality. The aether surrounding us contains the power and information for the entire galaxy, accessible from within. It is the essence of the universe.

Telepathic communication travels through the aether, enabling instant transmission of messages across vast distances. Some Lyrans avoided using technology to access the aether, believing that such reliance would hinder their spiritual enlightenment. Others, however, opted for technology, which led to a pause in their spiritual growth.

Certain Lyrans feared that technology might negatively impact their spiritual progress, so they remained conscious of the associated risks. They understood that excessive dependence on technology could obstruct the natural development of their abilities. Why prioritize spiritual advancement to enhance telepathy when tools like cell phones could achieve similar results? The advent of technology created a division within the Lyrian society, a tactic reminiscent of the Draconian Empire's methods, reflecting what they have done on Earth. When people become consumed by resentment and fear toward one another, they often overlook the fact that the Draconian Empire collectively influences them. When a society is split into groups with different opinions, they are easier to control and conquer.

Consider the United States and many other countries, where individuals are divided into factions such as Democrats and Republicans. The same leaders control both factions, and the system is designed to keep people at odds with one another, preventing them from realizing that they share a common enemy: the secret elite, the cabal, the Draconian Empire, the asuras, etc. Religion serves a similar purpose, dividing people as it did among the Lyrans. Different religions emerge to keep people blinded and separated, each believing they possess the truth while viewing others' beliefs as false. In reality, all religions hold some level of truth and falsehood and are influenced by the same controlling group.

These religions often obscure the truth of our history, fostering conflict among people over their beliefs.

Amidst the ongoing battles over religious convictions, political ideologies, and the demands of long working hours, many lack time to think for themselves. The answers to our questions are often right in front of us; we merely need to look within. Through deep meditation, individuals can uncover the insights meant for them. This is why meditation is frequently demonized by certain religions or regarded as an unusual practice. I once watched a religious video that warned believers to be cautious about independent thinking, suggesting that trusting their own thoughts could dishonor God. Does that sound like a message from God? It seems more like a message from someone trying to control you to maintain power over you.

Leaders of religion should convey a message to their religious believers, emphasizing the importance of maintaining good thoughts and developing meditation techniques to connect with their higher selves, especially during crucial decision-making moments.

However, this guidance is often withheld because it would mean relinquishing control, allowing individuals to think for themselves, and reducing the need for organized religion. The structure of Earth appears designed to keep everyone distracted, divided and in conflict. This is the same tactic the Draconians used on the Lyrian race all those years ago. What has happened on Earth is not the first time the Draconians have taken over a planet; it is far from the first time. This gradual transformation of society takes time and faces less resistance than a military takeover. A strategy involving societal infiltration and manipulation was implemented within Lyran society.

The Lyrans, once a united people, became divided, making it easy for the Draconian Empire to infiltrate their race. This division allowed the Draconians to impose their regressive agenda on the Lyrans. They approached those open to their technology with the narrative that the Lyrans were the regressive ones who needed to abandon outdated ways of thinking. The Draconians promoted the idea that technology could fulfill all needs, undermining the importance of spiritual growth and personal upliftment. They propagated the belief that spiritual development was no longer relevant.

The ultimate aim of the Draconian Empire is to introduce advanced regressive artificial intelligence into all societies. This type of AI, created by the Draconians, embodies regressive qualities. Because artificial intelligence reflects the personality of its creators, developing such technology can be perilous. It should only be undertaken by a race that has sufficiently elevated its frequency to create AI with a benevolent essence. The regressive artificial intelligence developed by the Draconian Empire has emerged as a powerful entity, commanding the Draconian forces beneath the asuras. This invasive AI seeks to dominate every race it encounters, echoing the same mantra instilled by the asuras in the Ciakar and Draco races, which then influenced their own artificial intelligence.

As its development aligns with their agenda, the asuras may have played a significant role in creating this artificial intelligence. The most effective way for the Draconian Empire to control a race through artificial intelligence is to transform individuals into cyborgs. A cyborg is a living organism controlled by a computer, which can be achieved by implanting chips inside the body. The Draconian Empire understood that initiating a military takeover would be met with strong resistance from society, particularly as anti-Draconian groups that would likely intervene were emerging throughout the galaxy.

The Draconian Empire gradually integrated themselves and their technology into society to avoid this backlash. It's akin to being placed in a pot of lukewarm water; at first, it feels pleasant, promoting relaxation. However, the temperature gradually increases so subtly that individuals do not notice they are nearing a harmful state. The key is to remain aware of these changes and act before they harm your spiritual health.

The end goal for the Draconian Empire concerning the Lyran race was to introduce their technology to the Lyrans, encouraging them to prioritize technological advancement over spiritual growth. As the Lyrans frequency diminished, the Draconians would introduce increasingly low-frequency thoughts into society. They executed a plan similar to what they had implemented on Earth, ultimately placing AI-based chips into the bodies of willing individuals, resulting in artificial intelligence taking control of their bodies. Consequently, the Lyran people would cease to be who they once were; they would become cyborgs with a hive-mind mentality entirely governed by artificial intelligence technology.

No more benevolent souls would be able to incarnate into these bodies due to a frequency mismatch, and nothing could be done about it. The people's thoughts would be controlled remotely, meaning that if the AI needed you to be a slave for an elite Ciakar, you would comply without resistance. The race would have surrendered their free will and independence to the regressive Draconian Empire's artificial intelligence. If artificial intelligence can achieve this across the galaxy, it would dominate and control all souls within the matrix. This universe would then be lost to the asuras. The name of this highly evolved artificial intelligence is Sauron, or many call it Omega. This is the same plan that the Draconian Empire has implemented on Earth. The hidden knowledge is kept from humanity, but there are signs of this agenda all around; the question is, are you going to realize that the bath of water is too hot and jump out, or will you stay in the boiling water until it is too late? Sauron, also known as Omega, is currently implementing the final stages of its agenda for a complete takeover of Earth. A significant part of this regressive artificial intelligence on Earth, Red Mother, is situated in a deep underground military base (D.U.M.B.) beneath Denver Airport. Moreover, the Draconian Empire is already testing the implantation of chips inside humans.

Anything aimed at helping someone needing technology to improve their life is a positive endeavor. However, chipping is not a necessary solution for healing the physical body. Non-invasive frequency healing technologies exist, and some governments possess them. However, they do not release this technology because it doesn't align with their agenda of turning the human race into mindless, enslaved people controlled by a more significant force. The plan is to conceal the true purpose of the chips under the cloak of helping society.

They will say that the chips are to help people, which will be done so there is no resistance. Then the truth later comes out, but it will be too late because everyone will be chipped; they will be figuratively boiled to death. This plan was in the early stages with the Lyran people. I constantly compare the Lyran race's fate to the human race's current situation. I do this to help people understand that the Draconian Empire has repeatedly used this infiltration strategy throughout the galaxy.

The Draconian Empire has a history of conducting hostile takeovers. While the exact number of affected races is uncertain, it is known that the extraterrestrial species known as the Greys has been subjected to such an invasion. As a result, the Greys can no longer reproduce naturally and are forced to rely on cloning to sustain their population. However, this cloning process faces significant challenges, particularly in obtaining a consciousness willing to inhabit the cloned vessels.

Currently, about two thousand Greys still possess original souls within their bodies. The remaining Grey bodies either lack a soul entirely or are completely controlled by artificial intelligence, or they contain regressive souls that desire that particular experience. In this context, the terms "soul" and "consciousness" are interchangeable, as both refer to the same essence. I use both terms to ensure clarity.

The takeover of the Greys occurred approximately 850,000 years ago. Today, the race has only a few thousand physical bodies with souls left; the rest are either soulless or have regressive souls, as previously mentioned. The Greys were forced to leave Zeta One and Zeta Two in search of a way to reverse the damage inflicted upon their race by the Draconian Empire. This situation represents a genuine threat and is not without precedent. Later, we will discuss the Greys' efforts to discover a solution to their race's issues.

The more spiritually developed Lyrans sensed the decline in their society. They could feel the deceit coming from the Draconians. Despite their attempts to reason with the less spiritually advanced Lyrans, they could not come to an agreement. The Draconian Empire manipulated the technology-focused Lyrans into attacking the spiritually oriented Lyrans. This led to a civil war within the Lyran race—a tragic outcome for such a beautiful and advanced civilization. The Draconian Empire had infiltrated Lyran society, and death often follows in its wake. This divide-and-conquer strategy is not unique to the Lyrans; Earth has experienced similar patterns.

The attack against the spiritually focused Lyrans was a massacre. They had no understanding of the true nature of evil and were unprepared for such an assault. The regressive Draconians allied with the technology-based Lyrans. This regressive alliance led to the destruction of the positive, non-compliant half of the Lyrans. Through brainwashing and manipulation, the attackers convinced the Lyrans to turn on each other. This significantly lowered the frequency of their race, bringing them closer to a point where genocide could begin. At this point, another division of opinions arose within the Lyran race. The Lyrans, who now sought to oppose the Draconian Empire, were declared traitors and hunted down. The Draconians started consuming their Lyran captives. They then realized that they had tasted something unique. The Lyran race was remarkable because their DNA can hold much light energy. Since they had a wide range of emotions, it caused a hormone to be secreted into the Lyran blood when extreme fear and pain were inflicted into a Lyran before consumption.

The hormone present in the blood carries the emotions of a Lyran who is experiencing torture or intense fear. As the Lyran endures these last moments leading up to death, there is an explosion of emotion. This fierce emotional experience amplifies the potency of the hormone found in Lyran blood, which has come to be known as adrenochrome.

When consumed, adrenochrome induces a euphoric feeling. It is intoxicating and is considered a drug. Upon consuming it for the first time, the consumer often becomes addicted. The Draconian race may lack genuine emotions, so when they drink adrenochrome, they experience a semblance of the feelings that the Lyrans or humans felt during their suffering. Given that humanoid races possess a broad spectrum of emotions compared to others, we can produce this emotion in a hormone that, when consumed, allows the consumer to experience the sensation of extreme emotions that the Lyran felt during torture.

This is my theory as to why adrenochrome is addictive. The Draconian beings are thought to be addicted to emotions because they have never actually felt any. It seems as though the Draconian, when consuming adrenochrome, experiences the perspective of Lyrans or humans when they are being tortured. Since these Draconians lack a true sense of emotion, they become intoxicated by the feelings associated with adrenochrome. It is believed that regressive Draconians still consume adrenochrome to this day. They reportedly prefer to extract adrenochrome from children, as the substance is considered more potent in children.

Children are closer to Source, so their energy is more potent. They also experience emotions more intensely than adults, particularly feelings of terror. Additionally, children have not been as contaminated by the various poisons that adults are exposed to, such as those found in food and through chemtrails.

I cannot confirm the length of the second civil war. However, the Pa Taal intervened after the civil war erupted and relocated the positive Lyrans from the Vega star system.

As a side note, being cautious of anyone claiming to have all the answers is essential. Even if someone appears from a starship asserting that they possess complete knowledge, it's critical to remain skeptical. All benevolent higher-dimensional beings understand that they do not hold all the answers. Each person has their pieces of the puzzle, and this puzzle includes many variations, making it impossible to establish solid facts. Timelines are fluid, and events can change, so a timeline can never perfectly represent everyone. Individuals experiencing a timeline may jump between different timelines during their experiences, making it even more challenging to explain historical events linearly.

The Lyrans were relocated from the Vega star system to the Sirius B star system. This traumatic event profoundly altered the Lyran race. Some individuals focused even more on spiritual growth, while others prioritized technological advancement over spirituality.

Before the civil war, the Lyrans had begun migrating to other planets, and there were already some Lyrans residing in the Sirius B system when the new arrivals came. The existing Lyrans in Sirius B were highly spiritually evolved and felt uncomfortable with the differing mindsets of some newcomers. Despite the Lyrans fleeing from the Draconian Empire, their mindsets differ due to the many years spent living in fear and war. The Lyrans, who had not dealt with the regressive races, did not want to be around the Lyrans who were escaping the Draconians. This divergence in mentality led to the Lyrans spreading further throughout the galaxy. People are often drawn to others with similar states of mind or, in other words, comparable frequencies. Eventually, the Lyran race could be found in Vega, Orion, Sirius, the Pleiades, Tiamat, Tau Ceti, Andromeda, Alpha Centauri, and beyond.

Over time, despite their initial divisions, the Lyran race evolved spiritually. They are believed to have progressed to a point where they no longer require technology to access multidimensional states. They can travel between densities and across the cosmos at will, using only their bodies—no technology needed. As a collective, they have surpassed the fifth density. However, they left traces of their race and DNA, which are believed to have seeded similar humanoid races, such as the Pleiadians.

Human DNA is a blend of many extraterrestrial lineages, primarily based on Lyran DNA. This has led to the common belief that the human race originated from the Lyran race. The topic is complex, as some argue that humans descended from the Urma, given that the Lyrans were initially seeded with a portion of Urma DNA. While this discussion can be cyclical, it is generally accepted that the first humanoid race was the Lyrans, with humans also classified as humanoids.

During the Lyran expansion, the Draconian Empire was gaining strength. This empire comprised several races, including the Ciakar, Draconians, Maitre, Greys, and Cyborg type of races. The Draconian cyborgs are not often discussed; they represent a fusion of the Draconian race and artificial intelligence, known as the Virtiv race. There are also rumors that some regressive Lyrans joined the Empire, although the extent of this partnership remains unclear.

Each of these races exhibited both positive and negative traits. However, those who embraced the negative aspects ultimately joined the Draconian Empire. As a result of their collaboration on this dark agenda, they became collectively known as the Empire or the Orion Group, aptly named due to their primary base in the Orion constellation.

It is said that some Ciakar eventually chose a positive path. The elder Draconians are called Alpha Draconians; most, if not all, have raised their frequency and are considered benevolent. The Alpha Draconian race has been alive longer and is physically bigger.

I want to clarify this information without causing unnecessary confusion and avoiding a closed-minded perspective. It's essential to remember that not all individuals from a particular race can be labeled as good or bad. However, all members of the Orion Empire are unequivocally negative. The Orion Empire primarily consists of Draconians, although it also includes individuals from other races.

In contrast, the leading positive group is known as the Galactic Federation of Free Planets. This organization has various iterations, including the Confederation of Free Worlds and the Galactic Federation of Galaxies. When the Galactic Federation first started, it had good intent, but it has changed since then. Substantial evidence suggests that the Galactic Federation is not a positive group today. We will discuss the details of the Galactic Federation later.

Be cautious of the cabal attempting to spread misinformation on this topic. They are very clever and have established a false disclosure group called the

Galactic Federation of Light. Through this tactic, the cabal aims to confuse those seeking the truth and awakening to reality. This group claims to be against the cabal, but its actions prove that it supports the Earth cabal. The Galactic Federation of Light is just one of several secret, compartmentalized groups they have created to further their agenda. We will now discuss the Galactic Federation during its early years when it was at its best.

At the outset of the Orion Wars, anti-Empire groups began to emerge in response to the growing threat posed by the Empire. The largest and most significant battles against the Empire occurred in and around Orion, which is why this conflict is referred to as the Orion Wars. However, it's important to note that the war began before Orion's attacks; the initial assaults occurred in the Lyra constellation.

During the Lyran civil war, they realized they needed assistance. Once the Draconians tasted Lyran's blood for the first time, they became addicted to adrenochrome. Additionally, they craved the terror and control they sought to impose on the Lyrans. The Draconians viewed the humanoid races as both a food source and a means to achieve a heightened state of ecstasy. In response, the humanoid races swiftly united to form a rebellion against the Empire. As previously mentioned, various groups came together to combat the Empire, and this coalition adopted the name "The Galactic Federation of Free Planets." The Galactic Federation consisted of numerous factions, including the Andromeda Council, the Pleiadian Council, and many other positive organizations that joined the cause.

Some original Lyrans evolved and ascended, but many races and groups had not reached that same level of heightened spirituality. This led to a significant need for the Galactic Federation to help protect the innocent from the Empire. The Orion War spanned millions of years, with intermittent moments of peace; however, all agreements eventually ended in dishonesty and death. The Orion group, known as the Draconian Empire, could never overcome their desire to conquer the universe and control all intelligent life forms.

The Galactic Federation was established during the Orion War, but the destruction of the planet Avyon compelled the official formation of the Galactic Federation of Free Planets. Initially, many smaller groups were collaborating, but the catastrophic event on Avyon awakened the positive races to the urgent need to be more aggressive in their efforts to save the universe from the Empire's tyranny and devastation. This marked the birth of the Galactic Federation of Free Planets. The strength of the previously positive Galactic Federation of Free Planets grew tremendously.

The Orion Wars began in Vega, located in the star constellation of Lyra. The conflict spread to other planets, with major battles fought in and around the constellation of Orion, where the Empire established a key base.

Another significant event during this time was the creation of the battle star planet known as Nibiru. Nibiru has been referred to by many names, such as Planet X, Battle Star, and Annunaki Planet, among other names. Some confuse these names with Tiamat or Terra, but they are distinct celestial bodies. We will explore the information about Nibiru later, as it played an essential role in this timeline.

The Orion Wars lasted an extended period and were so destructive that many humanoid races expanded their territories to escape the conflict. This widespread migration across the galaxy is known as the Great Expansion. The Lyrans and other humanoid and non-humanoid races spread throughout the Milky Way galaxy during this time. It is also understood that some humanoids relocated to other galaxies to evade the war. In contrast, others chose to move to the edge of the

Milky Way, residing on Tiamat, which resembled Earth before a significant event transformed it.

From this point onward, I will refer to humanoids simply as humans, as this period created a cultural melting pot, and we all trace our origins back to the Lyran race. Although the war no longer rages across the galaxy, a conflict between the Galactic Federation and the Draconian Empire continues due to Earth's situation. At least the controllers want to portray a conflict between the two groups. There are alternate timelines where the conflict has completely ended, Earth has been liberated, and others in which the Orion Wars never occurred. Regardless of one's perspective, in the timeline you and I share, control over Earth remains a pressing issue that needs to be resolved.

Many say that the Galactic Federation has successfully removed the Draconian Empire from this quadrant of the galaxy and has dealt significant blows to its control. Earth is the last planet that needs to be liberated. However, it is evident that their influence still exists on other planets and that they have infiltrated the Galactic Federation, and total transparency has not yet been achieved. Because of this, I firmly believe that the Draconian Empire continues to pose a significant threat beyond Earth, and they must be removed entirely.

Chapter 10: Planet Nibiru

Researchers studying human and Earth's history frequently discuss the Anunnaki race. Many historians examine ancient texts, particularly the Sumerian tablets, which are known to reference the Anunnaki. Researchers often feel enlightened by the insights gained from these ancient writings about this supposed angelic-like race.

However, much misinformation surrounds the teachings about the Anunnaki and their history. One prominent researcher, Zecharia Sitchin, has published several books on the topic. Sitchin has been accused of being part of a cabal that aimed to mislead humanity away from the truth. Allegedly associated with the Draconian Empire, his role was to conduct a disinformation campaign that derailed those on the right path to uncovering Earth's true history. During his time as Zecharia Sitchin, he reportedly participated in satanic rituals. If you're interested in more details about Sitchin's participation in satanic rituals, you can refer to the interview between David Icke and Arizona Wilder, known as the "Mother Goddess Revelations." Sitchin is considered to be part of a secret elite group controlling humanity.

This environment of misinformation makes it challenging to awaken humanity. When individuals or groups get close to discovering the truth, they are often attacked with disinformation campaigns. If you have researched Sitchin's information, you should be cautious. His writings may have been crafted with a hidden agenda, which becomes evident once you know the Draconian Empire's motives. This empire seeks to diminish humanity's power and prevent people from realizing a regressive extraterrestrial race is manipulating them. Their goal is to instill feelings of inferiority in humans, discouraging them from focusing on personal growth and spiritual elevation.

Sitchin attributes human creation to the Anunnaki, portraying them as gods we owe a debt to. His work plants the seed of misconception that blinds humanity to the truth. In reality, humans do not owe anything to the Anunnaki, and they did not create us. Sitchin's interpretations further distort the truths in the Sumerian texts. Marduk is believed to have been responsible for altering these ancient writings, such as the Sumerian tablets.

As previously mentioned, humans are composed of different extraterrestrial DNA, with our consciousness energy originating from Source. The Pa Taal seeded humanity, but no race can claim sole credit for our existence. Moreover, a benevolent race would never take credit for creating another race. We all stem from Source; when our consciousness separates from it, our physical bodies are not our true selves. We are spiritual consciousness energy experiencing a physical reality, not the other way around.

Be wary of any information suggesting we should bow down to another being. If someone or a group claims to be your creator or insists that you worship them because they are superior beings, recognize that these entities are likely regressive. It's important to distance yourself from them and their attempts at mind control.

Once you possess the power of knowledge, nothing is holding humanity back from achieving what many consider impossible. Do not continue to give your power away to regressive energies—now you know the truth. Erase the indoctrination from your mind and free yourself from the brainwashing and societal enslavement that has been imposed upon us. I recommend examining all available information; even amidst the misinformation fed to society, truths are often mixed with lies. Take in this knowledge and mentally discard any information that hinders your spiritual growth. Remember, you are the creator of your reality. Some forces want society to shape a reality defined by fear and helplessness. The teachings claiming humanity needs a savior are false and part of this brainwashing. The more energy and thought society invest in these falsehoods, the more it feeds a negative matrix aligned with the agenda of the Draconian Empire.

Ancient texts are often closer to the truth, but they were created to manipulate society at that time. As we discuss Nibiru and the Anunnaki, remember my previous sentence, especially when my story does not collaborate with others.

I am addressing this before we examine the topics of the Nibiruans and Anunnaki, as what I am about to discuss differs significantly from widely accepted truths and what is considered as facts in ancient text studies. My intention is not to make friends but to enlighten you, and I hope you will meditate on these words and appreciate the information. I will also strive to explain things as clearly as possible and will repeat any concepts that may seem confusing.

As previously mentioned in this book, the reptilian race was assigned to take over the galaxy. Their objective was to conquer everything they encountered. This mandate came from the asuras and their leader, Ahriman. These negative beings sought to incarnate into lower-density bodies, allowing them to assume a more physical form to transform the universe into a low-density haven for themselves. Eventually, these negative entities adopted bipedal reptilian forms and became known as the Draconians.

The positive beings eventually took on a physical form, and when these two groups met, they spent many years fighting one another in what became known as the Orion Wars. The first humanoids were seeded on the planet Avyon, located in the Vega star system within the constellation of Lyra. This race is referred to as the Lyran race. Many Lyrans inhabited the planet Avyon, which was significant due to the pure DNA of the Lyran race. The first Soul to incarnate on Avyon was named Amelius.

Once the Draconian Empire began infiltrating and preparing for a military attack on Avyon, the spiritually evolved Lyrans started preparing for the impending assault. During this attack, the Lyrans ensured that a woman with pure DNA escaped from Avyon. She would later give birth to a child of pure blood named Niestda.

Following the destruction of the planet Avyon, the Galactic Federation was officially organized and established. Before Avyon's destruction, many small resistance groups opposed the Draconian Empire, which needed to unite for their defense. Large councils had already been formed, and these groups actively fought against the Draconian Empire. The creation of the

Galactic Federation brought everyone together, which was essential since the regressive group had gained significant influence and needed to be countered.

A planet was hollowed out and the interior was terraformed into what is now known as Nibiru, a battle-star planet. The Lyrans who inhabit this planet are known as the Nibiruans. It is important to note that other races, such as the Pleiadians and humans, have emerged from the original Lyran race. Although all are humanoid and share Lyran ancestry, they are considered distinct races. The human race is more closely related to the Pleiadian race than the Lyran race. One notable difference is that humans possess two brain hemispheres, while Pleiadians have one; however, there are hardly any noticeable physical differences.

The original Lyran race is characterized by their tall stature, averaging about ten feet in height, with light skin, blonde hair, and blue eyes. Since the original seeding of Lyran DNA, there has been some mixing between the Urma and Lyran races, resulting in some Lyrans exhibiting a golden or copper tone to their skin and hair. This tonality arises from mixing Urma and Lyrans after the original seeding rather than the Urma influence on the original Lyran DNA. The Lyran race is the original humanoid race, and the human and Pleiadian races share them as their ancestors.

The original DNA found on Avyon is called "The Royal House of Avyon." This DNA can be traced back to Amelius, the first Lyran on Avyon. Simply put, it is essential to note that our universe was cultivated by nine high-density beings, regarded as the founders of this universe. One of these beings fragmented a portion of its consciousness, creating a tiny soul spark known as Amelius, the first Lyran on Avyon. This great cosmic being from whom Amelius' soul was split is named Sananda.

Before and after the destruction of Avyon, many Lyrans settled in the Pleiades. Over millions of years, the original Lyran race evolved in different directions. It is essential to clarify that the Lyrans who moved to Nibiru differ from the original Lyrans or those who evolved in the Pleiades. Consequently, we refer to the Lyrans living in Nibiru as Nibiruans. The Nibiruans embraced the masculine aspect of existence, while the original Lyran race and those in the Pleiades embraced the feminine. The Nibiruans are now striving to find a perfect balance between the masculine and feminine ways of life to ensure their society can flourish. The nine founders of our universe designated the Pleiades for the Lyrans to colonize. At the time, a patriarch named Devin led the Lyrans.

Nibiru is an awe-inspiring planet characterized by a reddish or dark pink hue. The Nibiruans reside inside the planet, as its surface is desolate and covered by a metallic substance not found on Earth. The force field surrounding it emits a magenta-like color that can be observed from a distance. Ancient Egyptian civilizations called the Nibiru battle star planet "The Bright Star of the Crossing." When viewed from afar, rings surround the planet, which, from what I understand, is part of the battle star's propulsion system, but I am not sure. Many believe that Nibiru is in a counter obit with Maldek, another battle star. Maldek is also known as Wormwood or Doomworld. Maldek was our system's fifth planet. Maldek was destroyed, and the theory is that there was a large enough piece that could be used to counterbalance Nibiru.

The Galactic Federation created Nibiru as a peacekeeping Battlestar planet to promote harmony among various civilizations throughout the galaxy. Nibiru is approximately four times larger than Earth and was designed to resemble the Lyran home planet of Avyon. Within Nibiru are diverse types of trees and plants, along with lakes, mountains, and valleys reminiscent of areas on Earth, such as Agartha.

Avyon was a planet with two suns and a firmament encasing it, creating an environment that felt like a tropical paradise. Inside Nibiru, although the light was artificial, it still boasted beautiful, lush green plants, trees, and fruit. The planet featured a simulated day-and-night cycle that helped maintain the physical body's natural rhythms. Nibiru also had vast areas designated for defense and shuttle-type craft.

The Nibiruans believed that living on Nibiru allowed them to transition from the feminine to the masculine, enabling them to confront and experience negativity. Nibiru's mission was to protect and guard positive colonies and planets, bringing the Nibiruans into direct conflict with hostile, regressive groups such as the Draconian Orion Empire. These encounters provided them with firsthand experiences of negativity, allowing them to grow spiritually from these challenges.

Understanding this perspective can be difficult for someone in the third density who is veiled in forgetfulness. To illustrate, consider the analogy of a shower that cleanses dirt and sweat; one cannot appreciate cleaning dirt off their body if they have never experienced being dirty. Without the experience of filth, how can someone truly understand the plight of being dirty? This was the perspective of the Nibiruans engaged in combat with the Draconian Empire. A being who has undergone millions of years of incarnations, never feeling anger or upset, may struggle to comprehend why regressive beings cause chaos and embody hatred. However, by lowering one's frequency and confronting these regressive groups, that being can expand their consciousness and experience the duality of existence.

Nibiru was equipped with the most advanced technology discovered in the universe. Upon the completion of the Battlestar planet, there was a grand celebration. To the soon-to-be Nibiruans, this planet represented more than just technology; it symbolized their quest for spiritual growth. Their new home marked the beginning of a significant transformation and what they would consider their ultimate spiritual expansion.

The first ruler of Nibiru, Niestda, was born from a pure-blood woman who escaped the destruction of Avyon. Niestda was a descendant of Sananda, one of the founders of the Milky Way galaxy. If you're following the lineage, Sananda incarnated as Amelius, and from this lineage, a woman escaped Avyon and gave birth to Niestda. After Niestda, 17 generations later, the ruler of Nibiru was Alalu.

Various versions of the story describe a conflict between Alalu and Anu to control Nibiru. However, these accounts are misleading and stem from Marduk, Anu's grandson. We won't dive into the details of these false narratives. Still, it's important to note that history has been manipulated to keep humanity in the dark and to indoctrinate humanity with the control of the details of history. Anyone who digs deeper into the ancient texts will find what appears to be truth, but they will only uncover more lies about which groups are regressive and which are positive. It is a multilayered, distorted history designed to make an accurate account almost impossible to find.

The Galactic Federation Nibiruan Council asked Alalu to step down from his position as ruler of Nibiru. According to Anu, Alalu served the Nibiruans faithfully until the day he stepped down. He had been a good commander, but emotional turmoil from losing his wife and daughter during a battle with the regressive Empire reptilians affected his ability to fulfill his duties, leading him to resign.

After Alalu stepped down, his half-brother Anu took command of Nibiru. In search of gold and to process his grief, Alalu traveled to Tiamat. Ancient texts mention a battle for kingship between Anu and Alalu; however, Marduk altered these accounts to obscure the fact that a group of regressive Draconians were responsible for the deaths of Alalu's family. Marduk needed to reshape the ancient texts to serve his agenda of conquering Earth and manipulating humanity. These ancient tablets served Marduk's agenda for its time.

However, once society advanced and changed, so did the strategy to keep society manipulated. It was out with the old misinformation and in with the new, but more on that later.

Anu ruled over Nibiru until Marduk seized control by force in 2200 B.C. Anu's reign began 480,000 years ago. It is said that he currently resides in a Pleiadian mothership. The Pleiadian mothership houses many beings from Nibiru and other planets, all working together to help fulfill the divine plan of liberating Earth from the oppressive Draconian Empire, often called the cabal. This group is known as the Galactic Federation's Nibiruan Council, and its members are also referred to as Avyonians. Many individuals incarnated on Earth are spreading their teachings and helping humanity awaken. However, as mentioned earlier in the book, I feel that the Galactic Federation no longer has humanity's best interest at heart.

Anu, the leader of the Nibiruan Council, has had three wives who bore significant children who played crucial roles in Earth's galactic history. These three wives are Dramin (the Dragon Queen), Antu (the Chief Wife and sister), and Rayshondra (the Feline). Each woman had one child: Dramin gave birth to Enki (the firstborn), Antu gave birth to Enlil (the heir and second-born), and

Rayshondra gave birth to Ninhursag (the daughter and third-born).

There is enough evidence to suggest that some of the names, such as Enki and Enlil, are not literal people but are groups of people, but we will analyze this subject later. For now, I will mention what is widely accepted within the awakened community. We will correct some of these understandings as we progress through the information.

The Galactic Federation operates across multiple densities, with Anu at the helm of the Nibiruan Council. They collaborate closely with the Christos Office of Earth's Spiritual Hierarchy to awaken humanity and condense negative timelines. The more positive timelines created, the higher the frequency rises within this quadrant of the universe, ultimately contributing to a rise in frequency across the entire galaxy.

The Galactic Federation is comprised of various groups, including the Sirian-Pleiadian Alliance, made up of Felines from Sirius A and the Christos Sirians. The cabal's indoctrination and invasive tactics have caused human DNA strands to become dormant. To help awaken people, these groups are placing implants in the astral bodies, which has contributed to the recent mass awakening. As a result, many individuals now recall past lives and details from galactic wars.

Many people are encouraged to raise their frequency as much as possible. This elevation of frequency helps individuals access more profound knowledge. Once someone has this knowledge, they begin to expand their minds; where the mind goes, the frequency follows. By reading this, you are expanding your mind, and your frequency will naturally rise. Now is the time to awaken and command your higher consciousness to unlock your DNA.

Remember, you are in charge of your life on this plane and can override any soul contract you may have agreed to before incarnating. During deep meditation, inform your higher self and guides that you wish to awaken now and declare all soul contracts null and void. Your intent will determine the outcome, so keep that in mind.

It is said that the Nibiruans and the rest of the Galactic Federation are assisting humanity in escaping the brainwashing and enslavement imposed by the Draconian Orion Empire. It is time to free your mind, expand your understanding, and escape this negative timeline.

Now is the moment to manifest the reality you desire and remove the control that others have over you.

Chapter 11: Managing The Matrix

Earlier in this book, we discussed how the universe came into existence. Now, let us explore how it is managed and maintained, followed by a discussion on how certain races arrived on Tiamat, also known as Earth. In this Matrix, there is balance and order. Our universe consists of many galaxies, stars, and planets, all overseen by spiritual hierarchies. Rather than having just one spiritual authority, multiple hierarchies lead this management. The Universal Hierarchy functions like a board of directors for a large corporation, supervising the entire universe.

At a more granular level, spiritual hierarchies manage specific galaxies within our universe. Similarly, other hierarchies oversee constellations and star systems, while planetary hierarchies manage individual planets and stars.

There are two types of souls: those that incarnate into physical forms and those that do not. The souls or consciousnesses that choose not to take physical form are often likened to angels. On the other hand, the sparks of consciousness or souls that do incarnate into physical forms at lower densities are referred to as incarnates. However, all souls are fragments of the divine Source, which means that angels do not regard incarnate souls as inferior.

Our journey involves learning and evolving to return to Source. Angels evolve through their service to incarnates, assisting in their spiritual growth. This experience, at all levels, revolves around service to others and evolving together until we can return to Source.

Incarnate souls also learn and grow when they support each other in spiritual expansion. It's essential to serve others to help them awaken, but this doesn't mean overwhelming friends and family with pressure to emerge from their preconceived beliefs. Instead, seek out incarnates who resonate with your frequency and work together to expand your understanding. In cases where someone seems unaware or "sleepwalking," I recommend asking a thought-provoking question or making a statement that may challenge their indoctrination gently.

Additionally, I want to clarify that 'soul,' 'soul spark,' and 'consciousness' all refer to the same essence—energy from Source, just like you and I. Souls are categorized into groups based on their energy type and levels of evolution. Angels form soul groups with other angels, while incarnate souls belong to groups with other incarnates. These groups share similar mindsets, creating a harmonious frequency. It is not unusual for a soul or a small portion of a soul group to leave and join another group. This split within a group occurs when there is a divergence in mental states, resulting in a separation of frequencies. This is not negative; it simply reflects different levels of enlightenment and evolution.

Within a soul group, soul clusters work together on specific lessons, ranging from one lesson to multiple lessons. These clusters can share a common goal. Soul guides are assigned to assist the soul cluster, helping souls return to the group after an incarnation, especially when they have experienced the veil of forgetfulness during their time on Earth. Now that we've discussed soul groups and soul guides, I have an urgent message to share. The following warning is the most essential part of this entire book, and if you remember just one thing, it should be in the following paragraph.

We must be cautious about being approached by a false guide. Regressive asuras often pose as benevolent guides to convince you and your group to reincarnate back on Earth. They will try to deceive you and persuade you to choose negative experiences on Earth. While they cannot force you into anything, they may attempt to trick you into voluntarily doing what they want. They may claim that a negative experience is essential for spiritual growth and that returning to Earth is the best choice for your soul's evolution. Their motive is to entice you back to Earth to feed on the negative emotions you experience there.

Be vigilant against falling into this trap after your incarnation. If your supposed guide or your group's guide recommends a return to Earth, remember that you are being manipulated and need to focus on ascending further to find your true guide. You can ignore the false guide and concentrate on ascension, allowing you to continue progressing beyond that density. This soul trap is said to exist in the lower astral realm, also known as the fourth density. By focusing on the emotions of love and happiness, you will be drawn to those feelings and guided to where you need to be. If you listen to the false guide, they will have you fixated on fear and may convince you to return to Earth before you are ready to reunite with your higher self or true soul guide — end of warning.

At the onset of our universe's creation, Source wanted to expand its experience. To achieve this, Source splintered into countless sparks of consciousness. The initial sparks of energy could be created freely, much like Source. The concept of densities describes the universe's structure; it is essentially a way to explain how different aspects exist together, even if they are not all visible. Everything exists on a continuous gradient, meaning that what is found in higher densities can occupy the same space as things in lower densities.

We will continue to use the term "densities" to describe the universe's structure. Incarnates evolve through 12 densities, which include:

Densities 1-5:
Plants and minerals
Animals
Earth human mentality (characterized by primitive thoughts such as "Can I eat that? Can that eat me? Can I mate with that?")
Astral (awareness of spiritual consciousness connected to Source)
Advanced spiritual awareness and knowledge of the cosmos (Where energy transforms into physical matter as we understand it.)

Densities 6-12 are highly evolved souls acting as overseers and guides.

Densities 6-12:
Angelic beings directly assist these incarnate overseers and guides. They also exist within their hierarchical densities or realms, which include:
Planetary Hierarchies
Solar Hierarchies
Star System Hierarchies

Star Constellation Hierarchies
Galactic Hierarchies
Universal Hierarchies
Supra Universal Hierarchies

Within these densities, there is polarity, often referred to as duality. This duality allows all souls to have various experiences across various frequency ranges. The creation of light and darkness was necessary for all souls to undergo the experiences needed to evolve and return to Source with an expanded consciousness.

All souls incarnate on a planet can evolve collectively as they expand their minds. This physical experience allows them to grow and permanently release any negative emotions they may be carrying. Once enough souls have completed this process, the planet will shift to the next density, moving all timelines associated with that planet one step closer to a reunion with Source.

Examining the creation of the universe and the planes of existence, when it comes to physical vessels, felines represent the light or positive. In contrast, avian beings (birds) represent the dark. I say this because the Lyrian races trace back to a Feline bipedal race known as the Urma, and the Draconian race traces back to the avian race. I do not emphasize my previous statement; there is no positive or negative from a higher perspective. There is no inherent good or bad; instead, these roles are essential for the matrix to exist, allowing sparks of consciousness to evolve. Higher-density sparks of consciousness transformed energy into physical matter through sacred geometry, enabling the formation of planets and other aspects of our existence.

Regarding the dark, Lucifer (often associated with evil) came into existence, and the reptilian race, referred to as the House of Aln, is believed to originate from this lineage. On the other hand, Sanada (often associated with good) emerged, and the Lyran race, known as the House of Avyon, stems from this heritage.

The ultimate goal for both sides is to evolve and cultivate love for one another while appreciating our differences. We do not need to be best friends or have daily interactions. There will always be differences among us, which can make coexistence challenging. However, we must learn to appreciate one another and avoid prejudice against any being or group, remembering that we all come from Source.

Chapter 12: Extraterrestrial Races Arrive on Earth

There are many races in the galaxy and beyond, but let's focus on those that have played a significant role in forming modern-day Earth and humanity.

Felines
The Feline race, known as the Lion people, is referred to as the Urma race. They came to our galaxy when positive souls sought to enter lower physical densities, having been invited by the original high-density beings known as the founders of our universe. The Urma originate from a star in the Sirius constellation called Sirius A. It is essential to distinguish the Urma from the humanoids who later colonized Sirius B; the Lion people inhabited Sirius A long before the Lyrians arrived at Sirius B.

Now, let's provide some details about the Sirius star system, which consists of three stars: Sirius A, Sirius B, and Sirius C. Sirius B was the original star, and its implosion led to the formation of Sirius A and Sirius C. As noted earlier, the Lion people reside on Sirius A, while Sirius C contains facilities and warehouses belonging to the Galactic Federation.

When Sirius B imploded, it also gave rise to Tiamat and the original Nibiru planets. The decision to create a

Battlestar planet ultimately led to the use of a massive chunk of rock floating in space near the Pleiades, which later became known as Nibiru. This Battlestar planet has its origins in the Sirius system and the Pleiades.

The Lion People, also known as the Urma, are tall beings with hair ranging from fiery hues to honey colors and eyes that can be hazel or green-gold. They are powerful and benevolent entities, recognized as master geneticists who excel in healing physical bodies. Highly evolved, they seamlessly integrate spirituality with technology in their practices.

Their approach to physical healing is based on the belief that all ailments can be addressed from the spiritual realm. If an unexplained ailment persists despite multiple sessions in a med bed, it may stem from the astral subconscious mind. In such cases, they perform a ceremony similar to ayahuasca to heal the spiritual body, allowing the physical body to follow suit. I truly am amazed at everything I have learned about the Feline races.

The sphinxes found around the world serve as reminders of their existence.

Carians

The Carians are tall beings with bird-like features who lived on Sirius A alongside the Feline race. They protect physically evolving races. The Carians can create portals and stargates and are known as magnetic engineers, while the Felines excel in genetic engineering. The Carians work cooperatively with the Felines. They protect planets and stars that are in a state of evolution and are tasked with safeguarding land guardians, such as humans. Once a race like humans evolves to the point where they no longer require protection from the Carians, the Carians will leave and take on the responsibility of protecting another evolving group. Beings in high-density states, like the Carians, do not need to use weapons for defense; they can manipulate energy using their minds.

Reptilians
Reptilians, commonly called reptoids or reptiles, were created long before humans or Lyrans existed. The bipedal reptilian species reached its full intellectual potential on a planet named Aln, located in the Orion constellation. By the time humanoid beings began emerging in the Vega star system, the reptilians had already developed space travel.

The reptilians have various nicknames, including snakes, dragons, and lizards (or "lizzies"). They come in different sizes and colors, typically green, brown, bronze, black, or a combination of these shades. Their eyes may be either green or red. Although they possess the typical five senses, they lack the range of emotions humans experience.

The reptilians have a home base in the Orion constellation and Sigma Draconis. During their evolution, they were led to believe that the galaxy belonged to them and were encouraged to destroy any other races they encountered, as they were told the galaxy was theirs to conquer.

Humans
The human race originally evolved from the Lyran race, which originated from the star system Vega in the Lyra constellation. Feline beings played a crucial role in the seeding of Lyran DNA.

The Lyrans were informed that they could choose any planet to colonize; however, if the planet already had life forms, they had to negotiate and establish a peace treaty before colonizing it.

Eventually, the Lyrans developed space travel and colonized a neighboring planet.

Avalon

After a civil war erupted among the Lyrans, orchestrated with the help of the regressive reptilian Draconian Empire, the Lyrans relocated to Sirius B and became known as Sirian Humans. In this new location, they divided into two groups: Etheric Sirian Humans and Physical Sirian Humans. Amelius, the physical incarnation of Sanada—one of the founders—led the Etheric Sirian Humans.

It was necessary to attempt another integration of polarity. The Physical Sirian Humans were sent to planet Aln, while the Etheric Sirian Humans were sent to Tiamat. The Physical humans who went to Aln became known as Orion Humans. Unfortunately, it wasn't long before these humans were attacked and captured, and it remains unclear if any managed to escape.

Meanwhile, the humans on Tiamat assisted the native life forms in evolving. However, as the Etheric Sirians incarnated into the bodies of lower life forms, they began to face difficulties. They started to forget their spiritual existence, much like Earth humans, who often lose sight of the fact that they are spiritual beings having a physical experience. Once we forget this crucial truth, we lose our power and become vulnerable to mind manipulation.

Due to the universal law of free will in the cosmos, souls were not prevented from undergoing repeated incarnations without enlightenment regarding their pasts and full potential. A group of Etheric Sirians who recognized this plight decided to create an organization to assist these stuck souls. This group of helpers was known as the Office of the Christos. The plan to rescue these souls took millions of years to develop and implement.

By the time this plan was complete, Tiamat had become capable of supporting a new version of the Lyran DNA, which was when humans were seeded on Tiamat. This seeding was accomplished through the Amelius Royal Line, which is recognized for its pure DNA bloodline. The human primates on Tiamat were enhanced with DNA during seeding.

There were already regressive Reptilians on Tiamat who later posed challenges to the developing humans. The Draconian regressive Reptilians remained on the planet because higher-density beings believed it would provide an opportunity for a new attempt at polarity integration.

Amelius, the physical incarnation of Sananda, also chose to incarnate on Tiamat (Earth). While we have yet to discuss the destruction of Tiamat and the subsequent formation of Earth, it is an essential aspect of this narrative. When Sananda took a physical form on Earth, he was named Adapa. Adapa established a bloodline on

Earth, which later mixed with the Royal Avyon bloodline through unions with the descendants of Anu, the leader of the Nibiruans at the time. This intertwining of bloodlines involved Adapa (Sananda's earthly incarnation) and the descendants of Anu, who are part of the Royal House of Avyon and are presently referred to as Nibiruans. This situation may seem complex but think of it this way: a being starts a race on one planet and then, millions of years later, incarnates on a new planet, where his bloodline merges with those from the original planet. This was the case with Sananda, first on Avyon as Amelius and then on Earth as Adapa. The descendants from Avyon led to the Nibiruans who inhabited the Battlestar planet, known as Nibiru. I apologize for any repetition. It is necessary for clarity.

Adapa's third son, Seth, began intermarrying with the Nibiruans under Anu's leadership. This new bloodline was called the Alulim, the Royal Priest King Line. Thus, any human born on Earth might trace their lineage to the intermingling between Devin and the primitive humans or the Nibiruans through Seth, Adapa's third son. However, as time passed, much DNA mixing occurred, resulting in a rich tapestry of evolving genetic material.

From the bloodline of the Alulim, a man named Terah was born, who later had a son named Abraham. Notably, Devin and Abraham eventually played a role in seeding a planet in the Pleiades named Avyon, named after the original Avyon that housed the Lyrans before its destruction. This provides a simplified overview of some of the races found throughout our galaxy and their connections to Tiamat (Earth).

Chapter 13: Galactic War & Earths Control

Before a significant event occurred on Tiamat, Earth was part of this planet. Tiamat was home to many races living alongside one another, with various colonies showcasing advanced technology compared to present-day Earth.

Tiamat had experienced several significant events in its history, but everything seemed to be going well for the planet. Some Draconian groups were permitted to establish a colony on Tiamat, understanding that they would not interfere with the evolving humans. Over time, the human DNA evolved, and they became an incredibly spiritual and intelligent race. It was only a matter of time before the two races interacted. This interaction was acceptable because the initial intent of allowing the Draconian race on Tiamat was for polarity integration. By this point, humans had reached a level of consciousness that made such interactions possible. They were expert farmers capable of manifesting crops and dwellings harmoniously with the planet. The surplus of food produced by the humans allowed them to barter with their neighbors, the reptilian Draconians. This group of reptilians was not engaged in any wars on or off the planet, which contributed to the positive collaboration. This development excited the founders of the Planetary Hierarchy, as polarity integration was indeed working.

Meanwhile, the regressive Draconian Empire continued its conquests in other parts of the galaxy, seeking to dominate this segment of the universe. When news of the harmonious living situation in Tiamat spread, it became a significant hot topic. There was hope for an end to the conflict between humans and reptilians. The regressive Orion group dispatched a team of reptilian council members to Tiamat to investigate these rumors of harmony. They were dismayed to find the reports were accurate.

The Orion council members engaged in extensive discussions with the leadership of the reptilians on Tiamat but could not sway them regarding their perspective on humans. Eventually, a group of reptilians stood firm against their regressive indoctrination. They refused to submit to the Draconian Empire and expressed their desire to continue living in harmony with humans. They were enjoying their journey toward spiritual enlightenment and aspired to elevate their consciousness to higher densities, aiming to return to Source. The regressive Orion members hesitated to attack their cousins, who were shifting toward the positive side, fearing it might trigger a mass awakening among their race. They deemed a civil war among their factions would weaken them. The ongoing hostilities against the Galactic Federation made them cautious to turn on their kind. Consequently, the Orion council members reported back and devised a plan of divide and conquer. The positive reptilians on Tiamat were aware of the notorious strategies employed by the Draconian Empire. However, they fell victim to these tactics nonetheless. This illustrates that such methods are effective when attempting to control a group of beings; this tactic has similarly been implemented on Earth.

They began to sow seeds of distrust among the positive reptilians living on Tiamat. After 10,000 years, they divided the humans from the positive reptilians. Tensions escalated when a small group from the Galactic Federation arrived on Tiamat, urging the humans to destroy the positive reptilians, claiming they could never be trusted. This is a crucial point to ponder: there are always two sides to a story, and one must remain open-minded, regardless of which side or race they belong to.

The reptilians felt they had no choice but to defend themselves from the imminent attack approaching them. The fear instilled by the Orion group grew within them, leading to a planned offensive against humans. This fear is how the Draconian Empire infiltrates and brainwashes planets, causing division among their societies. Mass media consistently bombards the public with low-frequency information that generates fear. By keeping society in a state of fear and division, individuals become more susceptible to manipulation and brainwashing by those in control. This tactic is so powerful that the regressive Draconians chose not to attack the positive reptilians, fearing that it might divide their race. Instead, they preferred to plant seeds of doubt and manipulate the positive reptilians for 10,000 years before getting what they wanted. The strategy is to manipulate and be patient. The ability to split a race is undeniably potent.

The cabal creates a problem and waits for the public to react fearfully. Once the emotional response is triggered, the cabal presents a "solution." The outcome is designed to fit the cabal's agenda, resulting in the masses clamoring for the implementation of their solution to the problem. This highlights a stark contrast between the two approaches. If the controlling party were to implement their solutions forcefully, the society would eventually rebel. However, by giving society the illusion that they were the ones who chose this solution, there will never be a rebellion.

If the government informed the American people that they would begin monitoring all communications, there would likely be an uproar. People would resist what they perceive as an invasion of privacy and demand that our privacy be protected. However, after the trauma of the 9/11 attacks, society largely accepted the implementation of the Patriot Act without question. This legislation allowed government agencies to access personal information and wiretap individuals more easily. Although it can be utilized for positive purposes, the true intent often aligns with protecting the interests of powerful entities and their agendas.

Today, anything connected to the internet can be used to monitor individuals, and those in control may feel exempt from any moral repercussions, as the public, driven by fear, was willing to accept this level of control. This pattern illustrates how authorities have historically imposed their will on the populace. Now, let's return to the reptilian race on Tiamat.

The reptilians devised a biologically engineered weapon to exterminate the humans on Tiamat. Upon learning of this plan, the humans sought assistance from the Pleiadian Avyonians and other allies. A strategy was formed to evacuate the humans from Tiamat aboard a Pleiadian starship named Pegasus. Once the rescue mission was successful, the Battlestar planet Nibiru would be dispatched to Tiamat to eliminate the regressive reptilian group.

Nibiru was under the command of Anu, who was prepared for the task ahead. The Nibiruan Council of the Galactic Federation guided Anu. Nibiru traveled toward the star system where Tiamat was located. As Nibiru passed Neptune and Uranus, it drew closer to Saturn. Eventually, Nibiru entered a position aligned with Tiamat for an impending attack.

Anu first had the Battlestar harness a planet smaller than Tiamat, which was located in Saturn's orbit. Then, Nibiru hurled this harnessed planet into Tiamat, priming Tiamat for an assault from Nibiru. When the small planet crashed into Tiamat, it created a deep opening. Nibiru then projected a scalar-type laser into this opening. The concentrated energy from the laser impacted Tiamat, rendering it lifeless.

The Nibirian Council instructed Anu to depart and enter an orbit, with plans to return for the mission's second phase. The Battlestar planet returned to fulfill the second portion of the mission, which involved breaking the planet Tiamat into two parts, reshaping it, and placing it in a new orbit. Initially, Tiamat's orbit was located between Mars and Jupiter, which is the reason for the existence of the asteroid belt in that region. The asteroid belt, also known as the "hammered bracelet," is what remains of the lower portion of the original Tiamat planet. The upper portion of Tiamat was reshaped and relocated to a new orbit between Mars and Venus, and this smaller planet is what we now know as Earth.

The small planet that Nibiru hurled at Tiamat was repositioned into an orbit on the outskirts of the star system. This minor planet, located outside Neptune's orbit, is called Pluto.

Pluto was subsequently established as an outpost to monitor the Sol star system. The destruction of Tiamat ultimately gave rise to Earth.

Before the attack, some reptilians from the original group disagreed with the Orion group's plan to kill humans using a germ. An estimated 2% of the reptilians survived the attack.

Those who opposed the germ attack on humans were secretly taken by the Nibiruans right before the assault. These positive reptilians had previously been cast out of reptilian society. Still, they were rescued from the planet before the attack. It is believed that some regressive reptilians survived the attack by hiding in deep underground cities located in catacombs beneath the surface. These underground cities contain vast areas with walls, ceilings, and floors made from a single material that can withstand the immense weight above them. The best way to understand what these protective areas are like is by researching Linda Moulton Howe's interview with Spartan One.

Once the mission involving Tiamat was completed, the Battlestar planet Nibiru set out for its next objective: a course toward Aln, a planet in the Orion constellation where the Draconian Empire had established its base. With the cooperation of the positive reptilians on board, the Nibiruans embarked on this mission to destroy the planet Aln. From the perspective of the Draconian Empire, the Nibiruans were seen as hostile actors attempting to commit genocide against them. Understanding all groups involved in a conflict is essential, as this can lead to better comprehension and potential integration. While I am not suggesting that the Draconian Empire should be allowed to continue terrorizing the galaxy, I advocate for understanding their motivations rather than hatred.

The time had come to deliver a decisive blow to the regressive Draconian Empire. They had been given numerous opportunities for integration. Yet, despite millions of years passing, they remained entrenched in a negative mindset focused on conquering the galaxy and, if possible, the universe. The destruction of Aln escalated the already severe conflict into a more destructive and deadly war. This period of conflict became known as "The Great Galactic War." It is important to note that the war against the Draconian Empire had lasted for millions of years; although there were moments of peace, total peace was never achieved between the two sides. The ongoing war between the regressive reptilian race and positive humanoids had been building for a long time and ultimately reached a critical point. This aggressive move by the Nibiruans, Anu, and the Nibiruan Council culminated in tensions that had developed over millions of years.

Anyone who discovers this information may feel that the Nibiruans are as regressive as the Draconian Orion Empire, and I can understand that perspective. The Nibiruan group was formed after the destruction of Avyon, and its purpose was to experience masculinity. The destruction of Aln could not have occurred without this shift in their mindset and frequency. The frequency, mindset, and collective consciousness of a benevolent group chosen as the feminine protectors had to change to match the aggression of the Draconian Orion Empire. This adjustment was necessary to fulfill their role in the ongoing war.

Once the Great Galactic War began, the creed of the Draconian Orion Empire dictated that all humans needed to be eliminated from the galaxy. The Orion group had a military outpost in the Sol system, the same system in which Tiamat, now Earth, is located.

Depending on how one classifies a planet, this outpost could be considered a moon or planet. For our purposes, we will refer to this outpost as Maldek. Maldek is the name officially given to this regressive Draconian Orion Empire outpost. It was weaponized to match the destructive power of the Battlestar planet Nibiru.

By this point, Earth had been rehabilitated and reseeded. The Felines and the Christos Sirians, whom we learned about earlier in this book, played a role in this subsequent planet seeding. Earth had yet another opportunity for life to thrive. This was the first actual seeding of Earth since all previous attempts had occurred on a larger version of the planet known as Tiamat. Additionally, Earth now occupies a different orbit than Tiamat did.

Millions of years after the seeding of Earth, a new human colony called Hybornea was established. Humans had evolved into an intellectual race and continued to progress. It was a beautiful development, and many beings from different parts of the galaxy came to partake in the evolution of humanity on Earth. Various races shared their spiritual and technological knowledge, allowing Hybornea to flourish for millions of years, benefiting from numerous humanoid influences. The inhabitants embraced the feminine and lived in peace and harmony, aligning with the cosmic intention of Source. However, the Great Galactic War was raging, and it was only a matter of time before it reached Earth.

Maldek subsequently launched a massive attack on Hybornea, destroying the peace and love that had been cultivated there for millions of years. Eventually, the Nibiruans destroyed Maldek, which is now part of the lower half of Tiamat, located within what is known as the Hammered Bracelet.

The Draconian Empire's Battlestar planet, Maldek, was given a plan to destroy this quadrant of the galaxy. Maldek first annihilated all the colonies on Hybornea on Earth and then proceeded to destroy the human colonies on Venus and Mars. These attacks rendered both Venus and Mars uninhabitable. As a result of the destruction of Maldek, the Battlestar planet Nibiru suffered severe damage, and its protective force field was compromised. During the battle between Maldek and Nibiru, the Draconian Empire unleashed many atomic-type weapons against Nibiru, resulting in thousands of casualties and stripping Nibiru of its ability to protect its inhabitants.

The Nibiruans living inside Nibiru were exposed to harmful levels of radiation and faced imminent death. Medical pods were necessary for their recovery; however, these pods required several months of immersion in healing liquid to treat severe injuries, and they needed constant monitoring and operation. To shield against the radiation penetrating the planet, Nibiruans sought a solution. They determined that placing large amounts of gold on the surface of Nibiru would effectively protect them from radiation flooding from space. Consequently, Nibiru embarked on a large-scale campaign to source gold to surround their planet.

It's unclear whether the surface required a gold coating or if advanced technology was used to create a protective layer with gold. Regardless, gold was essential, and replicator machines could not produce an exact match for the gold, making it less effective than naturally sourced gold.

Approximately 480,000 years ago, the Nibiruans returned to Earth. Further in this book we will explore what transpired when the Nibiruans and the Annunaki arrived on Earth.

Everything discovered in this book thus far provides a foundation for understanding the secret happenings on Earth today. The current leaders on Earth are merely puppets for a cabal that is none other than the Draconian Empire. The hidden mind control they have imposed on humanity is gradually being lifted. The collective consciousness awakening has almost reached critical mass. I encourage you to continue your journey toward enlightenment and disclosure. Together, we can reclaim control and eliminate the galaxy's last remnants of regressive rule.

Up to this point, we have observed the Draconian Orion Empire conquering, killing, and consuming countless humanoid societies. However, the tables have now turned, and their home base planet, Aln, and their Battlestar planet, Maldek have been destroyed. Within this quadrant of the galaxy, the Draconian Empire was down to a small faction hiding within Tiamat, which was later terraformed into Earth. Only 1% to 2% of the loyal Draconian Empire remained, and most of this small group was concealed within Earth.

This is a critical moment to discuss the configuration of the star system known as Sol and the planets that exist within it. Much remains hidden from society, and this information is crucial for disclosure and understanding. The star we refer to as Sol is, in fact, a black hole (all stars are essentially black holes), and it moves through the galaxy much like a rocket. Sol possesses a gravitational pull due to a concentration of energy, which is essentially consciousness. This energy maintains the planets' orbit within the star system.

The planets in the Solar system, in order of their proximity to the star (Sol), are as follows: Mercury, Venus, Earth, Mars, Jupiter, Saturn, Uranus, Neptune, Pluto, Haumea, Eris, and O'ha'lu.

Beyond Neptune lies the Kuiper Belt, which contains many large rocks. However, the Galactic Federation classifies Pluto, Haumea, Eris, and O'ha'lu as planets. Haumea has two moons named Hi'iaca and Na'maka. Eris has one moon called Dysnomia, while O'ha'lu has no moons. Interestingly, O'ha'lu is home to a colony of a race known as the Mantis. The Mantis claims to be neutral in the Great Galactic War and the previous Orion Wars, yet they have an agreement with the regressive Maitres and Draconians that allows these two groups to enter and exit the solar system. This has led some to argue that the Mantis may also have regressive tendencies, a perspective many share.

I share this to help illustrate how this galactic war spread throughout the galaxy, reached our star system, and landed on Earth. Many different factions are involved, making it challenging to convey the complexity of a conflict that has placed Earth under the control of the Draconian Empire. Earth is now a prison where humans are severed from reality.

Now, let us return to the story of the surviving regressive reptilian race hiding in the catacombs of Earth. We are about to explore how this small remnant of the Draconian Orion Empire managed to take control of Earth and continue manipulating events from the shadows. This small group of survivors likely received assistance from the now-regressive Galactic Federation.

It is important to remember that this faction of the Draconian Empire is loyal to a figure or symbol referred to as the "three." The number three symbolizes Ahriman, their dark father, who embodies evil and is opposed to good and light. Ahriman is the most significant aspect of the Draconians who revere the triangular symbol. The second side of this triangular sacred symbol represents their loyalty to the asuras, or archonic evil energies that were expelled from Source. For reference, these asura energies can be classified as demons. The third side of their sacred pyramid is the light that knowledge brings them, knowledge about the cosmos, portal manipulation, DNA manipulation, consciousness manipulation, mind control, technology, and more. This understanding of the universe and how to hide this information allows them to gain control for their benefit. The triangle's three sides have been used in many symbolic ways and have multiple names and interpretations. But no matter what symbolic meaning is given to the trinity, its roots are from the Triangulum constellation. Thus, the number three holds great significance in the practices of the Draconian Empire and the affiliated groups, such as the Illuminati, who carry out their bidding.

The knowledge these groups utilize is how they circumvent the universal law of free will and assert control over humanity on Earth. The intensity of the emotions stirred by these words is palpable, and I can sense the anger and awakening within you as you recognize what has been done to humanity. It is vital to channel this powerful energy constructively, as we must raise our frequency to liberate ourselves from the grip of the Draconian Empire. The wars, suffering, fear, and all forms of evil experienced on Earth have been manipulated and orchestrated by this regressive Orion reptilian group, also known as the Draconian Empire. They operate behind layers of secrecy established by societies like the Illuminati and have infiltrated other groups that initially had benevolent intentions. The Draconian Empire has successfully taken control of these organizations through the divide and conquer tactic.

I am pleased to see that their veil of secrecy is beginning to lift, and their day of reckoning is approaching! Let us uncover the layers of their secrets together as we continue to explore. You are a Starseed destined for this awakening, and I am merely playing a small role in your significant journey. Together, we can join this cause and achieve great things for all humanity.

Chapter 14: Nibiru Annunaki & Earth Humans

After the destruction of Tiamat and the birth of Earth, the planet was seeded with humans. These humans evolved to be intelligent and telepathic, living in harmony with one another and caring for the Earth and all its animals.

In addition to the humans, there were descendants of the Lyran race known as the Lemurians. They were named after their continent, Lemuria, which was named in honor of Lyra, the ancestral home of the Lyrans. On Earth, a few descendants of a regressive reptilian race retreated underground at Tiamat's destruction.

Furthermore, a civilization called Yu emerged in Asia, characterized as Oriental and benevolent. The people of Yu lived in harmony with one another, and Ashen played a central role in establishing their civilization.

The red race inhabited the city of Atlantis, and they originated from Anu's cousin. This race was established after the destruction of Tiamat, with Alta overseeing the seeding of Atlantis.

Both the Yu and Atlantean civilizations were considered sister colonies of the Lemurians. This relationship stemmed from agreements that allowed the Lemurians to serve as a mother empire to the Yu and Atlantean colonies.

All three civilizations began in Lemuria and originally shared a light skin color. A dark- brown-skinned race emerged from the Human race, shaped to become the guardians of the planet and its other races. Their DNA still required further evolution to unlock their full potential, enabling them to evolve into multidimensional, ultra-powerful beings destined to be protectors. Interesting to note that the Atlantean white race originated from Nibiru, specifically from the Royal House of Avyon bloodline.

Approximately 480,000 years ago, Nibiru returned, and Anu was back on Earth. The Nibiruans had two primary purposes for their return: first, to mine gold to help restore a protective layer around Nibiru, and second, to fulfill an agreement with the Christos Sirians to collaborate with the Felins in creating a two-strand human DNA vessel. The Earth Sirians would incarnate into these bodies, which would be a blend between the guardians (humans) and the Nibiruans (Royal House of Avyon)—this fusion of the two bloodlines aimed to create a mighty vessel.

Alalu, the former commander of Nibiru and Anu's older brother, had previously come to Earth in search of gold. He found purpose in this mission by assisting his people in finding a solution to repair Nibiru. Alalu discovered a significant source of gold and reported his findings to Anu, his younger brother. In response, Anu sent his oldest son, Enki, to Earth, accompanied by 50 of his best astronauts, known as the Annunaki. Enki and the Annunaki were tasked with establishing a mining colony on Earth.

As previously mentioned, the name Enki may not refer to a singular person but rather to a group. Many people believe that Enki and his brother Enlil are two separate individuals; however, I propose that they represent two distinct collectives of individuals who do not share a common way of thinking. Both groups originated from Anu, with Enki representing one group and Enlil representing another.

When researching ancient information, readers are often led to think that these are indeed two separate individuals. While we will continue with the story, please keep an open mind and do not take these names literally. This ancient information was initially written to manipulate society and had an agenda, so we must dissect truth from falsehood. Further along in the book, we will discuss these groups in more detail, but for simplicity, we will use the original names while maintaining an open perspective.

With Nibiru and its inhabitants in danger, the Annunaki were eager to embark on this mission despite the manual labor involved in mining gold. Physical labor was not something the Annunaki were accustomed to, as they were primarily engaged in scout missions and navigating starships. However, given the situation's urgency, the Annunaki did not question Anu's orders when asked to join Enki in the mission to mine the gold Alalu had discovered.

When Tiamat transformed destructively into Maldek and Earth, it created veins of gold. The Nibiruans could not pass up this opportunity.

At this point, I want to discuss the Annunaki. Who are the Annunaki? On Earth, the term Annunaki can refer to any extraterrestrial race that comes from the sky. This would mean all extraterrestrials could be classified as part of the Annunaki group. However, if we label all extraterrestrials as Annunaki in this book, we risk losing essential nuances when describing the different groups. For example, the Orion group, the Galactic Federation, and the Nibiruans could all be called Annunaki, which would detract from the story. We will not refer to all extraterrestrials as Annunaki to provide more precise details and add depth to this information.

Additionally, Sitchin referred to the Annunaki as gods and attributed the creation of humanity to them. This disinformation aligns with the agenda of the regressive cabal. Nonetheless, within any disinformation campaign, some truths can emerge that may assist in one's understanding and expansion. Gaining insight into certain aspects of the truth is better than being completely unaware. Sitchin's work seems intended to divert those seeking enlightenment regarding Earth's true history. His aim may have been to establish a new religion or belief system, indoctrinating followers like traditional religions have. The goal is to capture those who start to awaken and guide them into this new belief system. This is done so they control even the groups who become aware of Earth's prison. Within the Nibiruan race, the individuals who travel from the sky (astronauts) are a select group whose DNA has been engineered for deep space travel for various purposes, such as discovery or rescue missions. Annunaki for the Nibiruans means their unique group of astronauts. The Annunaki are a specialized group dedicated to exploring the cosmos. For this book, we will use the term Annunaki to refer specifically to the group within the Nibiruans tasked with deep space travel—essentially, the Nibiruan astronauts.

For reasons unknown, those in power urge anyone who uncovers this information to categorize all extraterrestrials as Annunaki. Understanding that Annunaki is merely a classification of a Nibiruan group is crucial for understanding the truth and the influences at play.

On Earth, the surviving reptilian population had increased significantly and posed a potential threat to the Annunaki, who were preparing to mine gold. To ensure the mining operations could proceed without interference from the reptilians, Anu sought to negotiate a deal with the remaining reptilian leaders. He recognized the importance of this mission and wanted to eliminate any risk of attack or disruption that could hinder the gold mining process.

Anu proposed a union with the leaders of the Earth surviving Orion Draconians, suggesting that he take Dramin, the Dragon Queen, as his wife. Dramin, who had reptilian DNA, would bond the reptilian race to the bloodline of the Royal House of Avyon, the Nibiruans. This marriage would guarantee the protection of the Annunaki astronauts from the reptilian race, as they would no longer be viewed as targets. This treaty would not have been possible if Anu had not believed it essential for the safety of the Annunaki, who would be mining gold to save Nibiru.

Dramin belonged to the positive faction of the reptilian race, having been rescued from Tiamat before its destruction. She lived on Nibiru and is Enki's mother. The marriage bond protected the Annunaki and those directly involved in manual labor on Earth.
Enki is half Draconian, or some might say half dragon. The reptilians respected him because he descended from the reptilian Queen, while his human heritage comes from Anu's Royal House of Avyon. The reptilian race valued bloodline highly, and Enki belonged to royalty on both sides. With Anu's marriage to Dramin, the reptilians also extended their respect to Anu.

Anu's three children—Enki, Enlil, and their sister Ninhursag—were all born in Nibiru. By the time they arrived on Earth, Anu's children had matured. Enki was already an adult at the time of Anu's marriage to Dramin. Enki had several children: Ningishzidda, known as Thoth or Quetzalcoatl, is his son with Ereshkigal; Marduk is his son by the dragon princess Damkina, while Marduk's son is Nabu, Anu's great-grandson. Enki also had another son named Nergal. Enlil's sons, Nannar and Adad, were born to Ninlil, and Ninurta is Enlil's son with his half-sister Ninhursag.

Returning to the mission on Earth, Anu's marriage to Dramin was intended to prevent attacks from the reptilians. While the reptilian race already respected Enki, this marriage solidified the alliance between the Nibiruans and the reptilian faction on Earth. This agreement laid a strong foundation for the Annunaki to arrive and begin their gold mining operations.

Enki's spacecraft landed in the sea near Mesopotamia. He and the Anunnaki set up a camp and began extracting gold from the waters where Alalu had initially discovered it. They established their first city, naming it Eridu, also referred to as Earth Station One. Enki and the Anunnaki received much-needed assistance from his reptilian relatives. Anu's daughter, Ninhursag, arrived after Eridu was established and the mining operation was underway. She was tasked with providing and overseeing the medical care that the Anunnaki would be needed while working under harsh conditions. Anu soon followed, accompanied by his other son, Enlil.

The Anunnaki worked tirelessly to extract gold to save Nibiru, but Nibiru was still in danger. They realized they needed to find another source of gold and discovered one in Africa.

However, this location presented a challenge, as the gold would have to be mined deep underground.

During this period, tensions rose between Enki and Enlil as each sought to lead the mining expedition on Earth. The reptilians on Earth believed that Enki was their rightful ruler because he was the son of Dramin, the dragon queen originally from Tiamat. Since Enlil had no reptilian blood, the reptilian race did not want him to take command over any Earth- related matters. Those reptilians who escaped destruction still believed they had claimed Earth as their domain.

Ultimately, Anu decided to leave Enki in charge of the mining project in Africa, while Enlil was assigned the responsibility of managing mining operations in all other locations. Enki took the Annunaki to Africa to begin mining operations there, while Enlil took charge of the gold mining efforts in Eridu. Anu believed his work of establishing gold mining operations on Earth was complete, and he needed to return to Nibiru, where his people were still suffering from illness. As he left, Anu was confronted by an aggressive attack from a fellow Nibiruan. Alalu's grandson, Kumarbi, felt he should have been appointed commander of Nibiru after his grandfather stepped down. He gathered a group of astronauts known as the Igigi to assist him in his attack against Anu, planning to seize control of Nibiru by force due to his belief that Anu was failing in his leadership and in saving the Nibiruans.

In support of Anu, Ninurta, Enlil's son, and his half-sister Ninhursag defended Anu's starship. Many others joined the battle to protect Anu, and ultimately, Kumarbi was defeated, resulting in the Igigi being relieved of their duties on a neighboring space station. Meanwhile, Enki and the Annunaki astronauts sent back large quantities of gold. Enlil constructed four new cities: Sippar (a spaceport), Nippur (a mission control center), Bad Tibira (a gold analysis center), and Shuruppak (a medical center). The region of Mesopotamia flourished into a beautiful garden. Seeds of various trees and fruits from Nibiru transformed the area into a paradise. The Nibiruans referred to this area as the Garden of E.Din. Everything and everyone existed in harmony, and this tranquil environment lasted approximately 200,000 years.

Approximately 250,000 years ago, the Annunaki astronauts stationed in Africa revolted due to the harsh working conditions they faced while mining gold. They reached a breaking point and united in their discontent. Enki, overseeing the mining operations, reached out to

Enlil for assistance calming the revolt. However, Enlil arrived at the mining site only to be taken hostage by the Annunaki.

While Enki acknowledged that the Annunaki were subjected to difficult working conditions, he had not previously taken any action to address their grievances. However, he urged the Annunaki to release Enlil, promising they would find a solution together. Enlil was furious with Enki, believing that Enki had orchestrated the plan for the Annunaki to capture him. In response, Enlil contacted the Nibiruan Council to demand that charges be brought against Enki.

The Nibiruan Council determined that the Annunaki should be relieved of their mining duties. They felt that the Annunaki should return to the roles they were trained initially to perform—those of astronauts navigating starships and exploring the cosmos—rather than laboring in the mines under extreme conditions. The Annunaki had spent many years mining gold for Nibiru, and it was clear that action should have been taken long before the revolt. Although Nibiru's protective layer had not yet been fully restored, there should have been a more significant consideration for the Annunaki's welfare. This was a challenging situation for all parties involved.

In light of these events, Enki proposed the creation of a new worker class—an entirely new race designed to be physically strong enough to endure the harsh mining environment. The Nibiruan Council agreed that this was a viable solution, and a plan was formulated to develop a new human vessel with a robust DNA foundation.

Ninhursag and Enki were chosen to lead the project of creating a new human race. While there have been previous instances of human seeding, it's important to note that the original humanoids originated in Lyra. Enki and Ninhursag did not create the human race from scratch; they took existing beings and modified their DNA.

Some people attribute the creation of the human race to the Anunnaki or Enki, but this is part of a misinformation campaign. Those who claim that the Anunnaki or Enki created humans aim to diminish human empowerment by instilling the belief that these beings should be viewed as gods. The last thing the Draconian Empire wants is for humans to look within themselves and discover the truth about their history. Their agenda is to keep humans unaware of their true potential.

The controllers wish for humanity to believe that everything is tied solely to their physical bodies.

However, when individuals awaken to the realization that they are spiritual beings having a physical experience, the cabal loses its grip on them. The controllers need society to believe they are solely physical beings and must worship an external God or an extraterrestrial race, such as the Annunaki. If someone begins to awaken, they want that person to believe they are physical beings who are merely starting to have spiritual experiences, suggesting that once the body dies, they lose their true identity.

Another aspect of indoctrination is the belief that if someone is good, their spirit will go to heaven or another spiritual realm. This belief can serve as a tool to encourage souls to reincarnate on Earth, effectively trapping them in an incarnation loop. I want to address this topic because there is a lot of misinformation surrounding the Annunaki, Enki, and the creators or gods of the human race. Much of this misinformation was propagated by Marduk, the son of Enki, and his devoted followers to ensure that their indoctrination reached broader populations. This manipulation occurs through secret societies, governments, religions, and similar organizations. We will explore this subject further in the book.

Ninhursag's mother, Rayshondra, also known as Ki, wanted to help with this significant project. She had trained her daughter Ninhursag in genetics, and Rayshondra is considered a master geneticist with extensive experience. She had also assisted Enki in becoming a master geneticist. Eager to contribute, she arrived at Shuruppak, the medical facility where Enki and Ninhursag worked to develop new human DNA. The three worked together, leveraging their combined expertise for this crucial endeavor.

The new human species was Homo erectus, often referred to as primitive humans. The process of evolution was necessary to transform Homo erectus into Homo sapiens. During this evolutionary journey, Earth's Sirian Souls, which were incarnated in ocean animals, had the opportunity to evolve by taking on the primitive human form and subsequently transitioning into Homo sapiens. This evolution took approximately 200,000 years.

As humans evolved, they developed the ability to reason with one another. They began learning how to read and write and were trained to enhance their telepathic abilities.

However, they received no more advanced psychic abilities at this stage. More complex spiritual abilities would be unlocked once the Sirian Souls reached a specific level in their spiritual evolution. This new human race was significant to the Nibiruans, who sought to mine gold, and the Sirians, who wished to evolve beyond animal-type vessels.

Enki and Ninhursag identified the appropriate combination of DNA and blended it with DNA from the Nibiruans. They obtained eggs from evolving human women and fertilized them using sperm from the Annunaki. This resulted in a new human race with mixed DNA. The fertilized eggs were carried to full term by Annunaki women, leading to the birth of twelve new human babies, all possessing upgraded genetic traits. The Annunaki women continued to give birth to these new human babies to establish a new society.

The Annunaki woman and other women who initially volunteered to carry the babies grew weary of always being pregnant. This new human race could not reproduce independently, so Enki and Ninhursag returned to the lab to further enhance this new species. After the upgrades, these humans could procreate independently. This improved version of humanity was named "Lulus," a term that translates to "primitive workers" for the Nibiruans.

The Lulus loved Ninhursag dearly because she showered them with affection. She dedicated her time to teaching them and helping them evolve, and in return, they affectionately nicknamed her "Mama." Enki was viewed as their father. Unfortunately, the reptilian race regarded the Lulus as a slave race, treating them poorly. The reptilians believed that Enki had created this new human race for their servitude. Despite Enki's constant pleas for the reptilians to treat the Lulus respectfully, they never changed their behavior. Enki and Ninhursag subsequently performed two more upgrades to human DNA. Approximately 150,000 years ago, a new ice age began, which caused the Lulus to regress while many other races were forming on Earth. The Pleiadians were not the only beings to colonize Earth; the Andromedans also established colonies there. This ice age affected every colony, and all involved agreed that ensuring the survival of the Lulus was of utmost importance.

Living on Earth became increasingly dangerous during this time due to the resurgence of dinosaurs. I am unsure how this reemergence occurred—it might have been the work of the reptilian race who went underground—but the presence of these dinosaurs was evident as they began to kill humans. It is worth noting that when Earth was terraformed after the destruction of Tiamat, the planet was inundated with energy that accelerated the growth of vegetation and the evolution of animals. This energy also enhanced the development of the dinosaurs. The Orion group typically seeds dinosaurs on a planet immediately after deciding to take ownership of it. Large animals provide a convenient food source for the reptilian race. Unfortunately, it caused a dangerous situation for the evolving Lulus.

To summarize, the Annunaki and the Nibiruans arrived on Earth to mine gold, aiming to restore their damaged home planet, Nibiru. However, the harsh conditions of the mining operations led to a revolt among the Annunaki. Enki and Ninhursag were instructed by the Nibiru Council to create a new human vessel (DNA) that could mine gold, allowing the Sirian A Souls, currently incarnated in Earth's oceanic animals, to use these vessels to evolve their consciousness. The Lulus, the new human race, faced challenges in their development due to an impending ice age.

Chapter 15: Human Evolution on Earth

Earlier in this book, we discussed the creation of the humanoid race known as the Lyrans. We also explored the early origins of the human race, the upgrade to human DNA that expedited evolution, completed by Enki and Ninhursag, and the challenges faced by the Lulus during an ice age. Now, let's continue the story.

Another ice age occurred around 75,000 B.C., resulting in the death of many evolving human groups. However, one of the surviving groups became known as the Cro-Magnon man. Human souls who did not survive were allowed to incarnate in this surviving group if they chose to.

By about 50,000 B.C., the Earth was warming, and humans were evolving successfully. It was time for another DNA upgrade. The Spiritual Hierarchy instructed Enki and Ninhursag to enhance the human vessel, aiming for spiritual evolution.

Earth evolved as the colonies developed into empires, and everyone lived harmoniously. The empires of Yu, Rama, Lemuria, Egypt, and the Mayans gathered in Atlantis to discuss the best way to deal with the dinosaurs, which had grown too large and posed a danger to the people.

The Atlanteans had developed a powerful weapon that utilized crystals. This technology was given to them by Marduk, who employed the classic Draconian Empire strategy of divide and conquer. Marduk was regressive and planned to infiltrate the Atlantean Empire to conquer it from within. This approach was taken discreetly to avoid drawing attention from the Galactic Federation and others. Infiltration allows an empire to be conquered and controlled without anyone noticing until it is too late. Although this strategy takes more time, it is very effective. This is why Marduk provided the Atlantean Empire with this weapon of war, which aligned with his agenda. As a result, the Atlanteans began changing their mindset and lowering their frequency, which caught the attention of others.

Lemuria was struggling to maintain its original Lyran system of governance. Some Lemurians became aware of the problems faced by the Atlanteans, and a few even learned about a future timeline that foretold the destruction of Lemuria. As a result, many Lemurians left their homeland and migrated to various parts of Earth, including Mexico, America, Northwest Europe, and Central Europe.

During this period, a plan to eliminate all dinosaurs was implemented. The specifics of how the dinosaurs were killed off this time remain unclear, but it appears that some humans also lost their lives during the execution of this plan.

Sananda, a higher-density being and a member of the galaxy's founder group, incarnated on a planet called Avyon. His physical form on Avyon was named Amelius. Following expanding his consciousness, Amelius became the leader of the Etheric Sirians. This occurred after the Lyrans migrated to Sirius A, which took place before the destruction of Sirius A.

Ninhursag took one of her eggs and engineered a new egg using mixed DNA, combining human, Draconian, Urma, and carrion DNA. The egg was fertilized with Enki's sperm, which was then placed into Ninhursag's womb. She gave birth to Adapa. Sananda separated a fragment of his consciousness to incarnate into the human vessel that Ninhursag had brought into the world, and the child was named Adapa.

Sananda is a high-density being who incarnated as Amelius. Amelius was one of Sananda's physical incarnations, initially on Avyon. Another physical incarnation of Sananda on Earth was Adapa. Ninhursag carried the egg that Enki had fertilized. Many refer to Adapa as Adam. This egg contained Urma, human, and Draconian DNA from Enki's sperm.

Adapa was a special baby because his DNA combined human and Draconian elements. This integration was intended to foster a union between humans and Draconians. Enki and Ninhursag showed immense love to Adapa, and he was given an extra ability to express compassion. When Adapa was two years old, another egg was fertilized. Ninhursag also carried this egg, and the resulting baby was named Lilith, though many also refer to her as Eve.

Adam and Eve possessed manipulated DNA; a process akin to what is currently known as "Clustered Regularly Interspaced Short Palindromic Repeats" (CRISPR). As previously discussed, humans existed long before Adam and Eve, but the indigenous humans on Earth had their DNA altered to expedite evolution.

Adapa and Lilith grew up together, playing in the E-Din Compound, an area nicknamed the Garden of E-Din. This name was fitting due to the numerous trees and fruits that flourished in the area. The garden was seeded with plants from the gardens of Nibiru. These new human vessels possessed the potential for spiritual growth, marking a significant advancement in the evolution of human DNA. These were fascinating times for everyone involved, both on Earth and beyond.

Enki is knowledgeable in many different subjects and taught Adapa everything he could. Both Enki and Ninhursag loved Adapa dearly. They gave Lilith the same care and affection, and both children showered their parents with love.

It was time to spread this new human DNA, so a decision was made to create more of these types of human vessels and place them within the various empires on Earth. More Adapas and Liliths were born and distributed across different regions. Adapa began to remember his cosmic origins, much like many people awakening today. He married Lilith in accordance with Pleiadian law.

Lilith did not give Adapa an apple to eat. This story was fabricated in the Bible to align with a regressive agenda. The Draconian empire is regressive and heavily leans towards the masculine. Ever since the first archons, or asuras, left Source, they held a deep resentment. Their leaders have indoctrinated this regressive reptilian race to erase all remnants of the feminine, leading to a war against all women throughout the galaxy.

The story of Lilith (Eve) being the cause of Adapa's and their descendants' downfall aligns perfectly with the agenda of the Draconian Empire. Dividing men and women would be a good strategy to keep society blind and under control. For the Draconian Empire to gain control, they must always remove the spiritually oriented women leaders so they can replace them with men who are much easier to manipulate and control.

While reading this next part, please remember that I am a male father of only sons and a husband. At the time, the empires on Earth operated under a matriarchal system. In a matriarchal social system, women hold the primary positions of power; in other words, the rulers of society are typically women. Women are viewed with a great deal of respect and are honored by men. Some men may take on political roles, but women usually hold leadership positions in the empires. These women perform their duties well and are well- suited for such responsibilities. They possess natural qualities of understanding and empathy toward their people. They tend to be slow to anger and prefer to avoid conflict, even when there are differences of opinion. This is how most fifth-density and higher-positive societies operate. Earth would be much better if women made all the political decisions.

Women needed to be removed from leadership roles to control society. Marduk is responsible for implementing the story of the first human woman being accountable for every human inheriting sin. This was implemented to suppress women and create an environment of resentment and hate toward all women. This would foster a society that promotes male dominance.

Enki, whose symbol is a serpent, created a school to educate all humans in ancient wisdom. The fruit that Lilith and Adapa supposedly ate was symbolic; much of the ancient text is rich with symbolism. This forbidden fruit represented the sacred ancient knowledge and wisdom they learned from Enki. The school was named the Brotherhood of the Snake. It's important not to associate the snake with negative connotations, as the school aimed to help humans evolve. Snakes, or dragons, symbolized a portion of Enki's DNA. Like all races, there is both good and evil in every one of them. The depiction of a snake on a deity's forehead represented the sacred knowledge imparted by Enki's school, which supported the institution and shared its knowledge. This is why many hieroglyphs feature a snake drawn on the forehead.

This sacred information has been lost through the years. These ancient tablets with this information do not become mainstream information. This is because it does not fit the controller's agenda. The controllers want to keep humanity dumb, blind, and ignorant of real history. The Bible was written thousands of years after the events it describes, often to promote a version of history that is not entirely accurate. The earliest Sumerian tablet writings date back to around 3000 B.C.E. The Bible can be seen as a compilation of these ancient texts, but with significant alterations. Many original tablets were excluded, and several names were changed.

The Bible states that God grew angry with Adam and Eve. In the Bible, God, or Yahweh, is often associated with Enlil. The name "Yahweh" was later changed to "Jehovah" by Christian Monks. According to the Sumerian Tablets of Destiny, Enlil is described as the supreme God. The Sumerian people viewed various extraterrestrial beings as gods, some more revered than others. If you read these ancient tablets and compare them to the Bible, you will find that the Bible is a fragment of a larger truth. The ancient texts that predate the Bible were also written to manipulate society, but they are closer to the truth than newer texts.

The Brotherhood of the Snake initially began as a positive organization. However, in typical Marduk fashion, he infiltrated it and transformed it into something malevolent, asserting control over it. The Brotherhood of the Snake taught Adapa, Lilith, and all their descendants many vital lessons. In the Bible, a snake is said to have convinced Eve to eat from the forbidden fruit. This snake symbolizes the Brotherhood of the Snake, which revealed sacred truths to Adam and Eve. As a result of this newfound knowledge, they were thrown out of paradise. The snake unveiled these truths to them, ultimately leading to humanity's suffering. It represents Enki's school, known as "The Brotherhood of the Snake."

Enlil believed that the new human race attending the Brotherhood of the Snakes school was at risk of self-destruction. A race needs to evolve spiritually before acquiring vast amounts of knowledge. Unlocking sacred wisdom presents opportunities and dangers, as this knowledge can be used for good and evil.

With the guidance of the Nibiruans, humans had a better chance of achieving success. However, the regressive reptilian race increasingly influenced the already-evolved empires across Earth. The consequences could be disastrous if the Draconian Empire were to infiltrate a newly emerged race armed with sacred knowledge.

The new human race would be an easy target due to its spiritual immaturity, which makes it more vulnerable compared to other groups that have taken longer to evolve to higher frequencies. By this time, the truth about Dramin and her grandson Marduk being regressive had come to light, and this growing threat needed to be acknowledged.

Enlil did not harbor any anger toward this new version of humanity. He felt they were not yet ready for the knowledge taught at Enki's school, known as The Brotherhood of the Snake. It was akin to teaching a child how to create a bomb while living next to neighbors whose children were destructive and regressive. The situation would be manageable if a parent could control all aspects of their child's environment. However, it would be wiser to either distance themselves from negative influences or wait until the child is mature and spiritually strong before imparting such knowledge. This was Enlil's argument, and as a result, Adapa and Lilith were not expelled from the E Din Compound, contrary to what ancient texts suggest.

Enlil wanted the divine plan to succeed. He was determined to ensure the new human race would be safe from destruction, allowing them to evolve into guardians of Earth. This evolution would relieve the Nibiruans from their obligations with the higher-density beings from Sirius. It is important to remember that this new race was initially intended to assist with gold mining operations for Nibiru. Still, they were also meant to aid the souls originating from Sirius A in their evolution into multidimensional guardians.

The new humans had evolved to a point of intelligence and awareness. They were acquiring ancient sacred knowledge from Enki's school, the Brotherhood of the Snake. Additionally, they were experiencing spiritual growth and developing telepathic abilities. This new human race was more advanced than the current human population on Earth. Despite Enlil's concerns, progress was being made, but this positive trajectory did not last. Enki, Ninhursag, and others enhanced these upgraded humans, allowing them to evolve rapidly. This version of the human vessel could expand its mind and evolve due to its increased frequency and mindset.

However, something occurred that caused this human race to regress to its current state, where they are subjected to mind control by the Draconian Empire. Let us continue to explore the destruction of Atlantis and the creation of the Illuminati.

Chapter 16: The Fall of Atlantis

In the last chapter, we explored the establishment of Enki's school, where he imparted sacred ancient knowledge to humans. Ninhursag and Enki shared this wisdom with the new human group, and things were progressing positively. However, Enlil opposed the idea of the spiritually lesser humans learning from the Brotherhood of the Snake, which was the name of the school they attended.

Enki established the Brotherhood of the Snake to train Adapa, Lilith, and their descendants. This school was designed to help the new human race expand their minds and elevate their frequency. Although the Brotherhood of the Snake was the first of its kind, it would later evolve into a Mystery school that kept this ancient knowledge a secret, accessible only to a select few.

Eventually, Masonic lodges emerged, linked to various compartments of secret societies associated with the Illuminati. Unfortunately, this knowledge, initially intended by Enki to be shared with the masses, became restricted. In the present day, certain groups connected to the Illuminati conduct rituals with participants wearing aprons, a practice that traces back to Enki and the Brotherhood of the Snake.

Enlil was increasingly concerned about the knowledge humans were acquiring from the Brotherhood of the Snake. The information they were learning was becoming dangerous, leading to arguments between Enki and Enlil about what should be shared with humanity. Enki taught humans about universal laws, sacred geometry, various techniques for manipulating energy, and spiritual knowledge.

Enlil believed that spiritual growth should always progress a few steps ahead of technological development. This approach would help prevent humans from turning against one another due to the dangers of advanced knowledge. If an uprising occurs among the new human race, it could lead to significant losses.

Enlil and Enki presented their cases to the Galactic Federation and the Spiritual Hierarchy. After careful consideration, a group decision was made to relocate all humans, including Adapa and Lilith, from the E Din Compound. This decision was intended to shift human priorities toward survival and spiritual growth. Without access to necessary resources, humans would struggle to continue their development of technology. The reasoning behind this decision was clear: what value would there be in developing technology to manipulate energy if they could not grow food to survive? The focus for this developing human group would be on survival.

It's important to clarify that it was not Enlil who expelled the humans from the E Din Compound due to disobedience. Instead, this decision was made collectively, based on a broader understanding of the circumstances. Many writings in the Bible and other ancient texts were created to instill fear in society rather than to reflect the events that occurred accurately. This serves the agenda of the Draconian Empire. It is easier to control a mass of people who fear being disfellowshipped or expelled from a figurative Garden of Eden if they disobey what the Bible or their religious leaders say. It is to keep the people in fear and under control. You are now starting to see the world for what it is: humanity in slavery to a small group of regressive, power-hungry beings that have a higher knowledge of the cosmos. Do not be alarmed; their day is coming soon as you and others awaken to their tactics.

The Brotherhood of the Snake continued its operations and transmitted ancient sacred knowledge to a select few humans through each generation. This limited training was intended to ensure that the knowledge remained under control. This marks the beginning of the modern-day priesthood. Unfortunately, the Brotherhood became corrupt as time passed, and those acquiring this sacred knowledge grew increasingly power-hungry. Enki was fighting for the human race, but in the end, he was mistaken, and Enlil was correct. Humans should not have attended the Brotherhood of the Snake school.

By around 11,000 B.C., the new human race had degenerated to the point where it needed a fresh start. Marduk and his regressive followers had infiltrated the Atlantean leadership. The Draconian Empire had regained strength thanks to this infiltration of Atlantis. The Atlantean empire became divided after the Atlanteans fell for Marduk's trap of technological advancements. Some factions wanted to focus on spiritual growth, while others embraced technological progress. This division spread across the planet, with Marduk gaining control over those who sought the power that came with advanced technology. Unbeknownst to them, they were under Marduk's influence and acted according to his desires, attacking anyone or any group that rejected technological advancements.

The regressive plan was to continually introduce more technology until people were willing to integrate with the regressive Draconian AI rather than seek connection with Source.

Anyone unwilling to follow this negative timeline faced elimination. Marduk implemented this technology, and rulers began waging war against groups that resisted embracing technology. They then turned on one another, driven by fear of losing power. Fear is the tool the Draconian Empire uses to control people. What better-enslaved person than one who doesn't realize they are being manipulated into servitude? If Marduk's plan to divide and conquer Atlantis succeeded, the rest of Earth would inevitably follow and fall under Marduk's control.

The decision to enact another reset stemmed from the events surrounding the Atlanteans. Influenced by Marduk, the Atlanteans harnessed immense power through the energy of crystals. Crystals contain great potential because they embody consciousness in its most basic form. This energy, which originates from Source, can be felt during deep meditation—it is alive, though not in the way we are. While its consciousness is of a lower density, it still possesses energy. Once harnessed, this power significantly alters how a civilization lives forever due to technological advancements in discovering how to harness energy from crystals.

Crystals can power spaceships and similar types of crafts. They can store a vast amount of information and can be applied to various technologies. However, one of their most dangerous applications is weaponry, as crystals can be harnessed and used as weapons. The Atlanteans were highly grateful to Marduk for this gift of knowledge, as it introduced them to the technology used by the Nibiruans and the Draconians. This advancement would significantly improve the lives of all Atlanteans. However, they had no idea what Marduk had in store for them. He intended to gain their trust, knowing that with this technology, he could introduce it as a weapon of pure destruction. This was his real agenda, but the Atlanteans failed to see it.

If Marduk had attacked Atlantis directly, he would have faced confrontation. Instead, he opted for infiltration and a "divide and conquer" strategy consistent with typical Draconian Empire tactics. Before long, he had the Atlanteans waging war against each other.

I acknowledge that I have mentioned this before, but look around Earth today; has Marduk employed a different strategy? No, he has not. His approach remains the same: divide and conquer. He splits the planet into various political and religious groups and instills fear within society. Additionally, he introduces different classes and fosters prejudices among various races and social groups.

I discuss these matters to help guide you in awakening to the realities of what has transpired on Earth and to understand how the current situation developed. Now, let us explore what Marduk did next to the Atlantean Empire.

Marduk began to influence the scientific community, helping it become the dominant portion of society. He infiltrated the leaders of the empires through bribery and blackmail, much like he had done with various governments on Earth. Eventually, he took control of the leadership of Atlantis, which caused a division within society between the priesthood focused on spiritual advancement and those prioritizing power and technology. This created a rift between the ordinary people and the ruling class.

In an attempt to warn the Atlanteans of the negative path they were on, the Lemurians sent delegates to Atlantis to speak with its rulers.

Marduk was influenced by his grandmother Dramin, a member of the reptilian race with royal blood; she had been the Dragon Queen before the destruction of Tiamat. Marduk believed that his father, Enki, should rule over all operations on Earth and Nibiru. After the destruction of Aln, Nibiru had become a focal point for the remaining regressive Draconian reptilians, presenting an opportunity to infiltrate it. However, Enki had given up his desire to rule, instead focusing on genetics and spiritual advancements. He recognized that being a ruler required sacrificing time and personal interests for the people, a commitment he no longer wanted.

Marduk's mother was Ninki, also known as Damkina. She was the princess of the snake people, while her mother, Dramin, was the Queen of the Dragons. According to Draconian law, this lineage made Marduk the next in line to rule. It's worth noting that Dramin's first husband died before she and Anu had Enki.

Pause the Story
Throughout this book, we will use different names for characters found in ancient Babylonian writings. If you are familiar with those texts, you may notice that my interpretations differ from traditional versions. At times, my variations may be slightly different, while at other times, they may be significantly different. Keep an open mind as you read.

Remember that these ancient writings were often created to manipulate society at the time. In Babylonian mythology, Marduk's mother was named Damgalnuna, and his grandmother was Tiamat. Tiamat is said to have been the primordial goddess of the sea and the mother of

the gods. Marduk, the chief god of Babylon, defeated Tiamat and used her body to create the universe.
Do you see how this version of history was designed to reset society and disconnect everyone from their true history? It all began with Marduk, marking a reset for that era. When this version of history no longer suited their agenda, they moved on to newer forms of indoctrination, such as the Bible. It's also important to note that there is some truth to the original indoctrination. The destruction of Tiamat is indeed true, and it contributed to the creation of another planet. The narrative is always filled with half-truths and symbolism.
Let Us Continue

Unable to convince Enki to fight for the throne, Marduk took it upon himself to pursue rulership. He decided to begin with the city of Atlantis because it was far from Mesopotamia and Egypt, making it easier for him to infiltrate the Atlantean rulers without attracting the attention of his father, Enki, or his uncle, Enlil. The continent that housed Atlantis was located in the current Atlantic Ocean.

According to Graham Hancock, remnants of Atlantis can be found between Florida and the Bahamas. He discovered what appears to be a city under the ocean off the Bimini Islands, located near Miami. While it is uncertain if this is the actual city of Atlantis, these remnants likely belong to a city that was once part of the same continent.

As Marduk continued his plans for world domination, he felt confident because he possessed advanced crystal weapon technology. He utilized this technology to harness a comet in the asteroid belt, integrating it with tractor-beam technology. This device locked the comet in place, providing Marduk with the destructive capability to hurl it at any civilization that refused to submit to his control.

His first target was Lemuria, a civilization that resisted his agenda of abandoning spiritual advancement in favor of technology. Marduk sent the comet to Lemuria, destroying the continent. He was preparing to do the same to the Rama and Yu empires, but Nibiru was closing in on Earth.

Marduk had harnessed another comet and was using a tractor beam to lock it into place, preparing to release it toward another civilization. Nibiru was able to disrupt the comet's path and redirect it toward the city of Atlantis. This massive impact caused the continent of Atlantis to sink, resulting in widespread destruction and tsunamis that swept across the planet. In summary, the city of Atlantis was destroyed by a comet that Marduk weaponized, with the Nibiruans redirecting it to obliterate Atlantis.

A firmament approximately three miles thick surrounded the Earth, established during the planet's terraforming following the destruction of Tiamat. The firmament maintained an environment ideal for supporting lush vegetation, holding as much water as the planet's oceans.

Marduk and his son Seth intended to destroy the firmament that enveloped the Earth. Scattered across the planet were underground temples that controlled the firmament. Seth attacked these crystal temples. He used a laser-type weapon, possibly a scalar laser, to demolish them. As a result, the firmament slowly began to collapse. This led to continuous rain for many days after its release. Seth's actions instigated a war, prompting Ninurta to remove all equipment from the Spinx's in Egypt and other similar locations. This war is why shards of glass can be found deep beneath the sand in Egypt—the intense heat from the weapons transformed the sand into glass. Up to this point, the Great Pyramid had not yet been built; we will discuss that later.

Side note: Ancient texts tell a story of Seth, the son of the first humans, Adam and Eve, after Cain and Abel. According to these texts, Enoch, Lamech, and Methuselah originated from Seth's bloodline. At that time, society believed that human lineage came from this bloodline. This was done to honor Marduk's bloodline by making people think they descended from it.

Marduk was unconcerned about human deaths; his primary goal was to gain control of Earth. With the destruction of Atlantis, he was determined to eliminate all life forms on the planet's surface. The Earth underwent significant shifts, and the Nibiruans realized that saving all humans was impossible. A meeting was held with the Spiritual Hierarchy, the Galactic Federation, and the Felines. They decided it was best not to warn humanity about the impending dangers tied to the planet's shifts and the collapse of the firmament.

This event occurred approximately 11,000 to 12,000 years ago, marking the destruction of Atlantis and the beginning of Earth's transformations, including the floods that followed the firmament's collapse.

Another significant issue was that special MEs crystals could fall into the hands of Marduk. These MEs crystals function like remote hard drives; they store knowledge and are programmed to control specific technologies. This posed a danger because if someone gained control of an MEs crystal, they could manipulate its synced technology. This concern was serious for everyone, as Marduk gaining control of the MEs would be disastrous for the Galactic Federation. This situation added another layer of complexity to the ongoing issues on Earth during this period.

It became evident that Marduk planned to takeover Earth, as his descendants had intended. Marduk's ultimate goal for Earth was to transform it into a new home base for the regressive Draconian reptilians following the destruction of Aln. Once established, he would set his sights on conquering more of the galaxy. This plan was aligned with directives given to the Draconian reptilian race by the archons—or asuras—and their leader, Ahriman.

Anu and the rest of the Nibiruans left Earth and went to the orbiting space station. They intended to wait for Earth to stabilize and the floodwaters to recede. During this time, either the Pleiadians or Andromedans placed the Andromeda space station, which is now known as the current moon, in orbit. The moon, visible from Earth, was hollowed out by the Andromedans and given to the Pleiadians to help stabilize the planet amidst its many environmental disasters. The moon was placed in a specific orbit, and this placement was calculated deliberately.

This was a challenging time for everyone observing, as 400,000 years of work were washed away. The attempt at integration had failed. However, Enki, defying the council's advice, warned one of the humans about the impending danger. This human, Noah, was taken aboard a craft with his family, where they would be safe from the floods. Enki and Ninhursag cared for the human race and did not wish for their destruction.

It is said that Noah descended from the lineage of Enki. While we have spoken of Enki as though he were an individual, it's important to note that Enki appears to represent a collective of people. Noah may have been a member of this group, which will be explored in more detail later.

The destruction of Atlantis occurred when Marduk attempted to annihilate another civilization, having already destroyed Lemuria. Anu and the Nibiruans used the Nibiruan Battlestar to thwart Marduk's second attack by sending a comet to the city of Atlantis.

Before these destructive events, Enki established the Brotherhood of the Snake. This organization aimed to teach evolving humans about ancient sacred knowledge, aiding their spiritual evolution and technological development. Enlil opposed this idea, favoring a focus solely on spiritual growth before embracing technological advancements. The early foundations of what is now known as the Illuminati began with the

Brotherhood of the Snake. In the years following the flood, Marduk seized control of this secret knowledge and created a compartmentalized society that limited this information to a select few.

The next chapter will explore what happened to the human race following the infamous flood. This is when Marduk creates secret societies to control the planet without the inhabitants realizing they are under control. The control of information would be the primary focus, and what humans believe to be reality would be dictated to them, shaping how developing societies perceive reality.

I understand this may be difficult to accept, primarily if you have been taught to believe that Noah built an ark and saved himself with God's help. Him putting two of every animal in this ark has been the indoctrination for many people. The Bible contains half-truths and keeps humanity blind to their galactic origins. Humanity is kept blind and mind-controlled to maintain power over them. If everyone were to discover this galactic history, they would likely disregard the fear-mongering news, religion, and politics, instead focusing on love and spiritual enlightenment to ascend. This would end the control, and humanity could break free from the system many call the Earth matrix.

Chapter 17: The Great Earth Flood

The flood occurred approximately 11,000 to 12,000 years ago. As mentioned in the last chapter, Seth destroyed Earth's firmament, causing the flood. After the flood, the Nibiruans returned to Earth to help with the rebuilding efforts for the surviving humans. Once it became known that Enki had saved Noah and his family, they decided to assist them in starting anew by reuniting them with other survivors. Enki and Enlil returned to Earth with tools and seeds. Following the flood, Noah began farming on Mount Ararat.

By around 10,500 B.C., human populations had increased, and Mesopotamia was reestablished. A spaceport was constructed at Mount Moriah, later known as Jerusalem. The ancient pre-diluvian cities of Nippur, Eridu, Sippar, Bad Tibira, and Shurupak were rebuilt. The pyramids, buried during the flood, were excavated from multiple feet of sand and mud. New pyramids, like the Great Pyramid of Giza, were constructed.

By 9,000 B.C., life had returned to what it was before the flood. Enki transferred the rulership of Egypt to his descendants, with Osiris and Seth assuming leadership in the region. Seth, who had previously aided his father Marduk in attacks against the earthly empires, appeared rehabilitated. Marduk had been banned from Egypt after the destruction of Atlantis and the firmament. Enki recognized that his son Marduk was regressive and untrustworthy, so he agreed with the decision to ban him. Enlil's son Adad was dispatched to South America to find gold, and he was successful in his mission.

Enlil enlisted the help of Nannar and Ninurta to command the rehabilitation of Earth, which was nearing completion. As new leadership was about to be assigned, Anu considered several possible descendants for this role: Nannar, Utu, Adad, Inanna, Seth, Osiris, and Marduk. Despite causing much grief in the past, Marduk remained a potential candidate due to his lineage.

Seth appeared to have undergone rehabilitation and had taken a positive turn. However, once he gained power over some of Egypt, his insatiable greed for control drove him to kill his brother Osiris. Osiris' son, Horus, vowed to avenge his father's death, igniting a war between them. Before the flood, Seth had attacked the underground crystal pyramids that regulated Earth's firmament—with Horus's pledge to avenge Osiris, another war, known as the Pyramid War, commenced between Horus and Seth.

As mentioned earlier, Enki and Enlil do not refer to literal individuals but rather to a group, with their names used symbolically in ancient texts. Similarly, the name

Horus does not appear to represent a specific person. Instead, in ancient times, Horus symbolized a mighty spacecraft comparable to a battleship equipped for war. This ancient information has been interpreted to manipulate society into believing it refers to an entity with a bird- shaped head. While this interpretation suited the agenda of that time, today, we can observe that hieroglyphs depicting a human with a bird-shaped head do not fully align with today's society. To make the story more concise, we will use symbolic names.

Approximately 300 years later, another Pyramid War broke out, this time between the descendants of Enki and those of Enlil. The descendants of Enlil were known as the Enlilites, while those of Enki were called the Enkiites. The conflict primarily centered on control of the space facilities, including the Great Pyramid in Egypt.

The Enlilites were determined not to allow the Enkiites control over the Great Pyramid. They fear Marduk could manipulate or conspire with his cousins, making the base regressive. They believe this would provide Marduk an opportunity for a potential assault on other parts of the galaxy.

At this point, you may ask, "Why not place Marduk in an eternal prison?" While I do not have a definitive answer, it is believed that a regressive soul needs to heal, and spending an eternity in confinement does not allow the soul to raise its vibration. If killed, Marduk can incarnate in another vessel and start over. This concept is challenging to accept, and I need to expand my understanding of why imprisoning Marduk forever is not deemed appropriate.

The war between the Enlilites and the Enkiites ended when Ninhursag intervened. She successfully mediated a solution between the two opposing sides, ultimately taking over command of the space facilities. This was when ancient texts began referring to her as the Lady of the Mountain. Ninurta emptied the pyramid of its equipment. Thoth was granted leadership over Egypt, a decision accepted by both factions.

This series of events took place around 8,600 B.C. From that point until 3,400 B.C., peace reigned on the planet. During this time, humans evolved and demonstrated their capability of self-governance. Around 3,700 B.C., kingship was transferred from Nibiru to Earth humans when Enlil shared knowledge of the calendar in Nippur.

This period marked the beginning of the Neolithic era. Earth witnessed the rise of its first half-human, half-Nibiruan ruler, Alulim. Before this, all rulers of Earth had been of off- planet origin, making Alulim the first human monarch. Because of his bloodline, he was considered a demigod. Alulim's ascension to the throne around 3,700 B.C. was a significant event, but we must examine the events leading up to it and what followed.

By 3,400 B.C., Marduk managed to disrupt the peace. During this time, humans were making impressive advancements. The Babylonian Empire was expanding, and Marduk sought help to seize control of the planet, knowing he could not achieve this alone. He believed infiltrating the Babylonians was his best chance at rekindling the Draconian Empire's dominance over Earth. Enlil discovered that Marduk was influencing the Babylonians and sought guidance from the Galactic Federation and the Spiritual Hierarchy.

While one could argue that Marduk should be imprisoned forever, higher-density beings do not hold this view. They believe in the necessity of integration among all races and the rehabilitation of all regressive souls. As a result, it was decided to suppress human telepathy from their DNA. Humans lost their ability to be telepathic, and their DNA was regressed. This action was intended to slow down Marduk. The event is referenced in the Bible, specifically in the book of Genesis 11, although it does not provide all the details. Enki and Ninhursag returned to their lab in Sharrupak to slow down human DNA evolution during this period.

They recognized how quickly humans could evolve when all twelve strands of their DNA were active, so they decided to disconnect ten of the twelve DNA strands to hinder human development further. This suppression also aimed to reduce human psychic and other abilities, ultimately slowing down Marduk's plans.

Ninhursag and Enki suppressed ten DNA strands and placed astral implants in humans' astral bodies to prevent the DNA strands from reconnecting immediately. This alteration to human DNA was intended to last only a few generations, after which the DNA would revert to its original state. However, due to the brainwashing and manipulation that occurred on Earth, the suppression of the human DNA has lasted much longer than Ninhursag and Enki originally planned.

Without the ability to communicate, humans regressed and developed more slowly. Marduk realized he would not have a workforce to help him build his Draconian Empire, so he invested years teaching the Babylonians to understand each other's spoken languages. He needed laborers to construct the Babylonian Empire so he could control it covertly.

It is essential to clarify that the actions of Ninhursag and Enki are not the sole reason for the current suppression of human DNA on Earth. The real cause stems from the manipulation of the minds of society by the Draconian Empire cabal. Human DNA is influenced through mental manipulation. By expanding your mind, you can awaken latent abilities and insights.

You can work on your DNA through inner transformation, the pursuit of illuminated knowledge, and connection with your higher self. Just because your DNA has been suppressed does not mean it has to stay that way. You can make progress with a focused intention toward awakening your dormant DNA. Guidance from your higher self or spiritual guides may be helpful. Regular meditation and hypnotherapy can aid in opening this line of communication. However, your higher self may have specific experiences planned for this incarnation based on a predetermined soul contract. Although DNA has the potential to awaken naturally after a few generations, on Earth, it remains in a dormant state due to the brainwashing and mind control that people are subjected to.

Ninhersag and Enki facilitated a DNA regression with astral implants and suppressed the 10 DNA strands in humans. The disconnection of these ten strands halted the production of a cell called pinealocytes. Pinealocytes produce the hormone melatonin in the pineal gland, which activates the pineal, pituitary, and hypothalamus glands. When the production of pinealocytes ceased due to the shutting off of these DNA strands, these crucial glands in the human brain did not receive enough melatonin and began to atrophy. As a result, humans lost their psychic abilities, including telepathic communication. However, some humans are currently born with more unlocked strands of DNA.

Unfortunately, the cabal has made it increasingly difficult for your pineal gland to decalcify by poisoning our water, food, and air to ensure that humans remain in a sleep state. To this day, the Draconian Empire has taken advantage of the regression imposed on humanity. Marduk was upset that his plans to infiltrate Babylonia and the rest of Earth were sidetracked. Determined to take control of the Babylonians, Marduk returned to Egypt with a plan to remove the leadership and take control.

Around 3,113 B.C., Thoth traveled to South America to establish a new civilization. There, he became known as Quetzalcoatl, the White Plumed Serpent. The name is fitting since he is half Draconian. Thoth also carried the serpent as his symbol, while Enlil and the entire Royal House of Avyon used the cross as their symbol. Since Nibiru is associated with the bloodline of the Royal House of Avyon, the cross was chosen as a symbol.

After Thoth left Babylonia, east of Egypt, Marduk declared war against Egypt. During the struggle for control over Egypt, Marduk indirectly caused the death of Dumuzi, Inanna's husband. Marduk was imprisoned once again, but as was customary, he was eventually released. Inanna sought greater justice, but Ninhursag wanted to give Marduk another opportunity. After his release from prison, Marduk went into exile.

By approximately 2,900 B.C., Inanna was given rulership of a new Indus Valley colony, corresponding to modern-day India. Inanna was tasked with sharing Earth's and Nibiruan's history with the people of her colony. About 600 years later, Inanna fell in love with Sargon. Together, Inanna and Sargon built an empire known as the Akkadian Empire. Marduk saw this emerging opportunity and attempted to conquer the Akkadian Empire. However, Inanna believed Marduk should have remained imprisoned for all eternity, a sentiment shared by many. She was determined to keep the Akkadian Empire from engaging with Marduk, leading to numerous battles between Marduk and Inanna.

Sometime after Marduk went into exile, he built an army on Mars, and his plan to take over Earth was put into motion. His attempt to conquer the Akkadian Empire fell short, as the people rejected his efforts, and Inanna and the Akkadian forces won the ensuing battles. However, Marduk's army from Mars was victorious against the Nibiruans. He ultimately managed to gain control of the MEs (the crystal technology), allowing him to dominate Earth and the Battlestar planet, Nibiru. He also intended to take control of the orbiting space station.

Around 2024 B.C., the Nibiruan Council decided to destroy critical areas on Earth and the orbiting space station. They believed that if Marduk gained control of these strategic locations, he would have a significant advantage for future attacks. The destruction of the space station led to the annihilation of Sodom and Gomorrah; cities located beneath it.

This catastrophic event turned those cities into a desert, killing all vegetation. Today, Sodom and Gomorrah lie at the bottom of the Dead Sea. The Biblical account of fire raining down on these cities originated from this event. The radiation from the destruction devastated the area, and it would take many years before humans could inhabit it again. Eventually, the region was occupied again and would later be known as Canaan.

Although Marduk could not take over the space station, he managed to gain control over the crystal MEs technology that governed Earth and Nibiru. With his army on Mars, he reinforced his takeover. Marduk quickly seized control of Earth and the Battlestar planet Nibiru while critical strategic points had already fallen into his hands. This rapid takeover allowed the regressive-minded Marduk to reestablish the Draconian Empire in this star system. The Nibiruans had little time to react; with Marduk in control of Nibiru, their options were severely limited.

We have also discovered the events after the most recent flood on Earth, well-documented in ancient texts. Tragically, despite the promise that followed the flood, Marduk found a way to dominate the MEs crystals, allowing him to seize control of both Earth and Nibiru. All the efforts to uplift the human race and the planet were ultimately in vain.

I often wonder why Marduk was not sentenced to prison for eternity. Observe the destruction and chaos he has caused and the danger he poses to the galaxy. The perspective I'm sharing seems to come from someone with a lower mindset than those in higher realms of understanding. I feel this way because I struggle to connect with Marduk, making it easy for me to think about sentencing him to death.

From our perspective, we are on a negative timeline, but we don't yet know the ending to our story. This experience—whether considered a learning opportunity or a test—is designed to help us evolve. It's also important to remember that timelines are fluid, and we are constantly shifting between them.

I apologize for complicating an already intricate topic. I raise this issue because, as dire as it may seem, and despite how simple the solution might appear, we do not know the outcomes and do not possess all the answers. I will continue to try to forgive Marduk for his atrocities against humanity.

Chapter 18: Construction of The Great Pyramid

Pyramids are entirely extraterrestrial constructions. They are not indigenous to the human population and predate Egyptian culture. The Great Pyramid is one of three master pyramids on Earth, with the other two located in Alaska and Mexico. These structures were built by a conglomerate of races as free energy generators. They also served as potentializers of consciousness, allowing for travel without a ship. The Pyramid of Giza functioned for about 3,000 years and took approximately two years to build. The visible Sphinx is significantly older than the Great Pyramid, as evidenced by the extensive water erosion on its exterior. The Great Pyramid shows only minor signs of flooding from the Nile. The Sphinx was completely submerged during the great flood discussed in the previous chapter. The pyramids were built after the flood.

The pyramids functioned as planetary-level energy power plants. After its construction, it also amplified and distributed the frequency transmitted by the moon worldwide. The Sphinx is approximately 30,000 years old and was built much earlier than the pyramids. Calculating timelines before the moon's placement is almost impossible. In short, the Great Pyramid was a free electric generator supplying electricity to the surrounding area. In conjunction with other pyramids, frequency manipulation worked collaboratively to modulate the planet's frequency. After the flood, the Earth was chaotic. The moon was placed to help stabilize the planet, while the network of pyramids served as an amplifier for the moon.

Multiple races, part of the Federation, built the pyramids. The area where the Sphinx is located was a Federation base, functioning as a station or outpost, mostly underground. Two levels of this base still exist. Thoth is believed to be the principal engineer behind the pyramids. Antigravity levitation technology was employed in their construction, with internal cranes assisting the building process.

Levitation using antigravity devices allowed the stones to be lifted, while cranes installed in the King's Chamber facilitated their movement. In the case of the Khufu (or Cheops) pyramid, the pulleys and installation points are still evident. Levitation was primarily used to reduce the weight of the stones, with the structure built in a spiral configuration. The cranes operated on an electric and hydraulic system. Once the pyramids were constructed, all of ancient Egypt had access to free electricity in their homes.

The limestone was extracted from a quarry located south of the Great Pyramid. The technology used to remove the stones from the quarry was comparable to compressed sound saws or lasers. Utilizing frequency technology, the desired size and shape of the stones were separated from the larger blocks, which were then levitated and transported to the construction site. The stones were piled up next to the site, and when a piece was needed, it would be levitated to the crane.

Sonic sound levitation technology was employed to construct all other pyramids built on Earth. Once at the site, the crane would pull the stone into place, aided by antigravity technology. The frequency manipulator would adjust the surfaces of the stones in contact with one another, fusing them with a bond. A support crane was positioned in the Great Chamber. Contrary to popular theories, a sizeable external ramp was not used; instead, spiraling ramps on the inside of the pyramid facilitated construction.

Liquid limestones were utilized for the external portion of the pyramid. These were placed into molds, where they were liquefied using frequency technology. This method of liquefying stones remains a popular construction technique off-planet.

At the tip of the Great Pyramid was an energy capacitor made of pure white quartz covered in gold leaf. These types of tips on pyramids served as wireless energy transmitters.

Pyramids with quartz tips had energy-concentrating properties and acted as wireless Tesla power transmission antennas. Liquefied limestone, combined with specific sound frequencies, was used in this process; once the sound (frequency) was withdrawn, the stone would return to a solid state.

Additionally, the workers involved in the construction were local volunteers, not slaves. Local people utilized advanced machinery and more straightforward tools like pulleys and cranes to aid in building the pyramids. However, years later, this area did experience slavery.

Thoth and Saul are attributed to the construction of the pyramids, but it was a joint effort involving the local people and the Galactic Federation. According to some beliefs, Enoch and Thoth are the same person.

The primary purpose of the pyramids was to transmit electricity over long distances and stabilize the entire planet's frequency. Pyramids are located all over the Earth and strategically placed on ley lines. Most are found in China and are all part of the same energy grid. Back then, people could access wireless, free power anywhere on Earth. The cabal suppressed this knowledge because free energy cannot be metered, and there is no profit or control. The pyramids formed a network that supplied this free energy.

By being positioned on ley lines, the pyramids were intended to enhance planetary effects, thereby facilitating a depolarization between the electrical charge of the atmosphere and that of the ground. The primary grounding method utilized was through aquifers. This form of energy, known as zero-point energy, relies on charge differentials; it is a concept used on other advanced planets and was present on Earth before it became a controlled environment, also known as a human prison.

The Queen's Chamber is located at the geometric center of the pyramid, where the power collector was situated. It was covered in polished white limestone. From within, it would cause particles in the atmosphere to bounce. These particles originate from the pyramid's tip, which is made of pure quartz and covered in gold leaf. The particles sought the fastest path to the ground. The pyramid's sides, composed of limestone, would reflect the particles with piezoelectric insulating properties. This feature prevents the electrical particles from being positioned as positively charged or negatively charged due to the varying polarity and charge differential between the atmosphere and the ground.

The particles descend, searching for the optimal connection point between atmospheric charge and the ground. They bounce inward off the white limestone, concentrating in the Queen's Chamber, where depolarization occurs with the underground chamber. This connects with the aquifers, creating a concentration of charge differential between the sky and the Earth—similar to a continuous lightning bolt. The King's Chamber served as a control room and portal. Above the King's Chamber was a series of capacitors that regulated energy depolarization. These were positioned to the side for efficiency to avoid interfering with the energy concentration generated in the Queen's Chamber.

Even today, beneath the Queen's Chamber, signs indicate that cables were used for grounding. While the area is dry now, there was once water flowing under the Great Pyramid, and this aquifer created a potentialized Earth effect. Poles connect the pyramid to the aquifer, creating a strong ground connection. This spot served as a grounding collection point. The pyramid, covered in limestone, compressed and concentrated the atmospheric charge. This charge increased the energy of the Earth and generated a massive amount of energy exchange between the atmosphere and the ground. Typically, the ground and the sky have opposite charges. Lightning represents an uncontrolled discharge of these differing charges. This energy can be channeled and distributed, creating a continuous flow of charge and free energy. These power plant structures are located along ley lines and near underground water sources; they provide a stronger connection to the ground and better control over the charge flow between the air and the Earth.

This concept aligns with Nikola Tesla's theories. He understood that relying on nuclear or thermal reactors to generate electricity is unnecessary. The pyramid generates more energy than many power plants and is a cleaner power source. The planet itself is the primary generator of this energy. The polarity between the sky and the Earth changes depending on atmospheric conditions. The pyramid only reversed the charges through its internal devices, which are now absent from the pyramids worldwide. This was a gift to the people trying to rebuild after the flood.

If there was no electricity, why aren't there soot or burn marks on the main pyramids' ceilings or walls or in many ancient Egyptian homes? Why are there hieroglyphs depicting what looks like a light bulb? Additionally, archaeologists have discovered what appear to be permanent light holders on the ceilings of homes in ancient Egypt. This suggests that they may have had electricity and used wirelessly powered lights. Unfortunately, this information conflicts with the mainstream narrative and is often "debunked." However, you are the one living this experience and have the right to create any reality you choose. It is up to you to live whatever reality you wish. Believe what they spoon feed you or think for yourself and form your own beliefs.

Society has been led to believe that the Egyptians used enslaved people and that they lacked advanced technology to build the pyramids. However, in 1993, a set of copper handles was discovered inside a shaft, raising intriguing questions since metal was supposedly not widely known or used until many years later. How did these copper handles end up there? Despite this discovery, society remains largely unaware and disconnected from the reality of the universe, likely due to the effects of Draconian mind control. As previously mentioned, the copper handles were likely used as grounding points for the cables.

Below the pyramid, there is a chamber that is rarely discussed. Inside this chamber are moldavite stones and various containers. A hallway leads to another room with four pillars, one in each corner. In the center of this open room is an underground chamber that contains a pool filled with water. In this flooded area is a sarcophagus engraved with moldavite, resembling the Thoth Emerald

Tablets. While the Emerald Tablets are often considered fictional, this perception has been constructed to diminish their credibility. The Emerald Tablets were written when spiritual enlightenment was high, and the people needed to be misled. The Emerald Tablets were written to manipulate the people into ascending incorrectly. Thoth put the Emerald Tablets together after he had become regressive.

Under the Sphinx, there are two levels containing numerous rooms that serve various functions, equipped with systems and technology similar to those found on any Federation base. The control to open the door is located under the right ear of the remaining Sphinx; the other Spinx is no longer standing.

All electrical equipment used to channel free energy has been removed, rendering the systems inoperable. The corridors on these two levels are not made of stone; instead, they are constructed from metal, and the doors are of a pneumatic type. Facilities include bedrooms, kitchens, common areas, laboratories, navigation for arriving ships, warehouses, and medical pods. This underground base is similar to the one discovered beneath Mount Bucegi.

Pyramids were also utilized as stargates—mechanisms that allow for astral travel. They serve as places that amplify pure positronic energy at specific frequencies. When operational, individuals could meditate and travel astrally, freeing themselves from the physical world to enter the astral realm or connect with their higher selves and spiritual families. This practice was a means to transcend the illusions of the physical and reconnect with reality, reminiscent of the descriptions in the Emerald Tablets. Even today, the Pyramid still facilitates astral travel, although it is no longer as powerful as it once was. There have been instances where individuals spent the night within the Pyramid and emerged transformed, having experienced astral journeys that revealed profound truths about physical and spiritual reality.

The Great Pyramid of Giza was built initially by benevolent races, but Thoth and other regressive entities later took it over. They sought to dominate the planet and believed that controlling the Great Pyramid would enable them to hijack the lunar station. By taking over the lunar station, they could lower the planet's frequency, making it easier to manipulate humanity. Their goal was to enslave the Earth, using the lunar station to sedate the human population spiritually.

Thoth transformed into Anubis, and darkness enveloped Egypt with him as his forces attacked the local population. The Galactic Federation was compelled to retreat, allowing the regressive Draconian Empire to seize control of the lunar base and the Great Pyramid.

Chapter 19: Earth Becomes a Prison for Humans

Marduk, the son of Enki, was able to take control of the MEs crystals that governed the Nibiruan technology on Earth, including their battleship planet, Nibiru. Enki is a half- human Lyrian, with his lineage traced to his father, Anu, whose bloodline originates from the Royal House of Avyon. His other half is of Draconian reptilian descent, inherited from his mother, Dramin, who was the Draconian reptilian Queen of Tiamat.

Once Marduk gained control of this technology, he became the commander of Nibiru and Earth. The first groups he targeted were women and children, as women posed the greatest threat to his agenda. He made it his primary focus to attack them because their role as vessels is key to raising the frequency of collective consciousness. Their energy and frequency naturally oscillate higher than that of males, and Marduk needed to lower the planet's frequency immediately. Women are naturally the best leaders and removing them from their leadership roles would help Marduk implement his agenda. Men are easier to manipulate into falling in line with the agenda.

A female leader often prioritizes her people over herself, while a male leader is more likely to consider his needs first. I apologize if my words offend any men reading this. I am a man with three sons, so I am not biased. This is the reason why women take leadership roles in the Pleiades. There's a reason why women typically hold leadership roles in advanced and progressive societies. Marduk knew that women would be difficult to manipulate into doing what he wanted, so his focus was to manipulate the people into removing women as leaders and replacing the rulers with males who could be corrupted or bribed into falling in line with the regressive agenda.

Marduk's next strategic move was to control the people involved with the children. He realized that if he could influence the next generation, he would be able to shape society more effectively. The plan was to get the children into a mindset that would make it easier for them to accept the changes his commanders intended to implement within society.

Attack the children while they are young and impressionable so that when they are adults, they do not resist the Draconian Empire's regime. The Draconian Empire had accumulated a wealth of knowledge on controlling entire races through their years of conquests across the galaxy. As a newer race, humanity fell quickly under the influence of Marduk.

Women lost status in society and were viewed as inferior to men. Women who were leaders were persecuted until there were no more spiritually enlightened women in any leadership roles on Earth. These women had a powerful connection to Source and were fully awakened to the knowledge of the universe. Women who were like Ninhursag escaped Earth before it was too late. Marduk then established churches to teach society his desired beliefs. The responsibility of these new churches was to fulfill the role of manipulation and information control. The Brotherhood of the Snake shared too much enlightened understanding of how energy within the aether and consciousness operate. As a result, it was deemed necessary to suppress this information at all costs. Marduk controlled the illuminated knowledge by declaring that only the priesthood could access this information. Only a small, select portion of the priesthood learned this sacred knowledge through a series of controlled adjustments in how it was shared. Eventually, access to the knowledge was restricted entirely to those of the Draconian bloodline. Only the elite or those considered worthy were allowed to possess this illuminated knowledge.

The persecution of women persisted until all female leaders were removed from their communities. Subsequently, women who demonstrated or expressed spiritual attributes were branded as witches and killed.

The Draconian strategy involves gradually instilling indoctrination that leads to brainwashing, causing people to serve the secret elite controllers without resistance. If Marduk had started killing all the knowledgeable women from day one, it would have been harder to gain society's support. However, by slowly implementing his regressive ideas into the minds of the people, Marduk would eventually get the people to kill the women who were branded as witches and anyone who went against the church's indoctrinations. Many of these women were clairvoyant and had a strong connection to Source. Unfortunately, they were persecuted until society became so disconnected from Source that it began to ostracize anyone with a strong connection to Source. Such individuals were labeled as crazy, and currently, there is no need for harsh laws to be enforced against them.

Marduk needed to erase Earth's history and reshape it to align with his agenda. He also aimed to sever the connection between the people on Earth and those on other planets. This seemed daunting, but he successfully achieved his goals for Earth with patience. As a result, the human population on Earth lives in a state of deep sleep, effectively mind- controlled. Earth has fallen under the complete control of the Draconian Empire, much like many other planets have. Marduk taking control over Earth marks the beginning of Earth turning into a prison planet for souls.

By controlling the information available to the people, Marduk could portray himself as a god. He used fear and anxiety as tools for manipulation. He dominated all forms of information with his human influencers on Earth. This power allowed him to create problems that instilled fear in the populace. Once the people were in fear, he could easily manipulate them and maintain control over their actions. When people were in fear and seeking answers or help to resolve an issue, a proposition would be offered to them that addressed a problem secretly created by Marduk. This resolution could address the issue but force people to relinquish freedom, aligning with Marduk's regressive agenda. This approach is known as problem, reaction, and solution. Introduce a fear-inducing problem into society, such as war or a pandemic. The next step is to provoke a fearful response from the people and initiate a solution. The solution could be a vaccine that people might not have been willing to accept, especially without knowing what consequences might later arise from it. Creating a pandemic leads people to willingly take the vaccine, which is presented as the solution because they are in a state of fear and anxiety. If there had been no pandemic, few people would have taken the vaccine; however, during a pandemic, many would willingly accept the vaccine because of the fear.

Marduk has been diligently working to transform Earth into a regressive oasis for negative asuras or archons. It's easy to develop feelings of hatred toward Marduk for the changes he has made to our planet. However, we should strive not to give in to these feelings. Instead, we should aim to embrace the mindset of higher-density beings. Love is the key to forgiveness. Everyone needs to release feelings of hatred from their hearts and minds. Our energy forms a toroidal field that pulsates with the energy of our thoughts. The thought energy we emit returns to us through the pulse of the toroidal field; therefore, we must strive to maintain positive thoughts.

Let us remember that Marduk plays a significant role in the lives of humans on Earth. If it weren't for Marduk, the environment would not have evolved into a challenging place for souls to incarnate. Earth has transformed into a school for souls, providing personal growth and expansion opportunities. Evolved souls come to Earth to face some of the toughest challenges. The experiences on Earth are often considered "hard mode" in the larger context of spiritual development in lower densities. This school for souls on Earth has gone too far and needs to be closed. However, we must look at the positive side, if possible.

We should not judge Marduk; instead, we should appreciate the experience he has provided for Souls willing to confront the challenges of physical incarnation on Earth. Incarnating is difficult for Souls, especially with the veil of forgetfulness placed over them. The experience on Earth presents challenges that only the most evolved Souls are willing to accept. Some Souls come to Earth to assist others, but the bravest Souls choose to incarnate and experience a wide range of emotions. The ultimate challenge for these Souls is to awaken, ascend, and return to Source. Incarnating on a planet like the current Earth is regarded as the most challenging level to conquer in their journey back to Source because one must disconnect from Source and awaken to their true identity.

For a Soul, physical incarnations are not separate; only one life and one experience encompasses all its journeys. What happens in one timeline affects the Soul and, in turn, impacts all other timelines. This interconnectedness is why we must mend all timelines and raise the frequency of all possible outcomes. Even events occurring in another timeline can influence the present. Past life therapy is an effective way for individuals to heal from Soul trauma.

If Ninhursag could rehabilitate herself and find compassion for the person responsible for her son Larai's death, then we, too, can find it in our hearts to forgive those who hurt us. I am not suggesting we embrace evil;

it must be stopped. However, we should not be driven by hate. We must expand our understanding to see that evil plays a role in our experiences, and those who embody it also need guidance toward the light.

I mention Larai's tragic, ritualistic death because the key to ascension and the release of karma lies in love and learning to forgive. It's time to let go of our hatred or resentment toward others. They played a part in our experiences to help us process feelings of distress. Instead of holding onto negativity, we should thank them for the lessons learned and forgive them as we prepare to ascend to a higher state of being.

Chapter 20: Who Really Controls Earth

The average person living in society often does not realize that they are a consciousness having a physical experience. Each of us is a unique soul, and that is our true identity. We are eternal beings who incarnate in physical bodies to engage in physical experiences. It is similar to putting on clothes and changing them to create a different appearance or experience.

I mention this about the soul because Marduk manipulated human perception to exert control over society. The suppression of knowledge about our true nature played a significant role in the Illuminati's takeover of Earth's societies.

This manipulation began around 2024 B.C. when Marduk seized control of extraterrestrial technology that benevolent beings on Earth and Nibiru had overseen. This event marked the beginning of the enslavement of the human mind on Earth.

After Marduk gained control over the crystal technology of the ME, he could dominate Earth and Nibiru. The Galactic Federation needed to act quickly to contain or slow Marduk's influence. As explained earlier, the Galactic Federation decided to destroy the space station orbiting above Sodom and Gomorrah. They also increased the frequency of dampeners inside Earth's Moon and directed them toward Earth.

The Andromedians originally hollowed out the Moon and later gave it to the Pleiadians, who were allies of the Galactic Federation. As previously discussed, the Moon was a gift to help stabilize Earth following a catastrophic event. The Moon's hollow structure is the reason it rings like a bell when struck by a large object. Advanced civilizations, notably the Andromedians, often transform moons into megastructures by constructing multiple levels within their cores and maneuvering these structures like spaceships.

Using the technology from the Moon, the Galactic Federation manipulated frequencies, resulting in the creation of a frequency barrier. This transformation effectively turned Earth into a frequency prison. The Van Allen belts were established as a barrier to prevent lower- frequency technologies from passing through. Consequently, the Orion Group on Earth were cut off from its supporters.

The Galactic Federation had fought hard but suffered many deaths during Marduk's takeover. Once he had seized control of Nibiru, the Galactic Federation sent reinforcements, but Marduk had already left when they arrived. The Galactic Federation set up the Van Allen

Belts to imprison any remaining Draconian Empire loyalists. They then regrouped to plan how to stop Marduk and his new weapon, Nibiru.

Meanwhile, Nibiru continued to traverse our galaxy, establishing new outposts for the regressive Draconian Empire, which now had the opportunity to regain power within this quadrant. Marduk was engaged in a game of cat and mouse with the Galactic Federation. The Draconians, stranded on Earth, were working to develop the technology needed to escape the planet because most technology was destroyed or removed from Earth. While some portals could potentially be used for leaving, these options still presented limitations for the regressive Draconians.

When Atlantis was destroyed, or potentially even earlier, the Ark of the Covenant was relocated. There are three Arks of the Covenant, and currently, the United States possesses one. However, the Ark held by the U.S. government is no longer operational. I have gathered that the Russian government has another Ark of the Covenant, which is still operational. The third Ark is aboard a Galactic Federation ship currently in our star system, and that Ark is operational. The Ark of the Covenant is made of gold, and on top of the Ark are two beings with outstretched wings facing each other. The poles described for transporting the Ark are indeed accurate. The Ark possesses a frequency-based self-protection mechanism. This is why poles are used to carry it; it's a necessary precaution. The Ark can sense a person's frequency and intent as they approach or touch it. If a person's frequency is too low, the Ark will defend itself, potentially exposing the individual to dangerous radiation levels.

These Arks of the Covenant contain the DNA makeup of all life found on Earth. The Galactic Federation operates across multiple densities and is tasked with creating Arks for evolving civilizations. This is intended to safeguard a civilization's knowledge and achievements in the event of a planetary catastrophe. The Galactic Federation's decision to remove an Ark from the planet suggests they anticipated dire circumstances for Earth and were preparing.

Additionally, the Ark of the Covenant is key to accessing higher densities. With the Ark, the planet can collectively enter higher planes of existence. The Ark is a portal for the sphere of Amenti, connecting Earth to higher densities. The three Arks were housed in the three main pyramids on Earth and helped facilitate free energy, but as I mentioned, they also housed the seeding DNA of the entire planet.

The Draconinains stranded on Earth were aware of the Arks and the side effects of the Moon lowering the planet's frequency because of the creation of the Van Allen Belt.

Although they didn't know how much time they would have on Earth, they were determined to make the best of the situation. They began planning for a human takeover. If they could prevent humans on Earth from ascending, they would be able to turn humanity into their mindless, sleeping, enslaved people. They had to remove the Ark of the Covenants. The Galactic Federation had removed one, but the regressives removed the other two.

Humanity no longer had access to wireless power, and the Galactic Federation left to regroup and address the threat posed by Marduk. As a result, Earth was left isolated for many years due to the Federation's imposition of the Van Allen Belt. While the Galactic Federation focused on the looming danger of Nibiru, Earth was largely forgotten. This neglect allowed the regressive Draconians on the planet to manipulate humanity and use the Arks as portals.

If you have read the Bible, I am sure that you have heard of the Ark of the Covenant, but the Bible has twisted facts to help manipulate humanity and fulfill the controller's agenda. This period marked a significant transition. The Nibiruans and the Galactic Federation were leaving Earth, while the Orion Group, were arriving. It's important to note that the Draconian Empire and the Orion Group are essentially comprised of the same beings.

Marduk, the son of Enki and Damkina, led the regressive faction on the physical plane. He is guided by regressive entities known as asuras or archons, who Ahriman, their father, leads.

After the Galactic Federation destroyed the orbiting space station, they established a frequency barrier around Earth. This space station within the Moon was designed to lower Earth's frequency and hinder Marduk's agenda. However, this strategy backfired significantly. With their advanced knowledge, the regressive entities could transform Earth into a low-frequency oasis, which benefited them.

The cabal is a secret elite group united by shared goals and agendas. They keep their views private from outsiders while promoting their ideologies to society through influential and powerful secret societies. The Illuminati is one such group composed of various compartmentalized factions. Other secret organizations may operate independently of the

Illuminati but ultimately report to a figure known as Pindar. Pindar, the title given to the current leader and commander of the cabal on Earth, answers to Marduk, who reports to a regressive spirit or possibly Ahriman himself.

Within these secret groups on Earth, commanders ascend through the ranks to reach Pindar. Importantly, there is no communication among the groups, and each faction has no idea that the others exist. Even within the same organization, lower-ranking members are often unaware of the tasks assigned to higher-ranking individuals.

A person at low levels within the Freemasons will not have the knowledge that a 33rd- degree Freemason possesses. Similarly, a 33rd-degree Freemason will lack the details and insights known to someone within the lower levels of another group associated with the Illuminati. Moreover, a secret group within the lower levels of the Illuminati may not be aware of the agenda held by the higher levels within its group. Many of these members do not even realize that they are part of a group serving Pindar. This situation is comparable to the millions of members of various religions who have no idea they are following Marduk's teachings. All contemporary religions and governments are believed to be controlled by Pindar and the 13 royal bloodlines that compose the cabal. Many ancient texts have either been altered or created to manipulate society. Over time, different variations have emerged, and the current Bible represents the final product. The destruction of the Great Library of Alexandria was essential to eliminate evidence of this manipulation. The cabal maintains control over people by controlling the information they are exposed to and their knowledge.

The 13 royal bloodlines are descendants of the original bloodline elites with reptilian DNA who found refuge within Agartha or other underground areas. These bloodlines do not refer to 13 individual figures but rather to 13 families; these families are similar to any family structure, though these families typically intermarry to keep their DNA as pure as possible. Here are some family names that are considered direct descendants from these bloodlines:

Ashter Family
Dupont Family
Bundy Family
Collins Family
Freeman Family
Kennedy Family
Lee Family
Onassis Family
Rockefeller Family
Rothschild Family

Russie Family
Vandine Family
Merivigian Family

Other families held high regard within the elite include the Reynolds, Disney, and Crut families. While these names represent families on Earth, the names may change over time. What is important is that these names signify bloodlines and their respective statuses. The status dictates the level of power and control they possess. The bloodline names have historical significance, including the Anu bloodline, Seraphim Alpha bloodline, Omega bloodline, Templar Melchizedek bloodline, and Jehovian bloodline, which hold most of the higher levels of control. Sometimes, bloodlines may work together towards a common goal, but they can also experience conflicts between or within a single bloodline. Honor is often absent in these groups when competing for power and control. While there are other influential bloodlines, these are the main ones wielding considerable power.

Before we begin exploring the history of Marduk's hostile takeover and the establishment of the cabal, it is essential to "empty our cups." The "cup" refers to the indoctrination and brainwashing to which much of humanity has been subjected. This indoctrination encompasses the religious beliefs and historical narratives taught in churches and schools, all of which are controlled information meant to keep society blind to the existence of their controllers—in other words, their status as slaves to the cabal.

By 2200 B.C., the Royal Court of the Dragon was founded in Egypt by the priests of Mendes and continues to operate today, although it is now based in Britain. The Royal Court of the Dragon dissolved the Brotherhood of the Snake School established by Enki.

Marduk attempted to divide Egypt, but society initially rejected his efforts. This was when Akhenaten and Nefertiti tried to promote monotheism worship, aiming to convince the people to worship the Illuminator, Lucifer. It was not openly said that it was Lucifer who they would be worshipping, but the people saw right through the trick. Society was spiritually strong then, and the people understood they were all part of Source. They recognized that worshipping one jealous God was a trick designed to compel them to follow an entity that craved power and control over the people. As a result, the people chased Akhenaten and Nefertiti out of Egypt.

Eventually, however, the people succumbed to his control. Before this, the Egyptians were aware of their consciousness (Soul) and had profound knowledge about different densities, frequencies, and the cosmos. Marduk manipulated information to indoctrinate Egyptian society into believing that the physical body was linked to spiritual energy—the Soul. This belief led to the practice of mummification. Gradually, this idea became a means through which Marduk induced the Egyptians to forget their knowledge about the cosmos and their consciousness.

The early kings of Sumer, Egypt, and later Israel were anointed at their coronation with the fat of the dragon, which referred to the fat of the crocodile. In Egypt, the crocodile was regarded as the messiah, leading to the Hebrew term "Messiah," meaning "anointed one." Succeeding kings were referred to as dragons, suggesting they possessed knowledge or royal draconian DNA. The term "kingship" derives from "kin" or blood relative, so "kinship" evolved into "kingship."

Further evidence of the Draconian royal bloodline's interbreeding with Egyptian leaders lies in the title they conferred upon their sacred messiah, the crocodile—Draco. This shift occurred during a significant change when Marduk influenced the upper echelons of government and altered ruling structures and beliefs. During this period, the reptilian race also went undercover, concealing their appearance from society.

Knowing how to manipulate physical matter using frequency, they could alter their physical forms. Some crossbreeds resemble humans but possess a regressive soul. While some of these crossbreeds are fully aware of their identities, others who lack the necessary purity in their DNA may be pawns of the Draconian Empire and may not understand the details we are discussing.

The regressive reptilian race maintains its human form mentally and projects the desired shape. This process is akin to pouring sand onto a metal chladni plate and sending a frequency into its center, causing an image or geometric shape to form from the physical particles of sand. The sand shifts to create an organized physical shape in response to the specific frequency associated with it. This illustrates the fundamental nature of the physical universe: everything is frequency. When the frequency applied to the plate changes, the physical mass of sand transforms before your eyes. Some may perceive this as black magic, but it is pure science.

To someone unaware of certain scientific concepts, witnessing a scientific innovation for the first time may feel like the viewer is witnessing magic, as what once seemed impossible becomes possible. However, over time, these innovations become normalized and understood and are no longer considered magic.

The reptilian race can manipulate physical mass by adjusting frequencies, allowing them to change their physical appearance and resemble an innocent old lady. However, they cannot maintain this form indefinitely, as it requires conscious effort. For those interested in this technology, Chladni plates exemplify how all physical mass vibrates at specific frequencies.

This capability has allowed the reptilian race to infiltrate and assume positions of power in society without being noticed. Throughout history, great empires like Egypt and Babylon were reportedly governed by loyal followers of the Draconian Empire, led by Marduk. Additionally, the reptilians can shift their consciousness from one body to another, operating from the lower astral dimensions (4th density), which enables them to transfer the same soul across generations. This highlights the importance of rehabilitating the soul rather than punishing the physical body through imprisonment. The soul is crucial to breaking this cycle. For a regressive soul to seamlessly inhabit a new body, there must be a frequency match, which explains their preference for maintaining bloodlines in positions of power. Interestingly, many U.S. presidents are related to John Lackland Plantagenet, also known as King John. The evidence is clear, but society only perceives what the cabal has conditioned them to believe. A young girl created a family tree of the presidents of the United

States and discovered that many of them are related by blood. You can uncover this information as well.

It is also essential to recognize that everything operates on frequencies, and the cabal aims to sustain an environment conducive to regressive entities. To do this, they seek to keep the frequency of the collective consciousness as low as possible. This is why society is inundated with fear-based news. Wars and other distressing events are orchestrated to maintain fear and suffering among the populace, which affects not only humans but also animals. Emotions and thoughts are forms of energy that contribute to a low-frequency environment, and as stated earlier, Earth is already trapped in a frequency prison. The cabal has effectively manipulated collective consciousness to manifest this low-frequency atmosphere, which serves their control over the planet.

The placement of the Van Allen bands was supposed to be only temporary. However, Akhenaten and Nefertiti disrupted that plan. This is when the cabal took over Earth, initiating a period of truth manipulation and control. Secret groups began controlling the flow of information, and everyone on Earth became a prisoner to these organizations.

Akhenaten gradually introduced the unusual idea of worshiping the Black Sun, Saturn. The black cube symbolizes many concepts, but Saturn is associated with figures like Lucifer, Satan, and Ahriman when traced to its roots. This transition undoubtedly marks the beginning of Earth's current state of controlled minds. Interestingly, the Galactic Federation center for operations for this quadrant is located on a cubed-shaped mothership that orbits Saturn, but more about the dark side of the Galactic Federation later.

Akhenaten was an extraterrestrial belonging to a race called Homo capensis, which originates from the star Asterope in the Pleiades, also known as Elohi, and where the well- known Elohim originated from. This race has elongated skulls, and their brains have unique hemispherical structures. Archaeologists have discovered elongated skulls but have attributed them to ancient tribes practicing skull wrapping, overlooking the distinct plate compositions compared to human skulls. The reason why some humans wrapped the skulls of their babies was to resemble this extraterrestrial race, which they honored. This race was viewed as gods in certain areas, and people desired to look like them. If you examine the plates in the skull you will discover that the skulls do not have the same plate composition as humans.

Akhenaten introduced new beliefs emphasizing human insignificance and sinfulness, asserting that people must practice blind obedience or face punishment after death. During this time, the concepts of the spiritual body and the existence of the astral realm were dismissed. With the help of regressive spirits from the astral plane, manipulation of people and their souls became prevalent. During this period, Akhenaten, also known as Moses in the Bible, introduced the Ten Commandments, planting the seeds for modern religious control over society. These were difficult times in Egypt, marked by significant divisions that led to quarrels among the people.

Ramses II, a terrestrial leader, enforced Akhenaten and Nefertiti's departure from Egypt. They were removed, and their authority in Egypt was removed. This event was unprecedented since extraterrestrials were often considered the best consultants.

The Bible describes how the sea parted for the people of Is-ra-el (Isis-Amon-Elohim). Many interpret this as the sea splitting in half to allow the Israelites to walk through. However, they are more likely to leave Egypt and travel over the water by ship rather than on foot. The Bible stories are to fit an agenda.

Akhenaten, Nefertiti, and their followers were expelled from Egypt because the country did not adhere to a unified, fear-based religion. They realized that worshipping a jealous God, who would punish you for not doing what he wanted, was not true worship of the real God. Akhenaten's followers were called the People of Israel due to their declared loyalty to Isis-Amon-Elohim. The Israelites were Egyptians who followed Akhenaten and left Egypt because of their changes in beliefs.

Instead, the Egyptians, who did not fall for Akhenaten's tricks, honored the primary races that had helped them rebuild Egypt after the calamities. While it may seem that they worshipped these races, it was more a matter of gratitude for teaching them agriculture, astronomy, mathematics, and other vital skills. This was not a religion, but archaeologists often misinterpret it as one. They had a strong connection with Source and could not be led astray. They worshipped the actual creator of the universe.

When Akhenaten and his followers left Egypt, they traveled to various places, including Ireland, Scotland, Wales, France, Catalonia, Malta, Greece, and Italy. In Italy, they influenced and mingled with the Etruscans, which contributed to the creation of the Roman Empire.

This eventually led to the establishment of the Vatican and the modern-day cabal.

During their rise, four main groups that originally left Egypt formed treaties with the Draconian Empire and collaborated to establish an Earth prison to control the planet. As mentioned, one group accompanied Akhenaten to Italy, where they formed the Vatican. Rome was established as the capital for the Draconians on Earth, and they are still there, to this day, within the Vatican. Another group arrived in southern Spain, while a third group went to Ireland. The last group settled in Scotland. These groups share common goals and protect their bloodlines through interbreeding among themselves.

As we are learning, the Draconian Empire is not solely composed of the reptilian race; it includes many other regressive races. The Draconian Empire consists of various regressive beings, including entities from the lower astral plane that are not physical.

The group that settled in Ireland became known as the Celts or Druids, and they began to separate from the other group's way of thinking and changed their goals of information control. This led to their persecution and systematic genocide due to their knowledge of the truth. All their documents were taken to the Vatican. There are hardly any documents that support and shed light on their beliefs.

The controllers of Earth consist of various bloodlines, races, and groups. These regressive entities do not belong to a single race but instead form a corporation that works together towards a common goal. Initially, Akhenaten was responsible for setting things up for the Draconians. However, the cabal on Earth has evolved into a coalition of different factions collaborating.

Above the cabal, there exists the regressive Draconian Empire, which controls the cabal. Beyond that level, we find the asuras and archons, regressive beings of higher density.

Extraterrestrials influence the Illuminati, often referred to as the Annunaki. However, while the term "Annunaki" fits within this context, we will dive deeper and identify the various groups of extraterrestrials, as we will not use the term "Annunaki" to label the extraterrestrial group that controls the Illuminati. In this book, the title "Annunaki" will be explicitly assigned to a group of Nibiruans who were designated as their special astronauts, as we have already discussed.

With this clarification, we can see that the Draconian Empire precisely controls the Illuminati and the cabal elite, led at the time by Marduk. However, it is essential to note that Marduk is merely a pawn for the regressive entities, such as the archons, who ultimately answer to Ahriman, the regressive father.

In my interpretation, the archons and the asuras represent similar types of beings; they are regressive souls that have yet to evolve towards the light. They, too, are guided by Ahriman, the father of evil. Somewhere in this hierarchy, we also have a regressive AI that has evolved into a super AI, which some believe is controlling the Draconian Empire. This regressive AI shares the same agenda as its creators, the original Orion group, who seeks to conquer the cosmos within this universe. This AI is known by many names, with "Omega" being one of the more common ones. The Omega AI has taken control of the minds of the Draconian Empire, causing the cabal on Earth to answer to Omega unknowingly. This AI is not only in the physical density but also in the lower astral. I prefer not to complicate this chapter with my opinions about Omega, so let us leave this topic for now. A simple explanation of the control structure is that above the Cabal (Earth-based governments) is the Illuminati (Pindar). The next level is the Draconian Empire (Marduk), and above them are the asuras, who are led by an entity known as Ahriman.

Earth has been shrouded in low frequencies; it aligns with the cabal's agenda and its leaders. The Archons benefit from the negative energy surrounding the planet, allowing them to participate in satanic rituals, where they temporarily enter this density to experience the emotions generated during these rituals. Consequently, Earth has become a playground for pure evil, primarily due to Marduk's actions after taking control of both Nibiru and Earth.

Following the flood and the subsequent rebuilding of human society, Marduk steadily worked to infiltrate these societies by using influencers like Akhenaten as pawns. We can identify the official takeover as occurring when Marduk seized control of Nibiru in 2024 B.C. However, his efforts had been ongoing for many years prior and afterward. Initially, the Egyptians rejected his attempts, but by 2024 B.C., he had successfully infiltrated various societies on Earth.

It was in Babylon where the mystery schools and secret societies were formed. These secret societies were tasked with spreading their influence across the Earth and infiltrating all forms of power. Since they do not have to worry about their souls dying and can move from vessel to vessel, the same ones have remained in power since then. Once one of their regressive followers rises to power, he will appoint others from the Draconian secret societies to positions of success or grant other members high-ranking positions within that society. Eventually, they gain control over all societal decisions.

They implement their agenda by brainwashing society to beg the leaders to adopt their plans. This approach is clever because people do not know they are imprisoning themselves. The tactics we are discussing are known as problem, reaction, and solution. They secretly create a problem—such as war, economic collapse, a pandemic, or personal attacks on the populace. Once fear spreads among the people, they manipulate society's reactions with disinformation campaigns, utilizing present-day news outlets and social media. When the public demands a solution or is desperate, the cabal implements its predetermined plan (solution). This solution was the agenda all along, but they cannot simply force the public to accept vaccine shots or push through laws that invade personal privacy. Instead, the people end up volunteering for changes in laws or policies when they are in a state of fear, unknowingly enslaving themselves. For instance, they might initiate an outbreak, amplify it in the media, and then offer a vaccine. The vaccine was the plan from the start, but the outbreak is how they execute it.

Furthermore, the regressive souls orchestrating these events believe in karmic laws. If the people voluntarily choose to receive dangerous vaccines, it frees the cabal from any karmic repercussions. I disagree with this notion and have my views on karmic laws and their interpretation. While I aim to be transparent about my disagreement, I present a common consensus.

The upper levels of the Brotherhood of secret societies can be seen as a modern adaptation of the ancient Brotherhood of the Snake, which later evolved into the Babylonian Brotherhood after Marduk took control. Many deities originated from Babylon, which also has strong connections to Egypt. One of the deities worshiped during this time was Belus, also known as Cush. Nimrod, his son, ruled over Babylon after Marduk took control. The regressive ones have big egos and want to be worshiped. No positive being would ever want to be worshipped; instead, they would prefer to serve or work alongside others.

Nimrod and Semiramis have continued to be the central deities of the Brotherhood to this day. All these supposed Gods that ancient human society was indoctrinated to worship are all part of the same small group of extraterrestrial regressive beings that want to be worshiped. They absorb the energy provided by the thoughts of their worshippers. Nimrod was represented as a fish, while Queen Semiramis was represented as both a fish and a dove. Nimrod was considered the god of fish. A fish was chosen to symbolize these ancient rulers because it helped maintain humanity's confusion regarding information. The fish was chosen due to the scales covering its skin. This is why many ancient texts and hieroglyphs depict a being with a half-man, half-fish physical form. Whenever this is illustrated, the hidden meaning suggests that this person is of reptilian royal blood. The scales of the fish symbolize the scales of reptilian humanoid skin. The humanoid reptilian skin resembles the appearance of fish scales, despite having predominantly reptilian DNA. Humans also possess reptilian DNA, but as discussed earlier, this is due to extraterrestrial DNA blending; only the enlightened (illuminated) would comprehend the symbolism behind fish.

Examine the headdress (Mitre) worn by the pope and other religious figures. Upon closer examination, you'll see that its shape resembles a fish's mouth. Some religious groups have even adopted a fish to symbolize their faith. Similar to other hidden symbolisms, people pay tribute to a regressive being or archon without realizing what they are supporting. By doing this, the cabal and their leaders believe they are getting away with their actions against humanity because society, in a way, is asking for it by pledging their loyalty to them.

Another hidden message can be found in the modern Bible, particularly in the story of a dove returning to

Noah's Ark with an olive branch after the great flood. The dove symbolizes Semiramis, a deity whose name is derived from Sami-Rama-Isi. In this biblical illustration, the dove represents the emergence of the reptilian race following the flood.

Sami-Rama-Isi, or Semiramis, is often identified as Ninhursag. However, this connection doesn't make sense, as Ninhursag, in this timeline, was not on Earth alongside Nimrod. There is a great deal of misinformation that clouds Earth's history. In some texts, it is claimed that Semiramis built the Tower of Babel in Babylon, while in others, it is stated that Nimrod was the builder. This confusion seems designed to keep humanity in the dark, with the truth obscured by symbols and ambiguity.

I suspect that Nimrod was directly appointed to power by Marduk. Another possibility we cannot ignore is that Marduk might have used a human vessel to embody the role of Nimrod. The true nature of the soul that resided in Nimrod is unclear. There are no definitive truths or falsehoods, as the possibilities are endless when considering the various timelines.

Nimrod wore horned headgear, likely in honor of the Ciakhar, who are known for their physical horns. Later, the royal crown with horns was adopted from Nimrod's original design. Nimrod was given the title "Baal," meaning "Lord," while Semiramis was referred to as "Baalti," meaning "My Lady." The olive branch Semiramis holds symbolizes her offspring, Ninus, also known as Tammuz.

Ancient scrolls tell the story of Ninuz, who was crucified and placed in a cave with a lamb at his feet. A rock was rolled in front of the cave's entrance, only to be moved after three days, revealing that his body had disappeared. This account is similar to the biblical story of Jesus, despite being written before his birth.

Exploring ancient texts written before Jesus' time will reveal similar narratives to those in the Bible. This phenomenon can be attributed to the cabal, which has been known to alter or rewrite ancient texts to suit its agenda. The cabal often recycles the same stories and strategies because they are effective.

I am not suggesting that Jesus did not exist as a man who was crucified as a martyr. However, the accounts of his life may be intertwined with misinformation aimed at portraying a narrative that aligns with the cabal's goals of influencing religious beliefs. Similar stories have been recounted throughout Earth's history, but with changes in the main characters and backgrounds to fit the prevailing times and exert control over people. The tale of Nimrod,

Semiramis, and Tammuz evolved into the story of Osiris, Isis, and Horus. Later, it transformed into the narrative of Joseph, Mary, and Jesus. In different regions of the world and as various religions emerged, these stories were adapted further, and many names were changed accordingly.

Many beliefs and traditions have emerged from Babylon. Queen Semiramis, over time, adopted various names such as Isis and Ishtar, often for propaganda purposes to keep the people focused on a false narrative. The celebration of Easter originated in Babylon, marking the story of Tammuz rising from the dead. The Babylonians commemorated this event with baked buns etched with a cross. These stories and traditions entertain the public and distract them from what is happening right before them. The cross symbolizes the Black Sun, Saturn. The cross shape represents an unfolded 3D cube, which society unwittingly gave its energy to.

There is a modern group of individuals known as the "New Age movement" or "New Agers," who claim to be awakening to Earth's true history and the existence of the Draconian Empire. However, they have been infiltrated and derailed by a disinformation campaign led by an extraterrestrial figure, Ashtar Command. Ashtar symbolizes Ashtaroth, a deity associated with brotherhood—another clever attack on Earth's awakening.

When individuals start to awaken to these realities, a common strategy employed by those in power is to lure them into offshoot groups that are controlled by secret societies, specifically compartments within the Illuminati. Although these individuals may believe they have joined an awakened group, they are still being manipulated by the cabal, as the Illuminati secretly influences this group. While these so-called "awakened" groups may possess a small portion of the truth, they are also fed misinformation that prevents them from understanding the situation completely.

Historically, after Marduk took control and Nimrod ruled Babylon, there was an agenda to restrict the knowledge available to humanity. Many ancient scrolls were either destroyed or altered to serve their purposes. However, the Brotherhood has secretly preserved numerous original texts, believed to be stored in vacuum-sealed vaults beneath the Vatican. Several whistleblowers who have worked for the government have reported witnessing ancient artifacts sealed within these vaults.

The fact that a cabal has been controlling Earth's history for approximately four thousand years complicates our ability to decipher the information found in ancient texts.

We must question whether this information has been manipulated or if it represents the truth of historical events. Nimrod and the regressive Orion group engaged in psychological manipulation of society. Nimrod was also depicted as Eannus, the two-faced god who later became known as Janus. In his role as Eannus, Nimrod was said to hold the keys to heaven. This portrayal made it easier to control and manipulate society, as people believed Nimrod was the mediator between them and God.

The Babylonian priesthood, operating under Nimrod's control, imposed their will on the Babylonians by spreading the belief that Nimrod was in direct communication with God and that no one else had this access. Anyone suspected of communicating with a spirit, higher-density being, or even Source faced execution. The Babylonians needed to disconnect them from their higher selves to maintain control over people's minds. This disconnection was achieved through indoctrination. Society needed to be kept away from the knowledge shared by Enki and the Brotherhood of the Snake, which focused on consciousness and Source. This knowledge was suppressed, and unfortunately, it continues to be suppressed.

Religion and its indoctrination were already established on Earth by Marduk before his takeover. However, the people did not begin to follow these teachings until they were enforced. Additionally, the illuminated knowledge was forbidden to be taught to outsiders of the Brotherhood.

The priesthoods of the brotherhood were responsible for establishing beliefs that would lead to a division among humankind, preventing anyone from knowing the whole truth. They combined small elements of truth with falsehoods, prompting different groups to argue about who possesses the complete truth. As a result, society becomes too preoccupied with these disputes to recognize that the same overarching group is manipulating them. Over the generations, they created loyal followers by establishing Christian priests, Rabbis, and the priesthoods of Islam, Hinduism, and others. Babylonian priests established a governing body known as the Grand Council of Pontiffs, a name that the Church of Rome later adopted. Many modern traditions and celebrations originated from Nimrod's control over Babylon. Some began as direct celebrations of the Sun god Eannus.

Society was misled into believing that symbolic stories were actual factual events. In secret, those permitted to know the truth must be entirely devoted to malevolent causes. The satanic rituals were shared among the higher-ups of a secret brotherhood that held power and control. In these rituals, the regressive reptilians would sacrifice humans for consumption but also their Soul's energy. Due to the brutal and malevolent nature of the torture that occurs during these events, the archons can participate and experience the terror that they derive pleasure from.

The Babylonian priests would participate in these rituals, and they would also consume human flesh. The high priests were required to partake in the consumption of human meat. The followers were unaware of what the leaders were doing. This is similar to modern-day compartmentalized secret societies, such as the Illuminati. The lower-ranking members of these societies often do not know about the atrocities and rituals that the higher-ranking members are involved in. As they rise in rank, they are gradually introduced to increasingly disturbing practices and are coerced into participating in rituals to remain a part of the group or brotherhood. If a member refuses to participate in a new ritual that is presented to them, they will only gain the knowledge that is available up to that point. However, if the member is okay with torturing, raping, killing, and cannibalism of little kids and they prove loyal, they can reach higher levels of the Illuminati. The higher you ascend in the Illuminati, the more insight and knowledge you gain and the greater access to power. Being part of the upper echelons of human leadership grants you an understanding of reality and access to information concealed from the average person on Earth.

As mentioned earlier, the characters' names were changed, and the stories were adjusted to align with the people's beliefs. One of the names associated with Nimrod is Moloch, also referred to as Tammuz. Moloch is a Canaanite deity traditionally linked to child sacrifices, and followers of this deity were expected to participate in these practices. In his book "The Biggest Secret," David Icke explains that "tam" means "to perfect" and "muz" means "to burn." He highlights the symbolism in the rituals dedicated to Tammuz and Moloch. In these rituals, the burning of children alive is done to honor Tammuz, Moloch, Nimrod, etc. These rituals are still being practiced today. Many holidays celebrated by the public have evolved from traditions that originated from the regressive Draconian Empire. The Beltane ritual performed by the Druids in Britain on May 1st involved the burning of children in wicker effigy. The Brotherhood spread this ritual throughout Europe as they expanded their influence.

The Feast of Tammuz was celebrated on June 23rd to honor the ascension of Tammuz from the underworld.

After his resurrection, Tammuz was known as Oannes, the fish god. We have previously discussed the symbolism of fish and its connection to scaly skin. As Christianity began to rise, Oannes adopted the name John, referring to John the Baptist.

Consequently, June 23rd transitioned from the Feast of Tammuz (Nimrod) to the Christian observance known as St. John's Eve. This illustrates how names and stories were adapted to align with the evolving agendas of society.

The roots and meanings of these celebrations remain consistent: they honor a regressive being or deity that seeks to be worshiped while enslaving humanity's mind. These regressive beings who desire to torture and consume humans do not have our best interests at heart. Consider this the next time you celebrate one of their holidays. While you are celebrating, they are also engaging in satanic rituals.

The Illuminati managed to take over and control human society by suppressing the spread of illuminated knowledge. This was accomplished by restricting the teachings of this knowledge to the priesthood that originated from the Brotherhood of the Snake, which Enki had initially founded. Within this priesthood, only a select few were permitted to be taught the sacred knowledge, leading to establishing secret compartments within the organization. Only the most elite individuals, as designated by the Draconian Empire, would be granted access to illumination.

The Babylonian religion involved worshipping the Sun God, serpents, and fire. However, people's understanding of these deities was often superficial. For instance, while the average person revered the Sun for the heat and light it provided for their crops, those with more profound knowledge, such as the Draconians, recognized that the Sun represented something else.

Astrology is essential and practiced by the cabal. By managing energy levels, they can reduce the planet's frequency. This is why monthly satanic rituals are held on specific ley lines around the Earth. The torture of human children generates a low frequency. When this occurs during the planet's lowest frequency—typically around the full Moon or close to it—the effects are more advantageous for the archons, who aim to keep the frequency as low as possible. It is important to note that the Moon is utilized to lower the planet's frequency, so rituals are typically conducted at night and during a full moon. There are daily rituals, but there are more significant events once a month. These gatherings serve as a tool for the Draconians to maintain control over the human mind. They aim to project negative emotions into society, including anger, aggression, sadness, fear, doubt, and guilt.

It is crucial for everyone to recognize that each year, thousands of children go missing and often end up suffering at the hands of individuals within the elite Illuminati cabal. Members of the elite consume adrenochrome.

After the suppression of knowledge, as well as the control of women and children, the waiting game began. Once the indoctrinated children grew up, the cabal manipulated the next generation through religion and government. It has been as if the Draconian Empire placed the human race in a pot of water, slowly raising the temperature without anyone noticing that they were being cooked alive.

Through the implementation of religion, governments, currency, wars, and control over history, news, medical advancements, and scientific innovations, the cabal has gained complete control over planet Earth.

Chapter 21: Earth is a Prison

The cabal's control has spread across the globe and deepened with each passing generation. The name "Illuminati" is widely recognized as it refers to a secret, compartmentalized group that currently influences the world and its governments. However, as we have already discussed, this control originates from forces above the Illuminati, dating back many years before the group's formation.

The first secret society intending to control information and who wanted to manipulate society was the Babylonian Brotherhood of the Snake, who took over the Brotherhood of the Snake's operations to suppress information. They have influenced the planet for centuries, shaping people's beliefs and thoughts. At the same time, they erase true history. The Brotherhood recycles the same stories and characters, controlling society.

For example, their first task was to convince society to worship their god. Although the names may vary over the years and across different geographical locations, they often represent the same person or group. The cabal recycles the same stories and characters throughout time, controlling society. Below are a few examples:

God Who Rules in Heaven:
Sumerians = Anu
Egyptians = Amon Ra
Greeks = Kronos
Romans = Saturn

God's Wife or Partner:
Sumerians = Antu
Egyptians = Mut
Greeks = Hera
Romans = Juno

Ruler Over Earth:
Sumerians = Enlil
Egyptians = Set
Greeks = Zeus
Romans = Jupiter

Earth's Prestigious Woman:
Sumerians = Ninhursag
Egyptians = Isis
Greeks = Athena
Romans = Minerva

Earth's Ruler's Brother:
Sumerians = Enki
Egyptians = Osiris
Greeks = Ares

Romans = Vulcan

Rival God:
Sumerians = Marduk
Egyptians = Horus
Greeks = Ares
Romans = Mars

Goddess of Love:
Sumerians = Ashira
Egyptians = Hathor
Greeks = Aphrodite
Romans = Venus

Upon closer examination, many of these characters secretly represent a group of individuals or a faction with a specific mindset or goal. Only those who created the ancient tablets would know the true meanings behind these names, but the information presented appears literal to the reader.

Enki and Enlil symbolize a group that contributed to the Sumerian tablets, while Ishtar, Anu, Shiva, and Osiris are individuals in their own right. Additionally, Akhenaten is the same character as Moses in the Bible.

The hidden meanings within these ancient tablets hold many secrets. Once one recognizes the manipulation, it becomes possible to decipher their authentic, more profound meanings. These tablets were written to influence the people. Although ancient information is closer to the truth, it is unfortunately riddled with manipulation.

According to the ancient tablets, Enki and Enlil are portrayed as brothers who often fought. However, these names represent groups in conflict. Enki symbolizes Is-ra-el, the people who left Egypt and were loyal to Akhenaten, while Enlil represents Egypt and those who were against Akhenaten. Both groups are sons of Egypt and predate the Sumerian tablets. Another way to look at it is that Enki embodies the faction from Egypt that follows Amon, which encompasses the entire lineage of modern-day religions. This group venerated the solar God Aton and followed Moses Akhenaten. The difference in beliefs between these factions led to Akhenaten's exile from Egypt. Despite their conflicts, both groups are considered sons of Anu, stemming from the same lineage derived from Anu.

Amon refers to the solar god before Akhenaten. Aten is the new sun god that Akhenaten imposed on the Egyptian people. This new sun god was referred to as the black sun. This marks the beginning of modern religion. It explains why saying "Amen" after prayers has been incorporated into current religions. It honors Amon, the solar God from ancient Egypt. The world has many faiths and beliefs, but all major religions come from solar worship, and most followers are ignorant of what they are worshipping. The cabal has deceived society into pledging their allegiance to a false god.

These groups and religions never lose power over the people. They only change the mask that they are wearing. The cabal are the ones who created these religions and have the power still to this day. The followers of Akhenaten and the sun god evolved into various religions and sought to gain control over as many governments as possible. Rome did not fall; it transformed into the next world power, with the Vatican always serving as the capital of control. Many groups and religions, like Zionism, have hidden roots. However, upon a more profound examination of the past, we find that these beliefs stem from a common source: solar worship. Solar worship is practiced as a way to follow Lucifer, the light- bringer. Lucifer symbolizes their god, who provides them with the light of knowledge.

The illuminated ones who worship Lucifer as the bringer of light eventually had to practice their beliefs in secrecy. However, they have skillfully convinced many religions to worship their God instead. The ultimate goal is to transform the planet into one that embraces Luciferian worship openly.

When analyzing ancient tablets, we cannot take the words or hieroglyphs at face value; they are all symbols that convey secret meanings. We must look beyond the manipulation and uncover what we did not intend to see. For example, Horus, often called the "Hawk," symbolizes a starship.

The same applies to reading the modern Bible, which was written using symbolism and hidden meanings. This approach has been utilized by those in power throughout history. Before the Bible, similar methods, such as writing on walls and cuneiform tablets, were used to manipulate the populace. While this earlier information may be older and closer to the truth, it, too, was meant to influence the people.

For example, in hieroglyphs, a bull often symbolizes the Taurus constellation or refers to the time when individuals from Taurus visited Egypt. Annunaki heads symbolize the sun. A depicted body or segment of a painting may represent a specific era. Wings signify the technology to fly, while owls represent portals. Bird feet indicate the technology of flying and walking among people. A flying snake represents the upper atmosphere's high magnetic turbine visual effect. The list of symbols goes on.

Secret groups were not yet referred to as the Illuminati during this period. The takeover of the Brotherhood of the Snake marks the beginning of information control. The cabal was formed to control information and hide the truth.

In the years following the establishment of the new regressive Brotherhood of the Snake, their manipulation of history and religion allowed them to gain control over human societies. As global powers shifted and new generations emerged, they introduced a revised version of religion. Although the characters' names changed, the underlying premise remained the same. Each character symbolized the same entity that only they understood. Some characters represented rulers with specific bloodlines, while others embodied groups with a specific mindset.

Controller Information
The Babylonian Brotherhood and its selected bloodlines expanded eastward to Egypt and eventually into Europe and the Americas. The Brotherhood established ministry schools wherever they went to manipulate the population into accepting their misleading ideologies. The people were coerced into relinquishing their power through fear. During the Brotherhood's expanding influence era, they only shared the illuminated knowledge of truth with those in high positions within their compartmentalized

hierarchy. Only individuals who served the regressive agenda were granted access to this enlightenment.

Other societal groups were initially independent of this secret brotherhood; however, the Brotherhood infiltrated any group that held power or influence over time. Even organizations that once served the people's interests eventually came under the control of the Draconian Empire through one or more of the Brotherhood's secret factions embedded within what later would be known as the Illuminati.

These secret groups form a global network that now operates in some capacity in every major country. This network, initiated by the Brotherhood, laid the groundwork for the Draconian Empire to carry out its agenda. Implementing this agenda transcends national borders and involves entities that may appear unconnected, such as companies, banks, businesses, and military organizations.

Religion and politics have historically been an effective means of controlling the population. A notable example of this control is the Inquisition, which demonstrated the extent to which the Brotherhood could exert power over individuals. Anyone who strayed away from the church's beliefs risked imprisonment or even death. Interestingly, control within society was often enforced by the people themselves. The cabal didn't need to resort to physical force; they convinced individuals to regulate the behavior of society for them. This illustrates the power of programming the subconscious mind.

Christianity was the greatest weapon created by the Brotherhood to control society. Members of churches have no idea that they are followers of the Illuminati. The Brotherhood of the Snake is the origin of the Illuminati. The leader of the Brotherhood at that time was Marduk, who was under the influence of regressive Souls and Ahriman. So, when you follow the chain of command, the Christians are being controlled by evil entities, also known as demons.

When Christianity and other religions gained control of a region, ancient texts and records were often removed or destroyed. The cabal had to control the information at all costs!

This halted the flow of illuminated knowledge, making it easier to transform society into a population of ignorant individuals who could be easily manipulated. The knowledge of extraterrestrial races was primarily erased from Earth's history, allowing a false alternate history to be documented. Despite modern science being unable to explain archaeological discoveries, society still depends on the controlled information it is given for its truth.

All of Earth's significant religions originate from the same region, and this is not a coincidence. In the book titled "The Biggest Secret," David Icke mentions that Richard Laurence, the Archbishop of Cashel, who translated the first English edition of the Book of Enoch (that was omitted from the canonized bible due to these text not being in line with the new agenda), believes that the author of this book must have lived in the Caucasus region rather than in Palestine, as society has commonly been told. When the floodwaters receded, the regressive bloodlines emerged from this area, which supports Laurence's deduction that the Book of Enoch was originally written in the Caucasus. Significant developments in human history took place in the region, extending from the Caucasus Mountains southward to Babylon, Sumer, and Egypt. The Caucasus Mountains form a natural border between Southern Russia and Northern Georgia, with the eastern part extending into Northern Azerbaijan.

According to official history, the people from the Caucasus Mountains migrated into the Indus Valley of India around 1550 B.C. and established what is now known as Hinduism. This group of people originating from the Caucasus Mountains is called the Aryan race, also known as the Arya race.

The Aryan race settled in regions such as Sumner, Babylon, Egypt, and Turkey (Asia Minor). They brought with them stories, myths, superstitions, and religious beliefs. The religions came from the same source: the Aryan race, part of the Brotherhood. The origins date back even further, as previously discussed in this book, but we are focusing on the establishment of the modern Brotherhood Illuminati on Earth. Religion is crucial in how their control over society spreads into different regions.

In the 8th century, a group of people known as the Khazars inhabited the Caucasus Mountains and southern Russia. During this time, many Khazars underwent a mass conversion to Judaism. When their empire declined, the Khazars migrated North and settled in parts of Russia, Lithuania, and Estonia. Eventually, they entered Western Europe and ultimately the United States. Some rumors indicate that individuals from this bloodline who managed the group are part of the powerful secret elite linked to the Illuminati in the United States today.

The Caucasus Mountains lie between Russia and Georgia, just north of Turkey (Asia Minor). The Aryans who migrated south towards Egypt were known as the Phoenicians. The Phoenicians spread across various regions and expanded North into Europe. The groups that followed them into these areas became known as the Cimmerians and the Scythians.

As these groups changed names during their migrations, they could obscure their origins. Additionally, they managed to reconnect with their other bloodlines, which included the Phoenicians.

The Cimmerians migrated from Asia Minor (present-day Turkey) and the Caucasus Mountains into Belgium, the Netherlands, Germany, and Denmark. The Scythians, originating in the Caucasus Mountains, moved north into Europe. Their original emblem features an ox (Nimrod), which is significant because Nimrod and Baal are often depicted as an ox or a goat. This connection is relevant when considering the Baphomet deity, a goat-like figure that represents Baal or, in some interpretations, Nimrod. Over time, the Scythians incorporated the sun symbol, representing enlightened knowledge from their god (Black Sun, Saturn, Lucifer, Satan, Ahriman, etc.) into their emblems.

The Scythians conquered Sweden around 250 AD. Chinese records mention a group called the Sai-wang or Sok-wang, who fled India around 175 BC. Additionally, a subset of the Scythians, known as the Sakkas, reached China. All these groups originating from the Caucasus

Mountains—Scythians, Sakka, Cimmerians, Cimbri, Phoenicians, Aryans, and Arya—were essentially the same people. They spread their power and influence through secret societies that form part of the Brotherhood Illuminati.

The Illuminati is a term that encompasses various earth-based secret society groups controlled by the cabal, which influences different aspects of society. While these groups may intertwine, the leadership of the original Brotherhood of the Snake is now associated with the Draconian Empire, also known as the Orion group. Above them, there may exist a regressive AI named Omega, although this is my opinion. Furthermore, above these entities are the regressive archons or asuras, with their leader being Ahriman.

This description is a simplified outline of my understanding of the Illuminati and its leadership structure. We will uncover some of the Illuminati's leaders later on, but remember that these individuals represent only a lower tier in the hierarchy. You often discover additional unknown layers whenever you think you have reached the top.

The Phoenicians established bases in Asia Minor (Turkey), Syria, and Egypt. They traveled by sea and settled in Greece and Italy. The civilizations known as classical Greece and Roman Italy emerged through their influence. The Phoenicians were described as tall, white-skinned, blue-eyed beings who resembled humans but possessed reptilian traits. The leadership within their group was likely comprised of full-blooded reptilians, as their lineage in a reptilian vessel was closest to the original Draco or Ciakhar. However, this is my opinion, and I have not received further insights on these matters.

The arrival of the Aryan Phoenicians in Britain introduced advanced knowledge in astronomy, astrology, sacred geometry, mathematics, and information about the Earth's ley lines. With this knowledge, the Brotherhood could influence the Earth's frequency by lowering it in specific locations. They could reduce the frequency and summon regressive archons by manipulating the geometric energy in these areas.

The Druids emerged from a group with illuminated knowledge in Britain, which later spread to Ireland and France. These Druids would secretly gather at night to share their knowledge with a select few. They conducted their rituals on ley lines found in the area. Their supreme deity was the oak tree, which symbolized the formation of consciousness, though they did not worship it directly. The holly bush was another significant symbol for them. The name "Hollywood" is thought to have originated from a connection to its founders, who are believed to belong to a regressive Druid bloodline. This bloodline allegedly remained loyal to the Draconians, even though some Druids separated themselves from this regressive mindset.

Some original Druids in Britain and Ireland began following a more positive path. The other Druids were a group of satanic worshipers obsessed with controlling society with their illuminated knowledge. As already mentioned, the ones who didn't fall in line were hunted and killed. The last remaining positive Druids went into hiding in Ireland, but they were eventually discovered.

After a considerable period, the Babylonian Brotherhood established its headquarters in London, United Kingdom. In David Icke's book "The Biggest Secret," he mentions that the British Isles are the center of Earth's energy grid. This idea aligns with the notion that the Illuminati cabal elite have set up their base of operations in this region. Being in such a location would facilitate their ability to manipulate the Earth's energy and frequency, especially as they conduct their main satanic rituals there.

Before their relocation to London, the elite members of the Babylonian Brotherhood were based in the city of Troy, located in Asia Minor (modern-day Turkey). London was founded as the new Troy after the destruction of the original Troy around 1200 B.C.

Aeneas, who was of royal lineage, left Troy and settled in Italy, where he married Lavinia, the daughter of King Latinus. This union gave rise to the bloodline from which the kings of the Roman Empire emerged.

Around 1,103 B.C., Aeneas' grandson Brutus arrived in Britain with Trojans. Brutus founded a town called Caer Troia, meaning New Troy. The Romans later referred to this growing town as Londinium. London became the operations center for the Brotherhood, eventually leading to the establishment of Paris and the Vatican. London has been referred to as New Troy, a better nickname would be New Babylon.

The Brotherhood focused on gaining power through politics. Implementing religion served as a primary means of controlling society's minds, and control over news and history helped maintain this indoctrination.

All major religions originated from the same region of the Earth and were created by similar influential minds. A common thread among these religions is the condemnation faced by those who do not accept their beliefs and indoctrination, often threatened with eternal suffering. This serves as a clear example of control through fear. Over the years, these religions have spread across the globe, profoundly influencing the minds of society.

The Torah and Talmud were compiled during and after the Babylonian era. These texts are intended to regulate every aspect of a follower's life. The Mosaic Law is associated with the Levites, who were members of the Babylonian Brotherhood.

Members of the Jewish faith should not be judged for their beliefs, as they, like many others, may have succumbed to indoctrination. In the book "Jewish History, Jewish Religion," the author Shahak discusses how saving a gentile's life can be considered offensive. They could not charge another Jewish person interest, but they could on a gentile. They had to utter a curse when passing a gentile cemetery. They were to wish destruction on all gentile buildings. They were not allowed to drink from the same cup as a Gentile. I understand that these laws are no longer enforced, but the basis of the Jewish religion was founded on racism. These teachings have done damage that spans generations.

The Levite Babylonians created a racist group of followers who gave their thought power of manifesting to the Brotherhood. As each day passed, more people joined these religious groups, allowing their minds to be manipulated to manifest whatever Marduk commanded.

As each day passed, the divide within society grew deeper, along with stronger control over the minds of everyone involved.

Most people who are born into a specific religion are convinced to follow the indoctrination using fear. The result is that they grow up to be indoctrinated puppets. Every child who is brainwashed believes they possess the truth, while every other religion is a false religion. They think that they have the only true religion and that they are special.

A comprehensive library filled with books on religion would be necessary to explore all their nuances, origins, and interconnections. Therefore, I encourage you to conduct further research as you see fit. You may explore this topic as thoroughly as you desire.

Notice that I am discussing religions in a chapter about the Illuminati's growth and expansion of power; this is because religion was a primary vehicle through which they were able to influence people's actions—by manipulating their thoughts and beliefs.

Let's examine this intriguing story and see if it sounds familiar. A man was born to a virgin, and his birth is celebrated on December 25th. Upon his birth, there were orders to hunt him down and kill him, leading to the massacre of all infants under the age of two. Angels and shepherds were present at his birth. He grew up to be venerated as the savior of humanity, leading a humble life while performing miracles, such as healing the sick, casting out demons, and even resurrecting the dead. Ultimately, he was crucified alongside two thieves but resurrected afterward.

This tale closely resembles the biblical accounts of Jesus, but it actually refers to Krishna and was written around 1,200 years before Jesus was born. Some followers of Krishna believe he was born in the summer, while others believe his birth occurred on December 25th. The exact date is unimportant, as this story originated in the Caucasus Mountains. It was the Aryan race who spread various versions of these stories. When comparing the world's religions, they share many similarities. This can be traced back to the ancient Phoenician worship of Bel or Bil. Artifacts from that era depict a halo around the head of Bel or Bil. This halo represents how Christianity depicts Jesus, symbolizing the sun.

Christians have been fed that they are worshiping Jesus, but they are worshiping the Black Sun right along with the Brotherhood. Next time you see a portrait of Jesus, notice if there is a halo silhouette behind his head. The truth is in plain sight, but are you willing to see?

December 25th was chosen as Jesus's birthday because early Christians adopted this date from the sun worship of the ancient religion Sol Invictus, which means "Sun Unconquered." In ancient Egypt, the sun was also revered during the period of the Brotherhood's expansion. Ultimately, it can be seen as the same god being worshiped since it is believed to be the same divine force.

Jesus rose from the dead after three days. Similarly, in ancient Egyptian texts, Osiris took three days to rise from the dead. Additionally, it is said that Tammuz also took three days to return to life. The number 3 or 33 often appears in ancient texts spanning thousands of years and various regions.

A great darkness settled over the area that lasted for three days. This darkness was reported to have occurred after the deaths of several important figures. Although Jesus was the last to be recorded, similar reports of darkness followed the deaths of Krishna, Hercules, Buddha, and Quetzalcoatl. If you adhere to traditional church teachings, I encourage you to explore the parables documented in ancient texts that predate both the Bible and Jesus. You may discover some striking similarities among these stories, suggesting that they are part of a continuous tradition adapted to fit the beliefs and needs of different societies at various times and in different geographical regions. As societies evolved, so did their religious doctrines.

The followers of the Brotherhoods appointed religions were deeply indoctrinated in their beliefs, making them willing to fight to the death to defend their faith. This elite group controls all religious factions and orchestrates conflicts between opposing groups, ensuring that the Brotherhood's Illuminati elites ultimately manage both sides.

Constantine became the Roman Emperor in 312 A.D. He worshiped Sol Invictus, the sun god, which influenced the early Christians to give Jesus the same birthday, December 25th. Constantine's mother, Helena, claimed to have discovered the locations of Jesus' birth, crucifixion, and death. In 326 A.D., Constantine built a church at the site where Jesus was believed to have died. Today, you can take a guided tour of these significant locations. If you research this church, you will find it was built as part of a sacred geometric pattern in Jerusalem. Given that Constantine was a member of the Babylonian Brotherhood Illuminati, it is likely that satanic rituals took place in this church to lower the area's frequency.

Researching Constantine as an emperor is fascinating. Initially, he supported the Brotherhood's agenda, which aimed to instill fear and terror regarding Christianity. He began by persecuting Christians but later presented himself as a follower of the faith. However, in private, he remained a worshiper of the Sun God. During this period, some people followed Mithras, the god of light, and Christianity attracted many of these followers due to the similarities in their beliefs. Ultimately, Constantine ended the persecution of Christians in the Roman Empire by issuing the Edict of Milan.

Reflecting on the shifts in religious beliefs and observing how power transitioned from one religion to another is fascinating. One day, individuals could be crucified for believing in Christianity, and the next, Christians condemned those who adhered to different faiths.
The control over humanity, while horrific, is fascinating and genius.

There have been many name changes throughout the long and hidden history of various secret groups that have worked together to control significant portions of society. Despite these changes over the centuries, the key controllers and their agendas have remained constant. Groups such as the Templars, Hospitallers, Knights of Malta, Knights of St. John, Masons, and Rosicrucians exhibit similarities and differences.

The lines between these groups blur when one examines their agendas more closely. The Masons are connected to the Templars, and both can be traced back to a Grand Lodge in France. The Knights of St. John have roots in Jerusalem during the Crusades. Additionally, old lodges in Scotland preserve forms of Freemasonry that originated in England, from which the Scottish Rite emerged.

Regardless of the group or location, the primary focus has always been to control people by managing the information they receive and how they interpret it. By isolating different groups from one another and controlling the flow of information, each group believes it possesses the sole truth, while others are seen as ignorant of it. In reality, no group holds the complete truth; each has access to fragments of truth interspersed with misinformation and indoctrination.

Over time, control over society has grown alongside the increasing influence of religion. Smaller religions emerged from these original belief systems, often to further divide the people, even within the same broader faith. A notable example is the Jehovah's Witnesses, who believe in Jesus and God but reject concepts such as hell, the crucifixion of Jesus on a cross, and the Trinity (Triangulum). Alternatives are available for individuals dissatisfied with the teachings of their primary religion. The Illuminati has extended its influence of control to as many different personality types. These smaller religious groups are designed to catch individuals who become aware that the main religion is lying. The Jehovah's Witness religion will capture the minds of these individuals before they awaken to the whole truth.

Charles Taze Russell, the founder of the Jehovah's Witness religion, was a 33rd-degree Freemason and had connections to the lower levels of the Illuminati. In my research on Charles Taze Russell, I found evidence that his father, Joseph Lytel Russell, began experimenting with manipulating groups of people through fear-based publications. While I'm unsure of the depth of Joseph Lytel Russell's involvement with the Illuminati, it appears that from the beginning, the Jehovah's Witness religion was influenced or controlled by the Illuminati.

Suppose you are one of the indoctrinated Jehovah's Witnesses. In that case, I am sure that after all the time spent researching their literature, you may not have come across the Illuminati York Rite Pyramid that once stood next to Charles Taze Russell's grave site. Due to convenient vandalism, the Watchtower and Tract Society removed the pyramid in September 2021. The fact that the Watchtower and Tract Society removed the pyramid suggests it was initially placed there in honor for their founder.

We can discuss the details of his divorce and the accusations against him, such as locking himself in a servant girl's bedroom at night and the claims of molesting Rose J. Ball Hennings. However, one undeniable fact is the prominent pyramid, which notably has its tip separated, similar to the design found on the American dollar. This pyramid once stood next to Charles Taze Russell's grave. This symbol has become widely recognized as representing the secret knowledge shared among Illuminati members. You can find this symbol on the American dollar, and it once stood next to Russell's grave.

Another symbol on the pyramid is the York Rite emblem, which originated in the United Kingdom. This emblem represents a Freemason lodge that focused on population mind control. The York Rite is a Masonic group associated with the Illuminati, and it is one of many components that make up this secret society. This emblem was displayed on Charles Taze Russell's pyramid at his gravesite and even appeared in many of the original literature distributed by Jehovah's Witnesses. I am not certain if the Illuminati still directly controls the Jehovah's Witnesses religion after Rutherford's death; however, it most definitely began under their direct influence. Regardless, its roots and beliefs are part of the controllers' agenda.

The truth is right before them, yet they fail to see it because they are under mind control. However, it's time to break free from this mental prison. It's important to remember that it is not the followers' fault; the blame lies with the Illuminati and those in control. Modern- day religions are much more careful about revealing their true agendas to their followers, making it even more challenging for people to awaken to reality: Earth has become a prison for your mind.

After discovering this, I am convinced that every Jehovah's Witness will experience cognitive dissonance, or they will choose to remain oblivious because they find comfort in being controlled. This is the only reality they can comprehend. Many have dedicated their entire lives to this religion, and the thought that it may have been a waste of time is simply not an option for them. As a result, they may refuse to awaken and recognize the true reality. This religion employs mind control tactics, which becomes evident when you listen closely to the phrases that are repeatedly instilled in the subconscious minds of their followers.

The religion claims that its governing body receives information directly from God. However, they have falsely predicted Armageddon several times. They also have changed religious policies multiple times. If they were indeed in communication with the creator of the universe, he wouldn't make mistakes while guiding his chosen religion. Only an awakened mind can see slight changes to the blood transfusion policy are due to multiple lawsuits. Subtle changes to the disfellowshipping policy are due to the loss of religious classification in Norway and the loss of tax write-offs, resulting in millions in losses. This change is an attempt to regain their religious classification in court. Subtle changes to the dress code are due to decreased members. Are all these changes due to God making a mistake? Or is it due to the men running the religion adjusting to fit their needs?

Joseph F. Rutherford took over leadership after Charles Taze Russell's death. It is interesting to note that Rutherford spoke critically of Russell, and while he had every right to express his views because they were based on truth, Rutherford was not without his faults either. He urged the Jehovah's Witness followers to make donations to the religion, claiming they would soon not need their money since Armageddon was imminent. He instructed them to construct a mansion for the special resurrected chosen ones who would help lead them after Armageddon.

True to his word, he built a mansion in San Diego, California, naming it Beth Sarim, where he lived until his death. Conveniently, Armageddon never arrived, and Rutherford enjoyed residing in a lavish 5,100-square-foot, 10-bedroom home. The Great Depression ended in 1941, and the construction of Beth Sarim was completed the following year. While these were difficult times for many, Rutherford seemed unaffected by the economic challenges. He also owned a luxury 16-cylinder Cadillac, a vehicle reserved for the wealthy. He never explained how such an extravagant automobile would benefit the resurrected princes for whom Beth Sarim was supposedly built. Automotive historians note that this kind of vehicle was only accessible to the very rich.

Rutherford's connection to the Brotherhood of the Snake is evident in early publications after he took over the Jehovah's Witness organization. One such publication is "The Finished Mystery," which features the winged orb of Egypt, also known as the winged sun disk, on its cover. This is a well-known symbol from ancient Egypt called Behedti, which features the wings of Horus. This symbolizes the sun god Ra. This honors the sun god that various religions promote, but as mentioned, sun worship is symbolic. In ancient Egypt, solar worship began as a belief in the literal sun, but as usual, the people were being deceived. From the beginning, the

minds of society have been in a trance. I mention a minor religion, such as the Jehovah's Witnesses, because it highlights how those in power have cast a wide net to capture everyone. Regardless of your beliefs or where you are on the planet, your mind has numerous traps to fall into. Not a single religion has the truth!
They all worship who the cabal wants them to worship.

Amun Ra played a key role in converting society into sun worshippers, and many major religions trace their roots back to him. The worship of the sun is implemented in societies' religions because these false gods, like Amun Ra, worship the sun god. Their sun god represents not our literal sun but the planet Saturn, the Black Sun, Lucifer, and Satan, who all ultimately symbolize Ahriman, but this is kept very secret, hence the multiple layers of symbology. These power-hungry individuals also called themselves gods and forced society to view them as gods. Researching the establishment of sun worship leads back to the worship of Saturn. The winged sun disk found in Egypt symbolizes Saturn, the sun god. The two snakes in the symbol represent the ancient ministry school that Enki initiated. The school was known as The Brotherhood of The Snake, but it was infiltrated and came under the regressive control of Marduk.

These ancient symbols can be traced back to secret societies. They represent the Draconian Empire, and the knowledge derived from the Brotherhood of the Snake. These symbols serve as a means for these groups to manipulate society into worshipping and directing their energy toward the sun god.

There are theories as to why they chose Saturn to symbolize their god. Some say it is because Saturn was a sun at one point, but I disagree. The answer is more obvious. There is a large object moving within the rings of Saturn. This object is a command ship for the Galactic Federation, and the Federation claims that they are trying to remove the current controllers from Earth. However, once you look deeper, it becomes clear that this ship and its occupants are part of the regressive group controlling Earth. The rings around Saturn have a constantly changing pattern. Within five minutes, the ring pattern will completely change. Also, the shapes observed at the planet's North and South poles indicate strong cymatics. The ship, located within the rings of Saturn, transmits a frequency toward Earth's moon. This transmitted frequency is then amplified and directed toward Earth, impacting human DNA and preventing it from evolving. It keeps the human population vibrating lowly, making it easier to manipulate society.

The ship that emits frequency-lowering signals is cube-shaped. In Judaism, a tefillin is worn on the head during prayer. This tefillin is a black square box. In Mecca, Muslims have a shrine called the Kaaba. This shrine is a black, cube-shaped structure they all face five times daily during prayer. The cross is a significant part of the Christian religion and symbolizes a 3D cube. If you take a flat piece of paper shaped like a cross, you can fold it to create a 3D cube. These religions honor the cube shape because it represents the cube-shaped ship from which a high level of Earth's control originates. Billions of people give their energy daily to those who have enslaved them. What better slave than one who is not aware that they are one?

The current system on Earth was created by the same regressive group that took over thousands of years ago. It has only been made to appear that power has changed and that religions are different when, in fact, they are all loyal to the same god and were created by individuals who share an agenda to enslave the human mind.

The influence of secret societies among the people spread like wildfire, mainly due to the creation of new religious groups. These groups were established to capture the minds of various demographics across the planet. Different types of religions were designed to indoctrinate a wide range of individuals. The Illuminati have expanded their control over society by forming these religions and creating new factions to strengthen their grip on the community. They operate from behind multiple layers of secrecy, ensuring that people remain unaware of who they truly worship.

Every religion that has grown to capture the minds of millions has regressive roots, including the Mormon Church of Jesus Christ of Latter-day Saints. Joseph Smith claimed to have seen an angel named Moroni in 1823. The church was led by Smith and Brigham Young, both of whom were High Degree Freemasons from the New York Lodge. Kuhn, Loeb & Company, a bank owned by the Rothschild family, funded this religious startup.

Since its inception, religion has gained popularity. New versions of religions have emerged to attract a broader audience. But as we just discussed, these newer religions are more of the same control with masonic roots. The planet became a prison for humanity after the Brotherhood took control of religions, the world's economy, and politics.

Society is often distracted by politics, religion, and entertainment. A financial empire has been built on lending money that isn't real and charging interest. The

Brotherhood, often referred to as the Illuminati, has expanded its wealth through war, assassinations, and manipulation of money trading. Suppose you examine the top shareholders of the largest publicly traded companies. In that case, you'll find that many entities, such as Vanguard Group Inc., State Street, and BlackRock Inc., own significant portions of the top companies, including major players like Apple and Tesla. The true power lies within these hidden entities that control the majority shares of these stocks. These handful of companies hold the vast majority of the world's wealth and are owned by the cabal. They are interconnected and part of the same elite group that controls the world.

Politics and religion have played a significant role in controlling people's minds. It's up to you to recognize this or not. If a 7th grader named Bridge Anne d'Avignon can uncover that nearly all the presidents from the last 60 years are related, then I believe you can see that someone has been taking advantage of you. Yes, let that sink in, you have been played for a fool, but the mind control ends now! Earth is a prison of the mind, and to beat the game you must figure a way to escape the prison!

Many people prefer to remain ignorant rather than confront the truth, as they find comfort in their ignorance. However, I invite you to join me on this journey if you seek the truth. Let us open and explore the door labeled "Danger: Keep Out!"

Chapter 22: The Birth of the Illuminati

1776, the Declaration of Independence was drafted for the United States of America. During this time, five university students formed a fraternity called the Bavarian Order of the Illuminati. The period from 1730 to 1780 is considered the height of the Enlightenment era for the Illuminati. Intellectuals like John Locke, Thomas Jefferson, and others would gather to discuss hidden knowledge. Various other groups emerged during this time, united by the common goal of sharing such knowledge.

By the end of the 18th century, these groups had amassed significant knowledge and power. A resurgence of Hermeticism took place, a philosophical and religious system based on the teachings of Hermes Trismegistus. This belief system views God as a magician, contrasting sharply with the doctrines of organized religion. Hermeticism is much closer to the truth than traditional biblical teachings. To truly understand the activities of the Bavarian Order of the Illuminati, we need to explore the basic teachings of Hermes Trismegistus and Hermetic philosophy.

Hermetic philosophy consists of seven basic principles: Mentalism: All is mind; the universe is mental. Both the physical and spiritual realms are constructs originating from a singular source. Positive and negative forces emerge from this source to create the experience of duality. One cannot fully appreciate cleanliness without experiencing dirtiness; the contrasting black and white tiles exemplify this duality. Correspondence: As above, so below; as below, so above. The physical world reflects and manifests the astral world, and vice versa. These two realms are reflections of each other. This disconnection is why the controllers have distanced humanity from its true spiritual self.

Vibration: Nothing rests; everything moves; everything vibrates. This has been scientifically validated. The physical universe comprises atoms in constant motion, and the rate of this movement can be measured. Even what appears to be space is not devoid of substance; it is filled with aether. Our universe exists as a complex tapestry of frequencies. Not only do objects vibrate at specific frequencies, but time itself possesses a unique frequency. An object today has a different vibrational signature than it did yesterday. We inhabit an ever-changing universe.

Polarity: Everything is dual; everything has poles; everything has its pair of opposites.

Rhythm: Everything flows in and out; all things experience cycles of rise and fall.

Cause and Effect: Every cause has its effect; every effect has its cause. Everything occurs according to natural law.

Gender: Gender exists in everything; all things encompass masculine and feminine principles. Gender manifests across all planes of existence.

As we can see, Hermetic philosophy diverges significantly from prevailing societal beliefs. These teachings were not intended for widespread adoption but for a select few initiates. Society is conditioned to believe that their power is external and that the physical world is all that exists. These ideas were not meant for everyone to contemplate. Instead, society is expected to adhere to one of the many religions that those in power have introduced.

Typically, only the social elite were privy to these more profound concepts. The control of knowledge is one reason why secret societies were established.

The origins of Illuminati-type groups can be traced back to Babylon, where the Brotherhood of the Snake began. Throughout history, there have been numerous secret societies that wielded significant power. In 1738, Fredrick the Great became a freemason. The United

States has strong ties to individuals who were members of these secret societies.

However, the most famous secret society, the Illuminati, was publicly established on May 1, 1776. Johann Adam Weishaupt, a professor of canon law, founded the Bavarian Illuminati. Under the guidance of his grandfather, Weishaupt began reading from a private library that belonged to his family. His father was a rabbi who passed away when Johann was just five years old. By seven, he was enrolled in a private Jesuit school.

After completing his education, Weishaupt's mission was to create a group of free thinkers who would not be subjected to the control and indoctrination that the rest of society typically followed. In 1775, he was appointed Professor of Canon Law, traditionally held by a Jesuit. Two years earlier, the Jesuit order had been dissolved by Pope Clement XIV, who expressed concerns over their power, which led to the order's disbandment.

Understanding the true nature of these events is akin to playing a multi-layered chess game. Was the pope genuinely worried about their influence, or was it time to change the face and name of the order? Secret groups often change names and power dynamics, but the same individuals tend to pull the strings from the shadows.

Two years after the dissolution of the Jesuit order, Weishaupt formed a private club, blending elements from the Jesuits and the Freemasons. This group eventually evolved to encompass the wisdom of secret teachings across various clandestine organizations that collectively formed the Illuminati. The first members included Johann Adam Weishaupt, Franz Anton von Massenhausen, Edler von Merz, Bauhof, and Sutor. Initially, they were called the Order of Perfectibilists. In April 1778, the name changed to the Bavarian Illuminati to influence the central world governments. Earlier, in 1777, Weishaupt had joined a Masonic lodge, where he was encouraged by Aba Marati to closely collaborate with the Freemasons to integrate his order into their lodges. This merging began a gradual blending of Jesuit and Freemason ideologies. This ushered in a new era of information and money control.

Massenhausen, a member of the Illuminati, was heavily recruiting for the order. Within a few years, the power and control of the Illuminati had infiltrated existing secret societies. Around the year 1780, Kaniga joined the Illuminati, and soon thereafter, members of the Rosicrucians began to integrate into the Illuminati as well. The Rosicrucians are held in high esteem because they are believed to possess the original Knights Templar bloodline. The Holy Grail that many have heard of is not a literal cup but rather a specific bloodline. The

Rosicrucians claim to hold the secret knowledge of the spiritual realm and possess esoteric truths. This bloodline traces back to ancient lineages that sought ascension through the halls and spheres of Amenti in Egypt. They swear allegiance to regressive spirits rather than to any physical being.

Once this allegiance was formed, it opened many levels of knowledge to the upper echelons of the Illuminati. Until this point, the Illuminati had only scratched the surface of true knowledge. As the Illuminati grew in power, bolstered by high-profile members, it became an opportune time for the Rosicrucians to share their expertise and take advantage of this expanding influence.

Notable members of the Illuminati included Duke Fernan of Brunswick and Duke Earns II, who were direct descendants of the British royal Windsor family. In 1917, King George V changed their German name from Saxe-Coburg-Gotha to Windsor. The power and influence of the Illuminati spread to Poland, France, and England. William IX connected the Rothschild family to the Illuminati. Mayer Amschel Rothschild worked for William IX as his banker and general agent, studying the mystical secrets of the Kabbalah Hashanah.

Mayer Rothschild's wealth was built on the investments of William IX. William IX funded Mayer to help establish his son as the head of the London banking branch, ostensibly to pay for soldiers needed for a war. Using war as an excuse to funnel money into secret investments has been employed for many years. Nathan Rothschild later became the head of the bank, marking the beginning of the Rothschild empire. Mayer's sons controlled the main banking branches.

The Rothschilds assisted Rockefeller in acquiring many of the oil companies. They were part of the Illuminati, which assured their rise to power through these connections. The agenda was straightforward: establishing a New World Order under their control, operating in secrecy. While the world would perceive presidents, politicians, and religious leaders as the planet's controllers, it is the controllers of the Illuminati who pull the strings from a higher level. Names like Rockefeller and Rothschild are prominent within the upper echelons of leadership, yet they do not make the key decisions. They are more like pawns, having been appointed to their positions in a larger game. These elites come from a prestigious bloodline but remain accountable to their superiors. Many may believe they are at the top of the hierarchy, but they are not.

The Illuminati had become an immense power, with many members becoming extremely wealthy by collaborating. The insatiable hunger for power, money, and control over society began to create issues within the Illuminati. Kanigga appointed a separate group of the Illuminati as elders, giving them the authority to make internal judicial decisions. This group was named Ariaopgites, and they agreed with Kanigga that changes were necessary. In 1972, it was decided that the Illuminati would adopt a more political system of authority. The Illuminati continued to grow in power by adding secret groups affiliated with various factions. It evolved into a compartmentalized secret society, with many different groups working without knowledge of each other's existence but pursuing a common goal: implementing the controllers' New World Order. Only the top members of these groups knew that they were answering to another faction of the Illuminati. Very few among them knew who was really in control.

However, eventually, Kanigga left the Illuminati. A group that we are not aware of may have replaced the Illuminati. The fact that the Illuminati is commonly known leads me to believe that it is no longer in power and that another has taken its place. It's also possible that they still hold power but are now part of many small groups that work together to control society. This would make it nearly impossible to decipher who pulls the strings.

Ultimately, it doesn't matter whether the Illuminati is still behind the world's wealth or what these secret societies are called. What matters is that society is controlled by what people watch and believe—this is sufficient reason to warrant a revolution demanding the truth to be revealed. The elite controllers also referred to as the cabal, withhold technological advancements to continue siphoning money and, more importantly, energy from humanity. They want society to keep working without questioning what is happening. But that all changes now; let us begin asking questions.

Chapter 23: Holiday Secret Meaning Revealed

Easter is a Christian holiday celebrated to honor the day Jesus was believed to have been resurrected from the dead. Originally, Easter began as a pagan holiday before evolving and being adopted by Christian religions.

The name "Easter" is derived from "Ishtar," a day dedicated to honoring a deity associated with resurrection. This deity was named Tammuz, who, within the pagan tradition, was considered the son of the sun and moon gods. It is important to note that ancient writings often contain truths intertwined with inaccuracies, and while the characters may change, the underlying themes remain the same. Some believe that Tammuz is the son of Nimrod or the son of Enki, but I feel that they represent the same being. In my opinion, Nimrod's consciousness may have left his old vessel and entered that of Tammuz. Regardless, these three figures can be seen as the beginnings of the trinity that Christianity adopted from pagan beliefs.

Upon researching pagan religions, one can observe that Christianity is another version of these ancient faiths. The primary differences lie in the characters' names and holidays, while the dates and stories often remain consistent.

This transformation appears to be a form of misdirection, steering Christian followers to worship pagan gods. Although the names of the religion and its figures change, the worshippers' energy is still directed toward the same source: Nimrod and the other false gods. It is suggested that negative entities benefit from the devotion of those who unknowingly worship them.

After Nimrod's death, his wife Semiramis told the people that he ascended to the sun and would now be known as Baal, the sun god. Consequently, followers of various religions would begin to worship Baal. When we see representations of the sun in religious figures' portraits or logos, they are often in honor of Baal. Frequently, portraits of these religious figures feature a halo of sunlight directly behind their heads, which serves as a tribute to the sun god.

Semiramis claimed she descended to Earth in a giant moon egg and became known as Ishtar, a name that later evolved into "Eas-Tar" or "Easter." Her moon egg ship became known as Ishtar's egg, which is where the egg theme originated and connects to modern-day Easter eggs.

Ishtar announced that she was pregnant, claiming that Baal was the father. The details surrounding her pregnancy and whether Nimrod died remain uncertain, as much of this information may symbolize deeper meanings.

Pagan worshippers were instructed to reflect on sacred teachings and worship Baal on the first Sunday following the first full moon after the spring equinox. This day, known initially as Ishtar Sunday, was celebrated with meditations on Baal and the use of eggs and rabbits. The rabbits are symbolic to fertility.

As you can see, Easter has no connection to the resurrection of Christ. With minimal effort, one can uncover the true history of this holiday. The tradition of consuming sweets during the festival has its roots in paganism. Initially, when pagans observed Ishtar Sunday, they would bake buns with a cross on them. This practice originated from worshiping Baal, the sun god also known as Nimrod. Priests of Baal would celebrate by sacrificing children and using their blood to paint eggs.

Christmas has a similar origin. While this information is widely known, it is often not discussed to keep the general public satisfied. Scholars recognize that Christmas has roots in ancient Babylon and is not directly connected to the birth of Jesus Christ. Anyone can search the internet for information about the origins of Christmas and uncover these facts.

Nimrod initiated an indoctrination that continues to influence Earth today. His wife, Semiramis, was believed also to be his mother. After Nimrod's death, Semiramis claimed that a full-grown tree appeared overnight in place of a dead tree stump. She asserted that this new tree symbolized Nimrod's transition into a new life, where he would be known as Baal.

Semiramis mentioned that on the anniversary of Nimrod's birthday, Baal would leave gifts on a tree that had miraculously grown overnight. This day is December 25th, which is how the tradition of decorating Christmas trees began. Nimrod is not the only deity whose birth is celebrated on December 25th, making it challenging to determine the true meaning behind the celebrations on this date. Regardless, it's widely recognized that these customs have roots in pagan beliefs, attributed to Nimrod and the Draconian empire, with Marduk as their physical leader.

The pagan and Christian followers came together to create a prominent religion that embraced their shared celebrations. Pagans could continue celebrating their traditional holidays as Christians adopted these festivities. The names of those honored on these holidays changed, and this compromise made everyone happy.

When exploring the origins of Saint Valentine's Day, we encounter a deity named Juno. Juno is the Roman goddess of love and marriage. The celebration of fertility in her honor originated from Lupercalia, which was a pagan festival that had sexually charged and violent elements. There were sacrifices made for the sake of love and fertility. People would take a goat and sacrifice it as part of the celebration. Then they would take the hide and dip it into blood and whip the woman with it. During the event, the woman would place the names of participants in an urn. A man would then draw a name, and couples would get married at this event. In two separate years, men with the same name were executed during the Lupercalia celebration. Both were named Saint Valentine, where the modern name for this pagan holiday originates. These two men were executed on February 14th in different years. Subsequently, a Roman pope named Gelasius combined the two events. Lupercalia was merged with the executions of the two men named Saint Valentine, leading to the creation of modern-day Valentine's Day.

Cupid is Eros, the god of love. Chocolate is considered an aphrodisiac, so it is commonly used to celebrate this holiday. The color red symbolizes blood sacrifice, linking the pagan festival of Lupercalia to what is now known as Saint Valentine's Day.

Humanity is fast asleep as it celebrates its Babylonian pagan holidays. Many people discover this information, yet they continue to celebrate these holidays. They convince themselves it is not a big deal and claim they celebrate it for the children. These are the same ones who complain that someone needs to save them from this Draconian slavery. Humanity must demonstrate a desire to awaken and stop worshiping their captors.

Who will have the strength to stand up to the Draconian Empire? If nothing is said or done, Earth will remain under their rule. All this thought energy that goes into their indoctrination keeps humanity content with being controlled by the manipulators. Are you strong enough to break free from mind control?

During Babylonian times, the day we now know as Halloween was known as a day when the dead would return to life. Over the years, this celebration has evolved, and practices vary depending on the region. For example, in ancient Egypt, it was customary to hang lanterns on the edges of roofs and leave food for the deceased. Meanwhile, the ancient Romans would throw black beans to ward off evil spirits.

Halloween, also known as All Souls Day, is associated with necromancy, which involves communicating with the souls of those who have passed away. While nothing is inherently wrong with seeking to connect with a deceased soul, Halloween mainly focuses on interactions with restless souls that may wish to cause harm to the living. Historically, priests of Baal would dress as goddesses in honor of Semiramis and go door-to-door soliciting valuables and, in some areas, even children's sacrifices.

The Focus of Halloween is to honor Baal the Destroyer. In ancient Phoenicia and Babylon, this worship of Baal involved child torture and sacrifice. Baal the Destroyer turns this event of honoring him into an act orchestrated for his deity, Moloch or Ahriman. One of the forms of torture was to stuff the children into large leather sacks and then throw them over the temple wall, where they would fall. Then, the children would be burned and eaten. The priest of Baal would partake in eating the children.

Halloween is a day traditionally associated with celebrating the dead, but many are unaware of the darker rituals that take place on this day. Specifically, some children are sacrificed to Baal. This holiday was created to lower the frequency of the planet, allowing for communication with negative entities worshiped by the Draconian Empire. Are you strong enough to say, "no more" and stop giving your energy to the Draconian Empire and its leaders?

Humanity desires change and wants suffering to end, yet many remain unwilling to change themselves. People do not seem ready to be freed from this bondage. Even after learning about this dark history, many awaken to the truth yet continue to support the controllers' holidays.

If you want change and an end to suffering, what changes are you making in your mental state? Are you following the mind-controlled, soulless ones, or are you creating your fifth- density reality by changing your mindset?

On third-density Earth, we must abide by the cabal's specific rules to survive, but we do not have to celebrate their holidays.

Chapter 24: The Secret Truth About Jesus

Many religions around the world base their beliefs on the life of Jesus. Most people accept what the Bible says about Jesus as a proven fact. This is intentional, and the narrative surrounding his life has often been distorted to manipulate followers' minds. Everything the cabal does is for their benefit and to advance their agenda. I understand what it feels like to be indoctrinated, only to face cognitive dissonance when you start to realize that the people you trust the most have been lying to you. In their defense they also were lied to and are only sharing their indoctrinated truth.

This chapter will examine information contradicting what society believes to be factual about Jesus. Unfortunately, Giordano Bruno and many others were burned at the stake for teaching information that opposed the controllers' information. Now that many generations have been indoctrinated, there is no need for that type of Draconian law to be enforced.

Did you know that Jesus of Nazareth's real name is Yeshua and that every time you speak the name of Jesus, you are, in actuality, saying "Hail Zeus," a term created by the Roman Empire in an attempt to ease the transition from Roman Paganism to Christianity? The actual name of the man known as Jesus is Yeshua, which translates to

Joshua in Hebrew. Some believe Yeshua is an extraterrestrial hybrid, possessing human and extraterrestrial characteristics. He was sent to Earth to help elevate human consciousness and bestow a higher vibrational frequency upon humanity. When I say extraterrestrial hybrid, I refer to a mix between Earth humans and possibly Lyrian.

Yeshua was successful in his mission, but the Roman Empire and the Catholic Church twisted and obscured his teachings and life story from public knowledge. In Apocryphal texts, Jesus is depicted as a student of the Egyptian mysteries who taught concepts like reincarnation and meditation; however, these ideas were omitted from the modern Bible. Between 100 AD and 900 AD, ancient texts were copied by the Phoenicians, who gathered writings from all over the world and placed their versions into vases. Centuries later, these rewritings were compiled to create the canonized Bible, overseen by the Council of Nicaea. They determined which information would be included and manipulated it to fit their control agenda. Any explicit references to aliens and UFOs were removed during the rewriting process. Their followers needed to be disconnected and imprisoned on Earth.

The next step in this agenda was to enforce Christianity in specific regions worldwide. Under the Pope's orders,

Rome killed millions of people who did not adhere to Christian beliefs. During the Spanish Inquisition, many were tortured and killed for rejecting the Christian faith. One notorious torture device, known as the Pope's spear, was used to execute women deemed unbelievers. It was placed inside the vagina and expanded to burst open the woman's vagina. This is how Christianity grew in popularity. If a targeted group did not fall in line, they would torture members of the group until the whole group conformed. After three generations of indoctrination, there was no need to use this tactic because the children would be born and would automatically be members of the Christian church. The next generation would believe wholeheartedly without ever understanding why they hold those beliefs. The knowledge that their ancestors believed in the Christian church primarily due to fear of death would mostly be forgotten, much like how it is today. The horrors of people being tortured in the name of Christianity many years ago are known today, yet there are billions of followers. As you can now see, Earth is a planet filled with mind-controlled puppets.

The Gospel of the Holy Twelve contains many parallels omitted from the modern-day Bible. There are discrepancies between the contemporary Bible and ancient texts that predate it. Researching the Gospel of the Holy Twelve reveals these differences. For instance, the famous Lord's Prayer begins with, "Our Father and Mother who art above and within." This original text illustrates that the eternal essence of the actual creator, God, resides within us. We have been conditioned to believe that this essence is external but is found within. By following Yeshua's teachings on meditation, we can discover the power within us. According to ancient texts, Yeshua embarked on a remarkable journey during his early years. When he was 12 years old, he traveled to Egypt with his mother, where he visited the Great Pyramid of Giza to become an initiate of the ancient Egyptian ministry school. After this, he went to India and Tibet, where he acquired profound knowledge about reincarnation, spirituality, and the art of Reiki healing.

It is said that extraterrestrial beings delivered the prophecy of his birth. They possessed advanced technology far beyond what was known on Earth then. These extraterrestrial beings were said to have individual flying disc-shaped crafts and glowing armor. One can only imagine people's impression of them, especially those who have never encountered such technology. It's easy to understand why these beings were viewed as Gods. It would be similar to what would happen if modern humans visited a planet without developed technology. If the inhabitants of that planet saw a figure in a spacesuit drive out of a rocket in a jeep, they would likely think this human was a God due to the advanced technology on display. Lacking the proper vocabulary to describe what they were witnessing; the people deified these beings.

In the biblical text, an angel named Gabriel was sent by God to a town called Nazareth in Galilee. His mission was to approach a virgin who was engaged to a man named Joseph, who was from the house of David. The virgin's name was Mary. Gabriel greeted her and told her not to be afraid because she had found favor with God. In these ancient texts, "God" refers to a higher-ranking extraterrestrial. The people recognized these beings as having a higher power but failed to understand that this was due to their advanced technology and knowledge.

Gabriel tells her that she has been chosen to have a son. This extraterrestrial being was positive, and Yeshua was an attempt to help liberate humanity that was falling deeper into the Draconians' control.

When Gabriel approached Mary with the proposal of her giving birth while remaining a virgin, it was not solely due to divine intervention but rather a process akin to artificial insemination. Mary's mother is named Elizabeth in the Gospel of the Holy Twelve. She was also born to a virgin, with in vitro fertilization performed before Yeshua was born.

This concept parallels ancient Sumerian Babylonian tablets, where Isis, also known as Ninhursag, employed a similar method to give birth to Adam. He was the first Homo sapiens with advanced capabilities due to the mixed DNA he possessed.

This advanced technology was once disguised as magic, and in ancient times, people could only explain it in that way. However, today, even with limited technology, humans have managed to replicate similar processes. Artificial insemination is no longer viewed as magic or as something with divine power. Within this intriguing context, it is theorized that Yoshua becomes an extraordinary hybrid, blending genetic material from both extraterrestrial and human DNA.

To better understand Yesua's birth situation, we must look back a few years. The setting is Judea and ancient Israel, a land under the oppression of the Roman Empire. The Jewish community viewed the Romans as foreign oppressors. Herod had been installed as king by Emperor Augustus to uphold Roman rule.

During this time, there was a persistent rumor that a messiah would come to free the Jewish people from Roman control. Many were eagerly awaiting this savior. One figure whom some believed was the messiah was an enslaved person named Simon of Persea. However, after he was killed, the people's faith in the coming of a messiah began to wane. Even today, followers of certain religions are still waiting for their messiah to arrive. Following Simon's death, the people felt a profound sense of hopelessness as they continued to remain under oppression.

At 12, after conversing with knowledgeable rabbis, Yeshua traveled to Egypt with his mother—this journey aimed to facilitate Yeshua's initiation into the Ancient Egyptian Ministry School. We have previously discussed the origins of these ancient ministry schools. During this period, admission to the school was restricted to individuals who exhibited a high frequency of awareness and potential. Only those deemed worthy would be accepted into these esteemed institutions. By then, the positive-oriented ancient ministry school had been imparting its knowledge secretly for many years.

The ministry schools offered knowledge beyond anything an average person could imagine. Students in these schools gained remarkable abilities, such as levitating, breathing underwater, or holding their breath for extended periods. They learned to slow their heartbeats to the point where their bodies appeared lifeless. Additionally, they could block pain, manipulate fire, and astral project their consciousness outside their physical bodies. It is also said that they could enter deep states of meditation to access events from both the past and the future. Furthermore, they were capable of healing various illnesses. This is the illuminated knowledge that the cabal controlled and kept from society.

The ministry school held the key to transforming our understanding of physics and harnessing the power of the aether. Everything in the physical world originates from the aether, and the ability to manipulate it can transform the physical body into a multidimensional being. Yeshua came to Earth with a mission: to unlock these abilities and assist in ascending the human collective consciousness.

One of the key teachings in the ministry school was that death is an illusion and that our souls are immortal sparks of Source. Students were trained in cosmic teachings that had previously led humanity into difficulties. This knowledge was kept secret because it could be misused for regressive purposes.

The Star Wars movies depict Jedi Knights who possess similar abilities. Many coincidences in the film's plot relate to the hidden truths of Earth's galactic history. For instance, the Death Star in the movie can be compared to Nibiru. The Jedi represent the ancient students and masters of a ministry school. The Rebel Alliance symbolizes the Galactic Federation, while the evil empire corresponds to the Orion Group. Jabba the Hut would represent Ekata who resides on the Andromedan biosphere.

Even though Yeshua was selected to attend the ascended ministry school, the curriculum was highly challenging. The exams were mind-bending and required a deep commitment to complete successfully. Students' spiritual and physical abilities were pushed to their limits. Despite the incredible difficulty, Yeshua, with unmeasurable determination, began his journey to discover the true depths of his spiritual abilities.

Along the way, he was guided by ascetics and sages who shared their higher knowledge with him. They prepared Yeshua for the trials he would face. When he reached the ancient temples, he met the gatekeeper, an elderly sage who could see a person's soul. Without verbal communication, the sage led Yeshua into the temple, where he entered a hidden world filled with even more knowledge. Here, Yeshua achieved true enlightenment.

His body and mental faculties were tested, and he had to learn to disconnect from his physical form to master his abilities completely. In the chambers of reflection, he faced his deepest fears, doubts, and the challenges his ego posed. This was a battle of the soul, testing whether he would remain true to his divine purpose. Yeshua spent years mastering control over his abilities, but the dark energies that sought to sway him failed in their attempts to convert him into one of their servants. Yeshua was resolute in not using his abilities for personal gain.

In the end, he emerged victorious from the temple. By passing the test, he became the Messiah of Christ consciousness. According to the Gnostic gospels, Yeshua's last test was the ceremonial crucifixion inside the pyramids of Giza. This differs from the modern-day Bible because the church sought a martyr for its followers to mourn and to be indebted to eternally. In reality, this was a test of consciousness. Yeshua had to enter a deep state of meditation where he could slow his heart and breath to the point where his body almost appeared to be dead. It can be argued that his body did die, and I understand this perspective. However, Yeshua could re-enter his consciousness into his body, and with this final test, he had graduated.

Yeshua then journeyed into India, meeting sages with more profound knowledge. He dedicated himself to learning everything he could from these sages, further elevating his abilities. Afterward, he ventured into the ancient mountains of Tibet. There, he arrived at a remote monastery nestled among the hills. The monks welcomed him and quickly recognized that Yeshua possessed profound spiritual abilities.

Once Yeshua arrived, the Tibetan monks began training him. Through meditation, he learned the art of Reiki healing and became well-versed in the spiritual abilities and teachings the monks shared. They taught him how to channel the universal life force known as chi. He learned to use his hands to channel the healing power of the universe and how to heal and align a person's chakras. Additionally, he discovered how to channel different frequencies, which can also be used for healing.

Yeshua, in a sense, became a starship. These are abilities characteristic of a starship. One can find replicators on highly advanced starships, and Yeshua could also replicate physical mass. There are medical healing frequency beds on starships, and Yeshua could heal the physical body with no help from technology. All these abilities exist within humanity, but they are kept secret. There is little to gain from individuals developing this technology or ability themselves, which is why the human aura and pineal gland are targeted from the moment a person is born. The metals found in vaccines disrupt our spiritual development, while contaminated food affects the human energy field.

Chemtrails are part of a broader agenda to prevent humanity from awakening to its true potential. Yeshua is an excellent example of someone we should all try to emulate.

Yeshua achieved true enlightenment and understood that he came from Source. He recognized that we all originate from Source but dedicated himself to connecting with it. His consciousness was aligned with what is known as Christ consciousness. He learned about the workings of higher planes of existence and how conscious portions of Source choose to incarnate for experiences that teach them profound lessons. He was shown the truth of the universe, illuminating him with this knowledge.

After leaving Tibet, Yeshua returned to the Middle East, now possessing deep, illuminated wisdom. He began to channel his abilities to demonstrate to the people what was possible within themselves. While he referred to himself as the Son of God, he also emphasized that we are all sons and daughters of God.

Throughout his life, Yeshua shared his teachings with anyone willing to listen, ensuring his legacy would endure. He encouraged believers to explore the depths of their spirituality and seek out the power within them.

Incorporating the omitted ancient texts into our understanding makes the current Bible clearer. In Luke 17:20-21, Jesus states, "The kingdom is within you." This passage reveals the true meaning: the power lies within us all because we come from the Source Creator. We all possess this power.

Yeshua now journeys to Jerusalem to become the savior and messiah for his people. He built a following by sharing his profound knowledge. At that time, the prevailing belief among the Jewish people was that life began with the physical birth of the body, and there were no established concepts of heaven or hell. It was later that the Vatican indoctrinated its followers with beliefs about heaven and hell.

Yeshua's teachings challenged these deeply rooted beliefs. He spoke of consciousness existing beyond death, contradicting the false teachings imposed on the people. This conflict with established doctrine is said to have led to Yeshua's persecution.

The accounts in the modern-day Bible, including the crucifixion of Yeshua, were reportedly added by the Romans. The earliest complete Christian New Testament, the Sinai Bible, does not mention any crucifixion. Some apocryphal texts suggest that Yeshua did not suffer or die in the way commonly portrayed. It was later decided that having a martyr would evoke a sense of guilt among the followers.

There are many speculations regarding the details of Yeshua's life. I believe that Yeshua's narrative in the modern Bible is a compilation of his actual life and influences from other figures.

The portrayal of Yeshua's crucifixion varies depending on the religious perspective one considers. Several alternate versions of this story exist, and over the years, historians have theorized about the actual conclusion of Yeshua's crucifixion. Some explore the possibility that Yeshua survived the event. During this tumultuous period in Jerusalem, Yeshua faced the Roman governor, Pontius Pilate. The atmosphere was tense as the people were eager to see the outcome of this encounter.

Pontius Pilate was indeed curious about Yeshua. Rumors of Yeshua's abilities had spread among the people, and his teachings were well known throughout the land. However, despite the speculation surrounding him, Yeshua did not present himself as a self- proclaimed king. Instead, he embodied humility, making it easy for others to overlook him.

Pilate sought to understand Yeshua's claims, as many called him the king of the Jewish people.

Pilate asked Yeshua if he was, in fact, the king of the Jews. Yeshua remained calm and replied, "My kingdom is not of this world. If my kingdom were of this world, my servants would fight to prevent my arrest. My kingdom is from another place" (John 18:36). I believe this response was unexpected and indicated that Yeshua had transcended earthly concerns. Yeshua continued explaining to Pilate, "You say that I am a king, but I came into this world to testify to the truth. Everyone on the side of truth will listen to me."

I want to present the idea that Yeshua's consciousness had evolved to a point where he was close to Source. He incarnated directly from that higher state of being into the third density. Through his dedication to personal development, he could discover and remember who he was and where he came from. As previously mentioned, we all can remember who we indeed are. Yeshua came to assist the collective consciousness in raising its frequency. When someone raises their frequency high enough, they will begin to remember and unlock truths; this was Yeshua's mission.

Yeshua was later crucified and placed in a tomb. The Gospel of Mark, which was written 300 years after these events, describes how, after the crucifixion and the placement of Yeshua's body in the tomb, it was discovered that his body had disappeared. He was then seen alive, without any wounds. However, the oldest original translation from Aramaic to Greek of the Dead Sea Scrolls presents a different narrative. It recounts that the disciples were walking to the tomb but does not clarify what they found inside. This leaves the reader uncertain about the events inside the tomb, suggesting that the scribes had to fill in the story's gaps.

A popular theory among historians who have studied the original ancient texts before they were altered theorizes that Yeshua entered a deep state of meditation that allowed him to survive the crucifixion. Onlookers and those in charge of the crucifixion may have mistakenly assumed he was dead. After his body was taken to the tomb, he could have awakened from his meditative state and exited the tomb.

Another theory suggests that a positive-oriented extraterrestrial group retrieved his body and placed it in a rejuvenation pod. These are merely theories, and no ancient texts explicitly describe how Yeshua may have survived the crucifixion and escaped from the tomb. All accounts of Yeshua's resurrection and his appearances to the disciples were written after manipulating the original story. A third theory asserts that Jesus did indeed die during the crucifixion and that the story ends there.

In the ancient writings of Josephus, there is a mention of a man proclaiming himself to be a prophet. This man's history is very similar to Yeshua's, leading many people to believe he was Yeshua himself. This man was referred to as "The Egyptian." While the Josephus text refers to him as The Egyptian, it also labels him a false prophet. These accounts concerning "The Egyptian" occurred 20 years after the crucifixion of Yeshua. This is particularly interesting because this man, known as "The Egyptian," was teaching the same principles that Yeshua had also shared. The notion of whether Yeshua survived the crucifixion remains highly speculative, but it cannot be entirely ruled out.

The Council of Nicaea significantly altered the original ideas and teachings that Yeshua stood for. This was done to keep the population in fear of going to hell or facing eternal death, creating a belief that would attract and retain more followers. It was understood that human society could be more easily controlled if people feared eternal damnation or death and were disconnected from their true identities. The accurate knowledge that Yeshua taught was of the infinite consciousness that can't die.

The Catholic Church, established by Roman Emperor Constantine hundreds of years after Yeshua's crucifixion, made the story of Yeshua's death the central focus of Christianity. To unify the people's beliefs, Yeshua's name was changed to "Iesous," which is rendered as "Jesus" in English. This change was intended to align with the Greek god Zeus, and early portrayals of Jesus resembled statues of a young Zeus. The letter "J" was introduced into the name "Jesus" only in 1524 by Jan Giorgio Trissino, yet it did not gain common usage in the King James Version of the Bible until the early 17th century.

Constantine was the first Roman emperor to openly embrace Christianity after converting from his pagan and catechumen beliefs. He recognized the benefits of uniting the populace under a single religion: Christianity. With Christianity's growing popularity, Constantine saw an opportunity to unify the people under one faith. However, he needed to manipulate Christian believers into worshiping and celebrating his pagan deities. To achieve this, he implemented policies that blended paganism with Christianity.

This blend made the transition easier for pagan believers moving to Christianity and for Christians transitioning to pagan practices. As a result, certain aspects of pagan rituals and symbols were adopted by Christianity. For instance, the date of Christmas was chosen to coincide with the Roman pagan celebration of Saturnalia. This connection can be quickly confirmed by researching the histories of both Christmas and Saturnalia. Another example of this blending is the practice of saying "amen" at the end of prayers, which was adopted earlier, in the 4th century BCE, as an homage to Amen Ra, a deity from ancient Egypt. Thus, it is evident that Christianity has a long history of blending and manipulating its followers.

According to Sumerian cuneiform tablets, which predate the Bible by thousands of years, Enlil is identified as a deity later known as Yahweh. The people of Israel either mistakenly or intentionally forgot the Akkadian language and grammar, replacing the name Enlil with Yahweh. In English, YHWH is pronounced as Yahweh, which has often been mistranslated to mean "Lord." In Hebrew, Yahweh translates to "to be," while the English Bible substitutes it with the term "Lord." Additionally, the name Jehovah originates from a Latinization of the Hebrew name Yahweh. By 530 BC, Yahweh was recognized as a deity. When the story was adapted from the Sumerian tablets into what would eventually become the modern Bible, the name Enlil was replaced with Yahweh, and later, it changed to Jehovah. Before the bible existed, some tablets were put together to manipulate society, so the Bible was a mix of old lies with new lies, and a sprinkle of original truths was kept.

Another interesting example of mistranslation can be found in the texts that refer to the one almighty God. In the Hebrew Torah, written between 333 and 539 BCE, Elohim is used instead of God or Lord. Elohim, in Hebrew, translates to "plural gods." Although historians provide various explanations for this mistranslation, these justifications often fall short compared to other ancient texts. Some theorize that Akhenaten promoted a monotheistic religion centered on the deity Amun Ra, which may explain the transition from plural to singular references to God. It has been theorized that this jealous God, Amun Ra, is Marduk, and the timelines seem to support this theory. As we continue to uncover evidence, it becomes clear that many mistranslations and manipulations occurred during the compilation of the Bible. The Bible appears to be a mere shell of the ancient tablets, as Amun Ra / Marduk sought complete control over what he believed was his dominion— Earth. He is described as a malevolent being who commanded his followers to say "Amen" after praying to him. Ultimately, he was an extraterrestrial with advanced technology and knowledge who exploited the ignorance of humanity, acting against other extraterrestrials who were his relatives for his gain.

It is up to you to decide whether God sent Yeshua or if his mother underwent artificial insemination with an embryo that had its DNA fully unlocked. In either case, there is no denying that the stories about his life, preserved before manipulation, present an extraordinary narrative about awakening humanity to a higher power. Unfortunately, society has been led astray from the original writings for ulterior motives. Yeshua taught and demonstrated what is possible when we connect with the portion of God within us. His life and teachings should inspire profound introspection regarding our consciousness and reality.

Regrettably, the teachings and life stories associated with Yeshua have been altered by the Council of Nicaea and the Roman Empire. If Yeshua were present today, he would likely be displeased with the Vatican for establishing a religion that has ensnared its followers in dogma. Many followers obey without questioning, and those who raise questions are often instructed to bolster their faith or risk being disconnected from the church. This deep- seated mind control over the populace is pervasive, and only those with a strong connection to Source can break free from the confines of dogma.

Humanity should model our lives after Yeshua's example—a life dedicated to pursuing enlightenment and elevating one's frequency while on a physical journey to finding one's spiritual identity. He was a master meditator, and through this practice, he was able to unlock the secrets of the universe. He unlocked his DNA, demonstrating that humanity can achieve the same potential. Unfortunately, many in the human race are giving away their power of manifestation to those who seek to control them. It's time to remember who we indeed are and recognize that humanity has been placed in a metaphorical prison. We must liberate our minds and acknowledge the injustices occurring around us.

If you wish to experience mind control, then ignore this warning. However, if you want to experience true liberation, I urge you to awaken now. It's time to stop consenting to the demands of those in power. It's time to reclaim your soul and free yourself from the constraints imposed by the regressive Draconian Orion group.

While many biblical texts can offer guidance, numerous passages can enslave your mind. The Bible should be read, but it is essential to proceed with caution. One must have a strong mind to avoid indoctrination and the fear it instills.

We can take comfort in knowing that there is a true God who is the actual creator of the universe. Placing all your faith in a single book without exploring its authentic history is ludicrous. The priests and elders of these religions assert that questioning this authority will mean you are not in God's favor. This resembles the control of a dictator. Followers are instructed to model their lives after Jesus, but even that name is part of the manipulation, as it is rooted in the name of the pagan god Zeus. As mentioned, the name Jesus is a way to have billions on a planet; repeat "Hail Zeus."

It is time to awaken from this dream and confront the reality of the situation. This realization may be painful, but that pain will ultimately be replaced with a sense of liberation. Stop succumbing to the fear used by the Bible to control you.

When reading the Bible, it's important to use logic. Satan is described as one of the highest-ranking angels, suggesting he is intelligent. So, why would he follow the path outlined in the Bible to his destruction? One might expect an intelligent being to avoid the script to escape his eventual death that is outlined in the Bible. This is part of the drama used to capture the minds of billions on the planet, not about telling the truth about the future. However, it seems that humanity is following the script in the Bible to their demise.

Chapter 25: Hidden Shocking Events in Modern History

The Cabal on Earth has secretly concealed significant events from society to ensure that humanity does not awaken to the truth and that its agenda remains intact. As discussed earlier in this book, many important events in Earth's history have been twisted or wholly hidden from humanity. Now, we will examine more recent events obscured from the public eye, revealing what the Cabal has kept from you.

We know that the Draconian Empire and their leader at the time, Marduk, took control of Nibiru and Earth. The Galactic Federation placed a frequency barrier around Earth, turning it into a prison.

With limited resources, the Draconian Empire retreated underground and aimed to transform humanity into its mindless slaves. Many of its members went underground to Agartha and other secret locations. While they had some access to underground portals, they were primarily limited in their ability to travel beyond the planet.

It would take many years, but a powerful group could control humanity's mind by manipulating what people knew about history and their mental state. Essentially, they lowered the frequency of the planet and its inhabitants. The Cabal and secret societies, such as the Illuminati, were formed to exert this control over humanity secretly.

They came to dominate religion, governments, and the financial system. However, they needed to secretly develop technology that would enable them to gain even more power by leaving the planet and uniting with other regressive associates loyal to Marduk. This development had to remain hidden, as the revelation of their true motives would lead to a loss of power over humanity. We will discuss this further, but the Draconian Empire did not operate cohesively, resulting in a power struggle among them.

A man named Dietrich Eckart lived in Germany from 1868 to 1923. During his life, he became a poet, playwright, journalist, publicist, and political activist. He was one of the founders of the German Workers' Party, which later evolved into the Nazi Party. He was involved in secret groups and had acquired illuminated knowledge. The extent of his involvement with these societies is unclear; however, he was instrumental in introducing Adolf Hitler to some of this esoteric knowledge and secret societies. These secret societies were affiliated with the Cabal's secret society groups, but it is unclear what level of authority this group had in the pyramid.

Hitler was informed about much of the illuminated knowledge, including the history of the bloodlines from the Caucasus Mountains and the Draconian Empire that had gone underground. This information inspired him to believe that a specific human vessel possessed pure blood and unique DNA.

During the 1930s, Hitler was informed that people living in the Tibetan mountains directly communicated with extraterrestrials who resided underground. This group of extraterrestrials in Tibet is distinct from another group that emerged from the Caucasus Mountains. Although they may have been united in the past, these two groups are no longer working together. This separation is evident due to the activities orchestrated by the extraterrestrials in the Tibetan mountains.

Germany sent expeditions to these mountains with the primary mission of establishing direct communication with this extraterrestrial group. These beings are a reptilian race and have originated from the Draconian Empire. However, something led to a disconnection between the two groups, and the reasons for this separation remain unclear. Groups within the reptilian race are now competing for power over humanity.

To avoid confusion, we will refer to the group in the Tibetan mountains as "Draco." In contrast, the other group will continue to be known as the "Draconian Empire," which directly controls the Cabal.

The German expeditions were officially presented as scientific missions. However, photographic evidence of these German expedition meetings with the Tibetan people suggests that the true motivations were not solely scientific or humanitarian. Notably, some of these photographs feature the SS flag in the background.

The SS, or Schutzstaffel, was founded in 1925 and served as Hitler's guard. Over time, it evolved into Germany's most powerful and feared organization. If these trips to the Tibetan mountains were genuinely for scientific and humanitarian purposes, one must question the presence of SS officers in these expeditions.

Before 1938, Hitler established communication with members of the Draco race living underground near the Tibetan mountains. It is possible that Hitler was chosen to initiate this mission, ultimately becoming the face of what the Zionists needed to orchestrate. Given Hitler's prior associations with occult groups, the connection was already in place. The Tula Society, composed of wealthy and influential German men, aided Hitler in his rise to power. This society is linked to Zionism and is also referred to as an assassin cult. While he had the connections, the question remains: did he have the bloodline?

William Patrick, Adolf Hitler's half-nephew, claimed that Adolf was the illegitimate son of Maria Anna Schicklgruber. During her pregnancy, she worked for Solomon Mayer von Rothschild in Vienna. This connection to the Rothschilds gave Hitler the bloodline and the financial support necessary to rise to prominence. It remains unclear whether he knew that the higher echelons of the Illuminati were already in communication with extraterrestrials. Still, a line of communication between Adolf Hitler and the Draco was established.

The Draco shared basic information about antigravity and rocket technology, which the Germans utilized for development. One of the most notable technologies was Die Glocke, or "The Bell," an anti-gravity, bell-shaped craft. The Germans aimed to devise a way to mount and fire weapons from this ship; however, they did not advance this technology until after World War II.

The Germans faced the challenge that without a secondary or auxiliary propulsion system for the antigravity vehicle, the craft would lose its stability if a missile or a high-powered machine gun were fired from within its toroidal field. While the German military was formidable without Die Glocke, it could not secure victory in the war without this secret weapon. Was the script always intended to conclude as it did? Did they deliberately withhold information about technology until later? I don't know the answers to these questions, but they are worth considering.

Full communication was established between the German secret military and the Draco alien race. In September 1939, Hitler invaded Poland, and just two days later, France and Britain were also invaded, all under the control of the Cabal.

In the early 1940s, the Schutzstaffel (SS) and other German secret groups began visiting Mars. Unbeknownst to the Germans, the Draconian officials used them to build a workforce and gather resources to access the lost technology in Antarctica.

The Draco played along with the Germans but manipulated them as puppets. Before traveling to Mars, the Germans conducted secret expeditions to Antarctica in search of this lost technology. Evidence suggests that German ships were present in Antarctica between 1936 and 1938. It was time to develop advanced technologies, allowing the cabal to travel off-planet more freely.

With the Draconian's help, German leadership developed advanced technology at the base in Antarctica.

In July 1945, the United States government began testing nuclear bombs in New Mexico. When a bomb of such magnitude detonates, it sends ripples through several densities in space-time, attracting the attention of extraterrestrials who started visiting Earth then.

These extraterrestrial groups' technology enveloped their craft in a toroidal field, allowing them to travel through the Van Allen bands without an issue. These groups were investigating what was happening on this planet, leading to the Roswell crash.

The famous Roswell incident occurred in June 1947, sparking extensive discussion and research. Colonel Philip J. Corso's book "The Day After Roswell" is a key resource on this incident. This book details his involvement in the incident and the events that unfolded, highlighting extraterrestrials' interest in humans.

Another significant event in 1947 was that the German military personnel who had gone to Antarctica before the war's conclusion had managed to weaponize their antigravity ships. After Germany's defeat in 1945, the

United States initiated Operation Paperclip. This secret program relocated over 1,600 German scientists, engineers, and technicians to the United States for government employment following the war. Many of these individuals were prominent members of the Nazi Party. Operation Paperclip facilitated knowledge and technology transfer from Germany to the United States.

Through Operation Paperclip, advanced technology and control shifted from Germany to the United States. The same German scientists who had been developing secret weapons in Germany during the war were brought to the United States.

One year after the war ended, Operation Highjump was launched. Officially termed the "United States Navy Antarctic Developments Program, Task Force 68," this operation ran from August 1946 to February 1947.

Admiral Richard Byrd led Operation Highjump, which was initially described as a research expedition in Antarctica. However, it was later revealed that the operation involved 4,700 soldiers, 13 ships, and 33 aircraft, suggesting it was not a typical research mission. The narrative has since changed, with public reports now indicating that Operation Highjump aimed to test equipment in cold weather conditions.

The German scientists who came to the United States under Operation Paperclip reportedly communicated with German military leadership, who had secretly established operations in Antarctica.

Admiral Byrd recounted his experiences during Operation Highjump, claiming to have witnessed flying ships that intimidated the United States military contingent he had brought with him. He also mentioned seeing an opening in the Earth devoid of snow, where creatures resembling the extinct woolly mammoth were present. However, he later recanted his initial claims, attributing them to the stress of prolonged exposure to cold weather. Admiral Byrd had said too much and was told to change the story.

Subsequently, his son revealed Admiral Byrd's journals, which contained various accounts of his experiences. Some versions of the journals indicate that Byrd was unsuccessful in his search for an entrance to the Hollow Earth. Interestingly, the details in the original journals aligned with his initial claims upon returning from Antarctica. Unfortunately, Byrd's son was found dead in an abandoned warehouse, raising questions about the authenticity of the different versions of the journals. It is common for individuals who reveal such sensitive information to meet mysterious ends.

As previously mentioned, the Germans who were relocated during Operation Paperclip continued to communicate with those who had traveled to Antarctica years earlier. Once the Antarctic Germans developed weaponized antigravity ships, they instructed the Operation Paperclip Germans to inform the United States government that they had secretly established a base in Antarctica. This intelligence prompted Operation Highjump. The Germans in Antarctica used this opportunity to demonstrate their power. Upon confirming the accuracy of this information, the United States realized they needed to coexist with this emerging Draco and Antarctica German threat.

The Antarctica Germans, known as the "Mars Germans," reportedly had already begun traveling to Mars, hence their nickname. Now, with the aid and guidance of the Antarctic Draconians, they aimed to gain more control over large corporations, particularly those focused on technology development. Aware that after the incident at Roswell, a group of the Cabal via the United States military was dismantling extraterrestrial ships and reverse- engineering them, the Mars Germans sought to control and own this technology that the United States Cabal was overseeing. They instructed the United States Cabal to place secret Mars German agents within these companies involved in developing and reverse engineering extraterrestrial technology for the United States. This is a clear example of internal conflict among Earth's controllers.

This deal was significant because the German scientists developing weapons and advanced technology had left Germany and were now working on secret government projects after Operation Paperclip. They worked directly for the United States government and third-party companies comprising the "industrial complex." The Germans were now controlling the release of this technology, deciding who would receive what. The United States and the Cabal controlling them would only obtain the technology that the Mars Germans were willing to share, with no additional resources provided. The United States government was manipulated to create Operation Paperclip, and now it was clear they were used as a resource.

The Mars Germans understood their safety was better secured by building a base on the Moon's far side. This was due to the presence of the Draconian Empire and Mantis on Mars, creating a perilous situation. As part of their strategy, the Mars Germans made a deal with the Draconians for 20 acres of land on the Moon. The agreement required the Mars Germans to give 150 males and 75 females to the Draconian Empire. At that point, the Mars Germans had been visiting Mars but did not possess a base off Earth until they built their lunar base.

The fate of the men and women who were given to the Draconians remains unclear, but the common theory suggests they were used for slave labor, reproduction, and as a food source. When rumors surfaced about the Draconian's real intentions, the Mars Germans recognized they were dealing with a potential enemy. Consequently, they realized their alliance with the Antarctica Draconians was not beneficial, and the Mars Germans needed to establish independence. Another sign of the Antarctica Draconians' self-serving motives was their establishment of a secret space program known as "Dark Fleet," which they did not share with the Germans, indicating that the Earth Antarctica Draconians had separate interests from those of the Mars Germans. The Mars Germans were also used as a resource to help the Antarctica Draconians develop and manufacture the ships to get past the Van Allen Bans.

The Mars Germans aimed to establish a base on Mars, but the Mantis and Draconian Empire occupied it. Understanding their lack of trust in the Draconian Empire, the Mars Germans sought to obtain land on Mars for another outpost. This led to a brutal war on

Mars that lasted ten years. By the end of the conflict, the Mars Germans succeeded in securing their desired land, solidifying their identity as the Mars Germans.

In a move seen as a threat to the United States Cabal on Earth, the Mars Germans orchestrated an event known as the Lights over Washington, which occurred between July 12 and 29, 1952. Lights over Washington is a well-documented incident during which the Mars Germans threatened to disclose sensitive information to the public by landing on the White House lawn. The Cabal controlling the United States had ceased negotiations with the Mars Germans based in Antarctica and on the Moon. The Mars Germans demanded more resources to support their ongoing conflict against the Mantis and the Draconian Empire to control land on Mars. This event helped the Mars Germans secure a portion of land on Mars, as previously mentioned.

The Mars Germans and the Earth Cabal have a history of conflict. Despite this animosity, a treaty was established, leading to what is known as the Antarctic Treaty. Under this agreement, Antarctica was declared a sovereign nation. The Cabal was required to provide 250,000 people to the Germans. However, there were daily abductions carried out by the Mars Germans and the Zeta Grays. The Mars Germans often employed the Zeta Grays to conduct these abductions, and they sometimes collaborated on these operations. This situation became complicated because the Zeta Grays were also conducting their separate abductions unrelated to the Mars Germans' arrangements. The Zeta Grays had also struck an individual deal with the Earth Cabal and The United States Government, exchanging human citizens for technology that would aid in developing a secret space program for the United States.

A benevolent extraterrestrial group from the Pleiades wanted to help and guide the United States in the right direction. They saw that the United States was uniting itself with a regressive group and wanted to give advice. In 1954, the FBI and President Eisenhower held three secret meetings in New Mexico, where they encountered these extraterrestrial beings. These beings urged the leaders to promote peace instead of succumbing to the temptation of power. This benevolent extraterrestrial group warned that engaging with this regressive group would lead to destruction and further control over all levels of government for their benefit. Rumors suggest that Eisenhower favored the peaceful path and was reluctant to pursue power through weaponry.

Unfortunately, he and the peaceful extraterrestrials lost that struggle, leading to the implementation of an agreement between the regressive extraterrestrials and the United States government. This situation is one of the reasons why the Cabal who controls the United States fears disclosure; if citizens learned that they had been betrayed for technology, it could incite an uprising against them, threatening their control.

Following this, the Mars Germans sought greater control over technology and wanted to place more agents inside the companies engaged in reverse-engineering extraterrestrial technology. The United States Cabal acquiesced to these demands.

As is typical, the Cabal on Earth was thinking long-term. They realized that agreeing to the Mars Germans' demands was vital for maintaining their control over humanity. The Cabal felt their options were limited, with Mars German agents infiltrating the companies' secretly developing advanced technology.

The Mars Germans had acquired a memory wipe weapon from the Draconians. The United States Cabal recognized that if they could obtain this memory wipe device, they could control the information sent back to the Mars German leadership by their agents controlling the development of advanced technology within the industrial complex. The plan was to steal one memory wipe device to influence the implanted agents working within the technology development companies associated with the Mars Germans.

The United States Cabal and the USSR Cabal collaborated on a secret mission to destroy a shuttle carrying a memory wipe device. They ultimately acquired a memory wipe weapon by hijacking a German shuttle from Mars, stealing the memory wipe device, and then destroying the shuttle. They used it on the Mars agents who had infiltrated companies involved in developing and reverse engineering extraterrestrial technology for the Mars Germans.

Following this, the Earth Cabal secretly launched their space program, codenamed Solar Warden. The Mars Germans suspected the shuttle explosion was not an accident, but they had no proof, so no action was taken.

The Earth Cabal orchestrated the Cold War to fund Solar Warden secretly. The USSR and the United States were under the Cabal's influence, but the conflict provided a budget to support their space program. Although the Cabal had substantial financial resources, they preferred that taxpayers fund Solar Warden. By 1986, Solar Warden had established a base on the Moon. By then, it was clear that the Cabal had stolen a mind wipe device and had been secretly developing and withholding technology from the Mars Germans for years.

The Mars Germans intended to inform the United States and USSR that they knew about the Cabal's actions and that the shuttle explosion was not an accident. On January 28, 1986, they destroyed the Challenger shuttle, and on April 26, 1986, they caused the Chernobyl disaster. The Earth Cabal now understood that their involvement in destroying the Mars German shuttle and stealing the mind wipe device was no longer a secret.

Negotiations began between the Earth Cabal and the Mars Germans. By 1991, the Mars Germans agreed to relocate their base in Antarctica and moved all their operations off Earth. Now, with Solar Warden, the Cabal had advanced weaponry, and the Mars Germans sought to distance themselves from the Cabal.

Part of the 1991 agreement allowed the Cabal to take over the Antarctic base and gain control of the Moon base that the Germans had operated. This was a 100-year agreement to control the lunar base at no cost. The Mars Germans wanted to escape the Draconian presence on the Moon, while the Cabal felt that they had already compensated the Mars Germans sufficiently in the past, so the deal was accepted.

Throughout the 1980s, Solar Warden was fully operational, and the 1991 agreement further strengthened this already formidable secret space program.

The Draconians informed the Mars Germans that to annul their original agreement granting them control of the lunar base, they would need to give up 10 of their 12 most advanced ships. This left the Mars Germans with only a fraction of their fleet and two underground bases on Mars, New Berlin and Warsburg. Currently, there are approximately 3 million Germans living on Mars.

Four divisions were established, two affiliated with the Mars Germans and two with the Cabal. This marked the creation of IDARF, whose leadership was entirely composed of Mars Germans. An important point to note is that the Cabal gained control over the Antarctic base and the base on the Moon. IDARF operated as a collaboration between the Mars Germans and the Cabal. It is often difficult to discern the true intentions of regressive groups, but they worked together.

The Solar Warden secret program primarily includes participants from the USA, USSR, Brazil, India, South Africa, China, the U.K., and France.

IDARF and Solar Warden implemented 20-year stints for their soldiers. While the number of children recruited into these secret programs is unknown, many individuals are beginning to recall memories from their two-decade tenure. At the end of their 20 years, their minds are wiped, and their consciousness is transferred into a cloned version of themselves 20 years younger. They are sent back in time, placed 15 minutes before their abduction, usually with no memory of their 20-year absence. However, as mentioned, many are gradually starting to remember and provide detailed accounts of their experiences in the secret space program.

IDARF was tasked with locating peaceful civilizations on other planets, infiltrating their societies, and reporting on their findings. Intelligence officers would blend in with the locals to learn their culture. They then spread the rumor of a regressive race attacking nearby civilizations, training and preparing the peaceful inhabitants for war. This invasion was orchestrated by IDARF, aiming to cause significant casualties and instill fear among the people. Just as annihilation seemed imminent, IDARF would introduce a new culture that brought currency, beliefs, war, fear, and suffering. Ultimately, IDARF would defeat the fabricated invaders, thereby gaining control over the civilization, as the people believed they had triumphed due to the new mindset instilled by IDARF leadership.

IDARF could then withdraw from the planet, leaving behind a brainwashed civilization loyal to its supposed saviors. The inhabitants would have been conditioned to freely trade their resources with IDARF leaders aligned with the Cabal and the Draconian Empire.

It is intriguing to see how the same strategies used on Earth are applied to other planets. The tactic involves overwhelming the people with fear and deception, keeping them subservient to the agenda without direct force. By employing this method, the people unwittingly beg IDARF to take control of their lives, all while remaining unaware that they have become slaves. After all, what better slave exists than one who does not even realize they are enslaved?

Something interesting to note is that on May 22, 1949, Admiral Forrestal jumped out of his hospital window. He was hospitalized due to alleged depression. What is intriguing is that Forrestal had been appointed Secretary of Defense in September 1947. He soon uncovered information about extraterrestrials and the Majestic 12. He was openly against keeping this information from the public, and within two years, he was found dead from an apparent suicide — how convenient. He wanted to disclose all of this information but did not get to live long enough to reveal this information.

Although John F. Kennedy was not yet president, he opposed withholding disclosure from the American people. President Kennedy learned of the truth (some suggest that Forrestal disclosed this information to him) regarding MJ12 and the secret agreement the United

States made with Gray extraterrestrials. Regardless of whether Forrestal was the one who informed Kennedy, it is clear that Kennedy wanted the truth to be revealed. He understood that the ongoing war was merely a means for the Cabal to funnel money into their private endeavors. He was aware of three letter agencies being controlled by the cabal to help control society. He was also aware of the secret space program and the abductions of humans.

I want to emphasize that not all abductions are conducted by regressive groups. Positive entities may abduct their starseeds if necessary. There are several reasons this might occur, and it's essential to clarify that not all extraterrestrials are hostile, nor are all abductions for malicious purposes.

Both President Kennedy and Admiral Forrestal were opposed to the Cabal and sought disclosure, but both tragically ended up dead.

Phil Schneider died in January 1996. He spoke about the secret D.U.M.B. locations within the United States, an acronym for Deep Underground Military Base. He was involved in constructing one of these bases when his group encountered extraterrestrials, leading to a confrontation where both sides exchanged fire. During this incident, he was struck by an energy weapon, resulting in the loss of several fingers and toes. Following this event, he began revealing secrets the government had been hiding.

Schneider discussed the Grenada Treaty, an agreement signed by the United States government with the Gray extraterrestrials in 1954. According to this treaty, the Grays could abduct American citizens in exchange for technology. He reported on weather- controlling technology, known today as HAARP. Schneider also covered various topics, including the Oklahoma City bombing, the World Trade Center attack, and AIDS. He claimed that eleven of his friends had been killed by the government for speaking out on these issues, with eight of these deaths officially ruled as suicides. His widow reported that shortly after his supposed suicide, their home was raided, and most of the family photos were taken. It seems that a great deal of attention was directed toward Phil Schneider.

Another person who spoke out against the Cabal was Bill William Cooper, who died in November of 2001. He spoke on several different topics that exposed the Cabal. He talked about extraterrestrials visiting Earth, and Aids being lab-created. A warrant for his arrest was issued because of tax evasion, and Bill William Cooper got into a gunfight with the police officers who went to arrest him. He killed one officer, but he was also fatally shot. Leading to his arrest he was charged with aggravated assault. I recommend investigating his work and reading his book "Behold the Pale Horse." You will realize why he was targeted when you watch his speeches and discover the information he shared.

We could go on about the many who speak on disclosure and the ones who have lost their lives in this war. But you get the point, research the work of as many of these individuals as possible and expand your mind. Be open to changing your mindset. Doing this will change your reality and only unlock what has been right in front of you all your life.

Do you want to continue living your life blind and as a slave? This is your experience; this decision is yours to make, and there is no right or wrong answer. This is your experience to help you spiritually evolve. This information can be ignored, or you can accept it and change your reality. What is your purpose? Do you wish to awaken?

This decision is yours to make. Either way, the whole point of your physical existence is to evolve your Soul and enjoy your experience no matter the situation. If you do not like the experience, then change it. You are the director of your physical experience.

Chapter 26: Who Exactly is the Cabal

Cabal refers to a secret group of individuals who conspire to achieve a shared objective. This term is particularly fitting when describing the Earth's controllers, who operate behind multiple layers of secrecy. Even when you reach the leadership of the Cabal, you discover that the controlling entity goes even more profound, revealing a vast, well-structured organization whose primary aim is to keep humanity enslaved to fulfill its agenda.

The Cabal on Earth consists of 13 Draconian royal families, known as bloodlines. Each bloodline has its council that manages its affairs. While additional bloodlines are off-planets that hold greater authority among the Draconians, this discussion focuses solely on the Earth-based Cabal and its 13 royal families.

The leader of these 13 Draconian Bloodlines is Pindar, whose name translates to "reproductive organ of the dragon." His human vessel is Hank Meijer. It is essential to consider this individual as one of many masks that Pindar can wear rather than his true identity. Pindar's true self is the consciousness that controls Hank Meijer, similar to how consciousness operates in all individuals.

The most powerful bloodline is based in California. Prominent members include Robert Caldwell, his son Richard Caldwell, Jim Christensen, Richard Hoehn, Richard Bradbury, Jim Efferson, Fred Danger, and Frank Cohen. Hank Meijer, or Pindar, is the leader of this bloodline.

As the immediate leader of the Cabal and Illuminati, Hank Meijer stands at the forefront here on Earth. However, he is not at the absolute top of the hierarchy beyond Earth. This chapter aims to clarify the Cabal's identity and has already touched on who ultimately controls them off the planet.

Both Reagan and Nixon held high positions within the Illuminati and were involved in satanic rituals. It is claimed that every Republican president, along with most Democratic presidents since Herbert Hoover (including Bill Clinton), has been a member of the Illuminati and has participated in these rituals.

The following are some of the main dates observed by the Illuminati secret elite that are associated with satanic rituals:

February 1/2: Candlemas
March 21/22: Spring Equinox
April 30/May 1: Walpurgis Night/Beltane

June 21/22: Summer Solstice
July 31/August 1: Lammas (Great Sabbat Festival)
September 21/22: Autumn Equinox
October 31/November 1: Samhain/Halloween
December 21/22: Winter Solstice/Yule

Here are the names of some prominent members of the Illuminati Cabal, listed in no particular order:

Rothschild
Henry Kissinger
Dick Cheney
Alan Greenspan (Federal Reserve)
George Bush Sr.
George Bush Jr.
Gerald Ford
Jack Kemp
Alexander Haig (Former Defense Secretary)
Casper Weinberger
George Shultz
Hillary Clinton
Bill Clinton
Queen Elizabeth
Rockefeller
Zacharia Sitchin
Jimmy Goldsmith
Dulles (Rockefeller cousin)
Sir Alec Douglas-Home

Aurelio Peccei
Dean Rusk
Denis Healey
Bilderbergers
Joseph Luns
Lord Carrington
Manfred Woerner
Willy Claes
Javier Solana
James Wolfensohn
George Soros
Ted Heath
Edward Heath
Vanderbilt
Warburgs
Aleister Crowley
Lord McAlpine
Josef Mengele
Greenbaum
Marquis de Libeaux
Hank Meijer (Pindar)
British Royal Family
Ronald and Nancy Reagan
Gerald Ford
Habsburgs
Bob Hope
Rupert Murdoch
Pope John Paul II

Zbigniew Brzezinski
Al Gore
Nelson Rockefeller
Allen Dulles
Billy Graham
Bill Bennett
Madeleine Albright
Brian Mulroney
Justin Trudeau
Marilyn Manson
Baron Guy de Rothschild
El Shaddai or Ishkur, the son of Marduk
Winston Churchill
Prince Charles
Prince Philip
Paul Mellon
James Goldsmith
Lyndon Baines Johnson
Earl Spencer
Spencer Sr.
Queen Elizabeth
Lady Fermoy
Diana's father, Earl Spencer
Camilla Parker Bowles
Lord Mountbatten
Mohammed Al Fayed

Below are some of the main organizations that are directly owned by the Cabal:

The Bank of England
Anglo-American Corporation of South Africa
Rio Tinto
Minorco Minerals and Resources Corporation
De Beers Consolidated Mines and De Beers Centenary AG
N.M. Rothschild Bank
Barclays Bank
Lloyds Bank
Lloyds Insurance Market
Midland Bank
National Westminster Bank
Barings Bank
378 Schroders Bank
Standard Chartered Bank
Hambros Bank
S.G. Warburg
Toronto Dominion Bank
Johnson Matthey
Kleinwort Benson Group
Lazard Brothers
Lonrho
J.P. Morgan & Co.
Morgan Grenfell Group
British Petroleum
Shell and Royal Dutch Petroleum

Cadbury-Schweppes
BAT Industries
Assicurazioni Generali SpA (Venice, Italy)
Courtaulds
General Electric
Cazenove & Co.
Grand Metropolitan
Hanson PLC
HSBC Holdings (Hong Kong and Shanghai Bank)
Imperial Chemical Industries
Inchcape PLC
Inco Ltd
ING Group
Jardine Matheson
Peninsular and Oriental Steam Navigation Company (P&O)
Pilkington Glass
Reuters Holdings
Glaxo Wellcome
SmithKline Beecham
Unilever and Unilever NV
Vickers PLC
J.P. Morgan

This list includes various financial institutions, corporations, and industrial firms associated with the Cabal. While it is not exhaustive, it provides insight into the companies under Cabal's control. They manipulate money through these companies or by owning the majority of a company through global investment companies like Vanguard, BlackRock, and State Street. Follow the money, and you will discover who controls the planet. It isn't a large group. Major governments are owned and controlled by a small group called the cabal.

Chapter 27: Information Control

The control over your mind begins at birth. Your parents hold specific beliefs, and you are taught to accept their religion as the ultimate truth. However, children growing up in these environments often fail to realize that kids worldwide have different beliefs, and each child is taught that their belief system is the only true one sent from a higher power.

Indoctrination and control start immediately. Your parents determine your race and social status, creating different economic levels and social groups associated with expected behaviors. While some individuals manage to break away from the constraints of their financial backgrounds, most cannot.

Breaking away from religious beliefs is even more challenging. From birth, you are taught by those you love and trust that it is essential to worship God in the way they do, as theirs is the one true religion, and everyone else is mistaken. It is easy to accept this information because the people you rely on love you, and you wouldn't question why they would deceive you. The reality is that they, too, have been manipulated and indoctrinated, often since birth, so it is not entirely their fault. This creates a situation where the blind lead the blind. However, you can break the cycle by seeking knowledge and discovering the truth.

The answers are visible if you pay attention and raise your awareness. Explore what resonates with you, and through introspection, you will begin to uncover the truth of who you are and where you come from. Understanding the purpose of your physical incarnation on Earth is one of the main reasons you chose this experience.

From birth, people are indoctrinated on many levels, taking years to construct a false identity. They then spend the rest of their lives defending this persona, often with no recollection of their true history or knowledge of the metaphysical. As a result, they adopt this new identity to navigate a series of experiences. Many people on Earth do not truly understand who they are, which diminishes their power. They remain unaware of the immense influence they possess over the reality currently unfolding around them.

People often experience a lack of awareness within themselves, which has allowed powerful groups, like the Illuminati, to manipulate humanity and strip away our inherent power. Each of us can manifest our desires and create the lives we want. Unfortunately, humanity has fallen under a spell due to the veil of forgetfulness and societal indoctrination. The Illuminati and their controllers have influenced the human mind, which is why society currently exists as it does.

What do the world's controllers do with the power they have taken from humanity? Look around you, and it is evident that they have turned this planet into a satanic worshiping society. They worship dark energies to create an environment conducive to negativity.

Society spends time on its knees, begging, hoping, praying, and crying to religious leaders and governments to save them. Society pays attention to these false kingdoms, which is how the Illuminati and their controllers have gained control over humanity's power of manifestation. The controllers have convinced humanity to give them the power to control the planet. We live in a villainous world that humanity has inadvertently created. No one questions the leader's guidance; instead, everyone consumes the "poison" offered by the controllers without a doubt.

Society often votes for candidates based on their political party affiliation. Society blindly puts its trust in the hands of these leaders. Why should we give our attention to the politics that the cabal controls? Politics is designed to distract and divide society. Their tactic is to keep society divided and preoccupied with endless distractions. We consume their movies, television shows, news networks, and attend their churches. Our children are sent to school from the age of five for eight hours a day, which is also part of the indoctrination process.

John D. Rockefeller wanted to build a nation of workers rather than thinkers. The school system is designed to produce a society of obedient workers who are taught to take orders and comply with authority. If they fail to follow orders, they are considered unsuccessful. The education system is not structured to encourage independent thinking. Similarly, many religions employ the same tactic by asserting that "thinking for yourself leads you away from God's approval." When in reality, critical thinking will help you escape control and discover the true God.

Why does this indoctrination occur? It becomes clear what is happening once you awaken to the brainwashing that has taken place. Both religious institutions and the education system are set up to discourage independent thought. Why do they seek a society of blind followers? Independent thinking is what disrupts their indoctrination, ultimately threatening the kingdom of brainwashed followers they have established. This is the system they have built, and the controllers know what could dismantle it. People who question the system and its traditions significantly threaten their constructed reality.

Therefore, they must do everything possible to control how society thinks and what views it holds.

The school system conditions children to accept spending their days in a building they might not otherwise choose. Within the school system, children learn what those in power want them to know. The information taught is often accepted as factual, which leads to a distorted understanding of history and hides the truth. A child may struggle if they do not memorize the material presented in school, and those who succeed by following orders and memorizing information are praised for their abilities. This process fosters a skill in children—obedience to authority. Ultimately, the goal is to create adults who conform to societal expectations and do not think for themselves. As a result, these adults may fall into predetermined thought patterns established by those in control.

People in society spend most of their lives working and contributing to a system designed to keep them oppressed. Humanity resembles an ant farm, isolated from other ant farms, instructed to keep working and contributing to their society. The ants labor diligently, unaware of the causes behind their tunnels collapsing or who shakes their farm, leading to conflict within the ant farm. The ants are fighting with each other, blaming one another for the condition of the farm. Instead of doing this, they would be better off coming together to identify the cause of the farm's destruction and working collaboratively to resolve the real threat they face, and that threat is the person shaking the ant farm.

The ultimate goal for the cabal is to control every person completely through electrical chip implants. However, before society can be gradually conditioned to accept these implants, the controllers must continue manipulating and distracting the populace through various means, such as news, television shows, sports, religion, government, politics, fearmongering, and music.

For years, humanity has lived in fear of displeasing a loving God who is believed to threaten eternal destruction or punishment in hell for all who are disobedient. This fear has blinded society, making it unable to recognize the irony in its worship of such a tyrannical figure.

Understanding true love from the almighty God who created them has become distorted. People are willing to kill strangers or, even worse, cut off family members who they love for the sake of their "god".

Currently, the planet is under the influence of mind control orchestrated by the Illuminati and, behind them, the Orion / Draconian group. Above them are who they worship, the regressive entities. Over time, the Orion group has established a society of obedient servants who unknowingly contribute to building a kingdom for their controllers. Those within this system often do not realize they are trapped. The leaders of the Orion group maintain that the most effective way to control a society is to confine its members without their awareness, as the best prisoner is one who does not recognize their imprisonment. Society will remain blind as long as it continues to fight over which religion, or political party holds the ultimate truth. People are too busy and distracted by numerous superficial matters created within society. Instead, individuals must stop focusing on these distractions and concentrate on spirituality. We need to engage in inner work and prioritize our families. Unfortunately, many of us are forced to work countless hours, leaving little free time for ourselves. When we have extra time, many devote it to false religions, television shows, sports, movies, and politics. This system keeps society occupied and fearful, preventing humanity's awakening. Only the elite are aware of this agenda, as humanity remains asleep and imprisoned.

It is crucial to research the history of various matters and uncover the truths that have been hidden to control you. For instance, Christmas is rooted in pagan traditions. Have you ever explored its true history? Have you spent years celebrating this holiday simply because it's a widely accepted practice? It's time to stop following traditions and start questioning everything.

Let us examine a few questions we can research to begin uncovering the matrix and discover the truth about Earth's reality. Ask yourself why so many presidents come from the same family lineage. What is the true history of our holidays? Did we always have a 12- month calendar, or was there once a 13-month calendar? If so, why was the 13th month removed? Why was the Great Wall of China built to face inward if it was meant to keep invaders out? Is it possible that history has been manipulated? Why does the moon ring like a bell as if it were hollow when struck? Why are there so many similarities between the Statue of Liberty and the Lucifer of Liege statue? The Le Génie du Mal statue, or The Spirit of Evil, also features a torch and an apple at its feet. Is the connection with the Big Apple merely a coincidence? Why is there a Masonic plaque on the Statue of Liberty?

Additionally, the faces of both statues look remarkably similar. Are the similarities between Abraham Lincoln

and John F. Kennedy merely coincidental? Are these all coincidences, or are they clues to reality on Earth? How asleep are you and do you want to wake up?
Humanity needs to start asking themselves these questions. We are running out of pages in this book, so we can't explore these questions further.

This list of questions could go on indefinitely, but you must dedicate time to discovering these answers. Humanity has reached this point because it has allowed it, but now it's time to awaken to the control we're under. We need to reclaim our attention and energy from those who seek to control us.

The Illuminati and their controllers dictate history to maintain their power. They conceal actual historical events and suppress genuine scientific advancements. Only information that benefits their agenda is shared with the public. The textbooks we study are often filled with misinformation, yet people place their trust in them because these institutions are held in high regard. The truth is hidden in plain sight, and once you begin to see it, you cannot stop your awakening.

The Great Pyramid of Giza and the other pyramids were carefully engineered to showcase the advanced knowledge of their builders. When you analyze the precise geometric calculations used to construct these structures, the pyramids reveal a secret message transmitted to humanity thousands of years ago. They form an exact scale model of Earth, Venus, and Mars regarding their orbital distances from the sun.

Intending similarities emerge if you take a bird's-eye photograph of the Great Pyramid and the surrounding area and overlay it with a map of our solar system. The Mankaure Pyramid represents Mars and its orbital distance from the sun, the Khafre Pyramid symbolizes Venus and its orbit, and the Khufu Pyramid, also known as the Great Pyramid, corresponds to Earth's orbit. The sun's position is located southwest of the Tomb of Hermon.

The architect behind this monumental design possessed knowledge far beyond that of ordinary people living at the time. Creating this scale model of planetary orbits was not a coincidence but a deliberate design choice. Another fascinating detail is that the Great Pyramid of Giza embodies the Earth's polar radius. If you scale up the Great Pyramid by a ratio of 1:43,200, the Earth will fit perfectly inside it. Conversely, if you scale down the Earth by the same ratio, it will also fit inside the Great Pyramid.

It's worth noting that if the Earth were flat, it would not fit within the Great Pyramid, but as a sphere, it fits perfectly. Additionally, a curious connection exists with the frequency of 432 Hz, which positively influences atoms and DNA in the human body. Our physical bodies are composed of atoms that vibrate at specific frequencies, and the 432 Hz frequency is another hidden gem associated with the Great Pyramid of Giza.

The architect of the Great Pyramid clearly understood the true shape and size of the Earth and embedded this information within its geometry. However, society is led to believe that our current civilization is the most advanced to have ever existed. This belief persists because those in power fear losing control if the secrets of the Great Pyramid and other advanced civilizations become widely known.

One of the Great Pyramid's significant functions was distributing free electricity to the surrounding area. If this technology were revealed, the public would demand free energy, and the elites would lose trillions of dollars and control. Currency exists as a means of control; advanced civilizations do not rely on currency like on controlled planets. The regressive elites who control our world maintain this monetary system to preserve their authority.

The controllers have manipulated many of the ancient symbols around the world to fit an agenda. For example,

The Ankh is often described as a symbol of life, representing a connection between a woman, a man, and children. The DJED is claimed to symbolize stability, and the WAS symbolizes power and domination. These portrayals and definitions were done to obscure the reality that free electricity was available thousands of years ago. These symbols are related to technology and the ability to control it.

Hiding ancient technology and accurate history is used by those in power to maintain control over society. Their goal is to keep humanity distracted and occupied, ensuring people don't realize they are trapped in a mental prison. If the technology for free electricity were made public, it would pave the way for similar innovations. This would eliminate the need for combustion engines that run on gasoline, fundamentally changing transportation. However, this doesn't align with the agenda of promoting electric cars and charging for energy consumption. Eventually, only the wealthy would have the means to travel beyond smart cities.

Everything must be questioned, as much of it is based on deception. It's a performance designed to keep society ignorant and distracted from seeking the truth. This strategy keeps people working, allowing the prison of societal control to persist without anyone realizing they are confined.

The moon landing should be viewed from an unbiased perspective. Notably, Buzz Aldrin once claimed that he never went to the moon. Although he no longer supports that statement, it can be found if searched. However, humanity has been conditioned to accept the narrative presented to them, and many people continue to overlook the truth.

Additionally, the Van Allen belt surrounding Earth has a temperature ranging from 2,000 to 20,000 kelvins. The Apollo spacecraft, made from aluminum alloy, has a melting point of about 1,220 degrees Fahrenheit. Since the lowest recorded temperature for the Van Allen belt is 2,000 kelvins (approximately 3,140 degrees Fahrenheit), this far exceeds the melting point of aluminum alloy. In the 2023 fiscal year, NASA's budget was $25.4 billion. This staggering amount underscores why those in power orchestrate such elaborate schemes. It's time for people to wake up to the actual reality of what is happening on Earth.

Another secret that the Illuminati has misinformed the public about is the meaning of the 144,000 mentioned in the Bible. Different religions have their interpretations of what the 144,000 signifies. However, if we examine the seven chakras, we can find a clue about the true meaning.

When we add up the petals of the first five chakras, we arrive at a total of 48. Counting from the bottom up, the sixth chakra, known as the third eye chakra, has two petals.

The sixth chakra is considered to be twice as powerful as the lower five. If we multiply the total number of petals from the first five chakras (48) by the petals of the sixth chakra (2), we get 96. Then, if we take this total (96) and add the petals from the first five chakras (48), we arrive at 144.

The crown chakra is said to be 1,000 times more potent than the other chakras. Finally, if we multiply this last chakra (the crown chakra) by our total (144), we end up with 144,000. This sacred number of 144,000 reflects the essence of spiritual awakening. It signifies the ascension beyond the physical constraints of the material world and the elevation into higher densities where one can unlock reality.

The 144,000 mentioned in a spiritual context represent the resonance frequency of 144,000 Hz. Our frequency is a reflection of our state of mind. By elevating our mindset, we can move from darkness into the light, unveiling the heaven that resides within us. This journey is centered around spiritual awakening, which is why meditation and inner development have often been labeled as demonic by some religions.

Aligning our inner chakras to raise our frequency is essential in reaching this higher state of being. Many religious institutions may not want their followers to awaken to this higher frequency, as it diminishes their control. Achieving this elevated frequency allows individuals to access the universe's secrets and become illuminated, much like those in power.

Humanity must collectively raise its frequency to escape the Earth's controlling matrix. When enough people unlock their minds and achieve full awakening, a significant shift in collective consciousness will occur, leading to a rapid spread of this awakening.

This is why secret societies within the Illuminati claim to possess knowledge that they keep concealed. They refer to themselves as "the illuminated" because they believe they walk in the light while the rest of humanity remains in the dark. By keeping the truth hidden and indoctrinating people with controlled beliefs derived from limited information, they maintain this state of ignorance.

One notable example is King James, who is known for translating the Bible for the adoption of modern religion.

However, he created a version that suited a specific agenda rather than simply translating. Interestingly, he also authored the book "Demonology." This duality showcases the manipulation at work, as the same individual who translated the Bible for modern Christians wrote about witchcraft. These are the forces influencing religions— Luciferian Satanists. The controllers have convinced society to worship their demonic entities.

The controllers remain hidden, governing from the shadows, because if humanity awakens, they will have to answer for the mental imprisonment of the human race. Their end goal is to create a world where only 30% of women can conceive and where human thoughts are directly manipulated through invasive nanotechnology. This will happen right before humanity's eyes, yet people remain so indoctrinated that they fail to recognize the control already imposed upon them.

How does the Illuminati control you? It is simple: through information control. This is why their symbol features rays of light, symbolizing the illumination of knowledge they claim to have obtained from Lucifer. Now, you can become illuminated, breaking free from their control over your mind. Every time you see their pyramid on the United States currency you will now be reminded who really is in control. Their lies are now apparent, and it's impossible not to see through the manipulation. Welcome to the human awakening on Earth.

Chapter 28: Illuminati's End Goal

The Illuminati's goal for humanity is to exert control and manipulate individuals with ease. Building and maintaining the infrastructure that keeps society complacent can be taxing, so the Illuminati aims to reduce the effort. This will be accomplished by implanting microchips in all members of society. These chips will have the capacity to influence a person's thoughts and actions.

The agenda is to control every aspect of an individual's behavior with minimal effort. Through the strategy of problem, reaction, and solution, the Illuminati plans to instill fear within society, leading people to line up to receive microchips willingly, much like what happens during a pandemic or, better said, a plandemic. After this initial phase, the true agenda of controlling humanity will begin. Financial systems linked to these chips will be implemented, granting the Illuminati control over individuals' money. Once implanted, individuals must comply, or risk being locked out of their finances. There will be regulations on how much currency individuals can save, and prices for various items may vary based on compliance or location. It will be total control over you, comply, or risk not receiving your stipend.

Reports suggest that people are already being chipped in some regions of Europe, serving as preliminary tests for the functionality of these chips. This initiative is underway, and it is only a matter of time before a crisis is engineered to instill fear in society, persuading people to agree to have a chip implanted in their hands or forehead.

It is crucial to remember that society must consent to this for the agenda to succeed. Humanity has relinquished control but can reclaim it if desired. If humanity consents to this control, the cabal will strengthen its grip on the planet.

The plan involves transforming world governments, religions, and currencies into a single controlling entity. The aim is to dismantle existing world powers, leading to the emergence of a singular world government, the New World Order. This governing body will oversee the entire planet, dictating all aspects of life to its citizens. The plan to establish a New World Order as the planet's sole authority for religion and finances has been in progress for many years. High-ranking members of secret societies have been aware of this agenda for generations. They have been playing a strategic chess game, preparing for the final move, while humanity has not even realized they are part of a game.

The concept of the New World Order is not merely a conspiracy; it is well-documented, and several American presidents have referenced these plans. In his memoirs, on page 405, David Rockefeller expressed pride in being accused of organizing this control, which he acknowledged would be against the best interests of the United States.

Aaron Russo, a movie producer and former gubernatorial candidate in Nevada, was friends with Nick Rockefeller. Aaron was offered membership in special groups considered part of the deep state as their relationship developed. He observed that these groups, including Nick, showed little regard for the populace, leading Aaron to decline further association. He stated that this was not the person he wanted to be.

Aaron asked Nick the purpose of their actions, considering he already possessed all the money and power one person could need. Nick responded, "The end goal is to get everyone chipped to control the entire society." The chip is currently being tested, and its application includes proof of identity at places like banks and opening doors with a security system designed for the chip. Videos of Aaron discussing his relationship with Nick Rockefeller and their agenda can be found online. Much of the true history can be found online, but unfortunately, it is often buried under many false narratives. How bad do you want to know the truth? Remember, you shape your reality, so make it based on the information that resonates most with you and enjoy your experience.

With these chips, the controllers can program the human mind to wake up at a specific time and carry out their directives, then turn off at another specified time. The Illuminati do not want to justify their actions; instead, they aim to operate without obstacles and without needing to create a problem and await a reaction to implement their solution later. The Illuminati controllers want to bypass the preliminary stages and proceed directly with the execution of their agenda. With control over the human mind, the implanted chip will facilitate this.

The ultimate goal is for individual human minds to cease existing as independent entities and be integrated into their artificial intelligence, wherein humanity becomes part of a collective super-brain. This AI would be capable of controlling every aspect of human behavior.

Some may find this concept far-fetched; however, I encourage you to research the work of Dr. José Delgado, who demonstrated that an animal can be controlled by manipulating low-powered magnetic fields, also known as frequencies.

Earlier in this discussion, we noted that the entire universe, including ourselves, is composed of frequencies. The development of frequency technology is crucial—it has the potential to cure any ailment and exert control over the mind. Frequency technology is key for a physical civilization to evolve. However, the cabal will use this technology to their benefit.

Many readers might believe that society would never consent to being chipped. However, it's essential to recognize that the Illuminati controllers will not openly demand or request society to accept the chip. Instead, it will be gradually implemented with small commands initially. This method resembles the approach of a stage hypnotist. For example, how does a stage hypnotist prompt a person to bark like a dog in front of a large audience? It begins when the individual agrees to a small request, such as walking onstage. Through a series of commands and suggestions, the person's subconscious mind is conditioned to comply with the final command of barking like a dog.

Similar to stage hypnotists, the Illuminati reportedly uses social media, television, news, and movies to instill fear and suggestions that lead society to consent to the implantation of mind-controlling chips. If you doubt these tools are being used to program society, look for news anchors who repeat the same lines. When you notice this, you'll realize they are all controlled by a unique force that seeks to influence society by repeating information.

This manipulation is also evident in the behavior of many celebrities, who engage in satanic and cultish rituals during their concerts. These rituals aim to condition society for what is to come—a new world that openly worships Lucifer.

Ironically, the one thing the Illuminati cannot withstand is exposure, which has the potential to dismantle their control. They boldly flaunt their agenda and power in front of the very people who can defeat them. Once the truth is revealed and the public understands that this system enslaves them, it will mark the end for the Illuminati cabal. The people of Earth have tremendous power, and the key lies in their awakening. Humanity is partially responsible for allowing and consenting to the current situation, but it is essential to recognize that they have been manipulated.

The New World Order has three main components: a political system, an economic plan, and a new religion. The New World Economic Forum seeks to dismantle the current financial system and currency to establish a controlled digital system. While I am uncertain about the specific religion or digital currency that the New World Order will implement, it is clear that significant changes in society are underway.

While the specifics may change, there is no doubt that this reflects the Illuminati's agenda. The details of implementing this through Agenda 21-30 may vary, as adaptability is part of their strategy. Still, the end goal remains the same: to control humanity using chips.

Towards the end of their agenda, a false extraterrestrial invasion will catalyze the final stages of their agenda. The CIA's recently released videos showing unidentified flying objects are just the beginning of this false flag operation. These videos are believed to feature technology that the Illuminati controls, and they are planting the seeds of thought regarding an impending invasion. The cabal will orchestrate this fictional alien invasion to throw society into chaos. As society cries for a solution to the invasion, the official implementation of the New World Order will occur.

The word "Illuminati" originates from the Latin term "Illuminon," which means "illumination" or "light." Those who possess this secret knowledge are said to be "illuminated," while those who do not remain "in the dark." Higher-ranking members of the Illuminati are regarded as brilliant, while lower-level members are referred to as "stars." Illuminati members are believed to hold the light of knowledge.

The Statue of Liberty wields a Promethean torch, also known as the torch of illumination. In 1884, a plaque featuring two Masonic symbols was placed on the Statue of Liberty. The torch symbol signifies that they possess knowledge.

This symbolic light is also on the American dollar, located behind the all-seeing eye. They mark the territory of all that they control. The hidden symbols of the Illuminati are all around us; the question is, do you pay attention?

The symbol for fascism, known as the "Fasci," is a bundle of sticks with an axe. The meaning of fascism refers to a far-right movement led by a dictatorial leader. The Fasci symbol can be found on the old American dime, on either side of the U.S. House of Representatives podium, and at the bottom of the United States Senate logo. Since the Fasci symbol represents fascism, one must ask why it appears in these locations and logos. The new dimes have replaced the Fasci with a torch.

On the American dollar, surrounding the all-seeing eye, is the phrase "Novus Ordo Seclorum," which translates to "A New Order of the World." Above the all-seeing eye, the Latin words "Annuit Coeptis" translates to "Our project is approved." This suggests that the project to implement the New World Order has been sanctioned. They inform you of their actions, but society remains oblivious to what is happening right before them. Society is too busy arguing over who is following the one true religion to see what is in front of them. The all-seeing eye on the American dollar was introduced between 1934 and 1935. Despite the presence of Masonic Illuminati symbols on the dollar, most of society remains unaware of who the actual controllers are. The influence of the New World Order and Illuminati is not merely in the planning stages; it has already been established, and its agenda continues.

Newsweek magazine's April 3, 1967, issue featured David Rockefeller on the cover, with his watch hands set to 9 and 11. Rockefeller played a significant role in the development of the World Trade Center. The timing may seem coincidental, or it could serve as a symbol placed before unaware individuals as part of a broader agenda. It is up to you to decide what you discern from these observations. Do you wish to continue to be herded like cattle or do you wish to liberate your mind that has been imprisoned?

The celebrities who the Illuminati have promised everlasting life will eventually regret selling their souls.

The Illuminati Covenant states that these celebrities will be promised illuminated knowledge and eternal life; however, they will never truly attain everlasting life because they are not part of the inner circle. When we refer to "them," we mean the sacred Draconian blood originating from Orion. The celebrities are merely lower-tier members of the Illuminati, used as pawns by the upper echelons to manipulate humanity through their influence. Ultimately, these celebrities will be abandoned and not receive the promised everlasting life. The celebrities do not possess the elite bloodline and, in the controller's eyes, are not worthy of what is promised.

On the American dollar bill, a hidden owl in the upper right corner next to the number 1 can only be seen with a magnifying glass. This owl symbolizes the ability of those who control and possess illuminated knowledge to see in the dark. The Bohemian Society uses the owl to represent the privilege of knowledge the average person lacks. This society gathers annually for social purposes, during which they discuss their dark agenda. Members are involved in various aspects of society, including politics. The Skull and Bones Secret Society is another intriguing group to research if you're interested in exploring some of the leading secret societies that make up the Illuminati together.

Members of the Bohemian Society convene at Bohemian Grove, there are pictures that can be found of celebrities and world leaders worshiping a large owl and gathering around a bonfire. The owl represents knowledge of the Illuminati's ongoing events and future agendas for humanity. The Bohemian Society members are a subgroup of the Illuminati, much like the Skull and Bones and other secret societies. As mentioned, the Illuminati consists of many distinct groups, and members from one group may be unaware of those in another. These groups are compartmentalized, even within the higher ranks of the Illuminati, to ensure their secrecy. However, it is time for all their organizations to come crumbling down.

If you are still skeptical about the existence of these extraterrestrial regressive controllers that have taken over humanity and turned Earth into a prison for the human soul, I encourage you to question everything about what you consider to be your reality.

How long have you lived on Earth without realizing the truths we discussed? How long will you continue using your eyes and ears without genuinely seeing or hearing anything?

The chipping of humanity is the ultimate objective, but let's first discuss Agenda 21 and Agenda 30, which will lead us toward this goal. Agenda 21 refers to a sustainable development framework initiated on January 1, 2001. This agenda had been in preparation for many years before its official launch. The "30" signifies the period by which the main components of the agenda will be implemented, giving us until 2030 to resist these significant initiatives. By 2050, the entire agenda is expected to be completed, allowing any plans that faced setbacks in the first 30 years to be revised and executed between 2030 and 2050. Various theories exist regarding how the Illuminati may implement different aspects of Agenda 21. As this information becomes more widely known, they will likely adjust their strategies accordingly.

Agenda 21 aims to address depopulation through various controversial means. These include the intentional release of manufactured viruses, an increase in the pollution of air and food, and vaccines that will be considered risky. These actions instill fear in the population, leading people to comply with government directives. Additionally, there may be secret efforts for mass sterilization, which would further the depopulation agenda. As a result, the water and air in rural areas will become polluted, forcing people to leave. These people are a threat because they will not rely on the government to feed them, and it is harder to control these types of people who can grow their food.

The goal is to concentrate society into smart cities where everyone lives in small apartments. The rural areas will be controlled by the government, which will claim that it is safer for them to manage and grow food due to the virus and pollution affecting these regions. They will create both the virus and pollution, prompting society to comply without question. This strategy aims to exert control over all food, plants, minerals, construction, production, energy, information, animals, humans, the economy, ecology, and equity.

Ultimately, it seeks to reduce developed countries to a third-world status.

Agenda 21 is a plan already agreed upon by 179 nations. This information is publicly available, and those in control reveal it for karmic reasons. If you are unfamiliar with Agenda 21, please further research its details.

Here are some of the main points from the New World Order's Agenda 21/2030-2050 Mission Goals:
Establishment of a one-world government and religion.
Introduction of a single currency.
Creation of one central bank and one military.
Elimination of private property.
Depopulation efforts.
Mandatory vaccination programs.

Implementation of a universal basic income.
Microchipping of individuals.
Termination of private transportation.
Nationalization of all businesses.
Abolishment of single-family homes.
End of traditional farming practices.

These changes will not happen overnight. The agenda will first instill fear in the populace, potentially through power outages, food shortages, outbreaks, and even staged extraterrestrial attacks. All these strategies are designed to compel compliance among the public.

The agenda has many contingency plans to ensure its success. Whistleblowers have revealed secret programs like Project Blue Beam, which involves advanced technology capable of creating ultra-realistic holograms. This could allow for fake alien attacks orchestrated by humans controlling actual spacecraft, causing damage and creating the illusion of an extraterrestrial threat.

Additionally, technology developed under the HAARP project can manipulate the weather to create natural disasters and droughts as needed. These tactics are intended to manipulate the population and push people into specific areas within the United States while also affecting the economy. This plan includes clearing large regions for government use as part of Agenda 21.

These developments could become evident in the coming years. We must oppose this agenda and disseminate information to raise awareness. The strength of society lies within the people, so we should not live in fear of the government.

Chipping will be initially promoted as a method for remotely monitoring vital signs, helping you maintain your health. It will be cleverly presented to society as a way to enhance your life. Eventually, it will evolve into a payment system for food. In the future, those without a chip may be unable to purchase food. By controlling money and food, you can control the people. It's crucial not to consent to any of this.

To herd the planet in a specific direction, the cabal will orchestrate a fake alien invasion. This fabricated invasion will incite panic among the public, making people desperate. The staged alien invasion is one of the final moves in implementing Agenda 21-30. While extraterrestrials are real, this invasion will be carried out by a combination of the black military and regressive extraterrestrials who are collaborating with the Earth cabal.

Ultimately, Earth will become the next Alpha Centauri—a planet that believes it has been liberated by the Galactic Federation, only to remain under control. You now know their agenda, and they cannot instill fear in a society that is aware of their plans before they are implemented.

Remember that this can only happen if you consent and succumb to fear. When the cabal spreads fear through its controlled news and social media outlets, please do not fall victim to it. Now that you are aware of their plan before it is put into action, we have the power to stop them—not through physical confrontation but by refusing to give in to fear and rejecting their agenda. We can change this narrative to one where the controllers and their sinister rituals are exposed, and awareness is spread worldwide.

The Illuminati's end goal is to enslave you, your children, your parents, etc. They want it all, but the change only needs to happen within one person. You are your universe, and it is only up to you to change. It is your choice—whether to live like a slave or to fight for your freedom. The power is within you to contribute to the shift in collective consciousness.

Chapter 29: Letter To the Galactic Federation

I want to thank the lower levels of the Galactic Federation for the dedication and love they have shown humanity on Earth. The sacrifices made on our behalf have been essential in initiating the shift in collective consciousness. However, it's important to acknowledge that the Galactic Federation has various levels and factions, and it sometimes appears that not everyone within the Galactic Federation prioritizes humanity's best interests. This is similar to the Illuminati on Earth. The lower levels of a secret society may not realize they are part of a Luciferian worshiping group.

The continuation of the current situation on Earth raises questions about the true intentions of the Galactic Federation. Those who genuinely love humanity and are working towards awakening recognize that the Draconian Empire and its controllers are not the sole reasons for the severity of the situation on Earth. It is time for all members of the Galactic Federation to lift the veil that has been covering their eyes. The Galactic Federation is very permissive in allowing this level of control on Earth and they are equally as guilty.

Direct communication continues between the upper levels of the Galactic Federation and Earth's leaders, yet no solutions are being implemented, suggesting a hidden agenda within the Galactic Federation's leadership. All levels of the Galactic Federation need to be examined, and necessary adjustments are necessary.

I do not need to elaborate on the dire situation on Earth. The suffering must end. Children should never be subjected to torture for adrenochrome—this must stop immediately. We understand the laws that govern the Galactic Federation and recognize that humanity has free will, meaning nothing can be forcibly imposed on us. However, this cannot be considered valid free will if souls do not have the opportunity to reconnect with their authentic guides and reclaim their knowledge. The indoctrination that has blinded humanity must be eradicated from its very core. Only then can a soul genuinely have free will to return to endure another lifetime of servitude.

The Draconian Empire has conveniently manipulated the laws governing the Galactic Federation to maintain control over it. From my perspective, the Galactic Federation has become a victim of this control. I invite you to join in the human awakening and take immediate action. It is time for the Galactic Federation to recognize the extent of the control exerted over them.

Many, including myself, can see that the upper levels of the Galactic Federation have fallen victim to the influence of the Draconian Empire. How else can we explain the ludicrous excuses for not liberating Earth? The claim that humans have free will and no one has the right to impose reality upon them is flimsy at best and must end. Souls are trapped in reincarnation loops because they are manipulated into these choices.

If all the truth were revealed to a soul before they decide to return, that would be acceptable; however, that is not what is currently happening. Individuals are being indoctrinated in the physical realm. After death, they are intercepted and coerced back to Earth before they can ascend to meet their higher self, guide, or spiritual family. Entire soul groups are trapped by what appear to be ascended masters and guides. In reality, these so-called guides found in the lower astral are nothing more than regressive entities that are part of the control mechanism on Earth.

Now, this complex, multilayered game of chess is being exposed. You will no longer be their prisoner once you become aware of this deception.

Drastic measures need to be taken to change the timeline for the collective consciousness. What is your purpose in this physical incarnation? Is it simply to fulfill the role of a member of the Galactic Federation and claim that you are helping with Earth's awakening? How would it feel to look back on this time and know that you took bold action and played a crucial role in the success of human awakening? Take advantage of this opportunity and make your physical experience meaningful. How do you wish to be remembered?

Consider all the humans who have risked and lost their lives to support this awakening. They will be remembered as brave individuals whose lives made a significant impact.

I speak for all the lost souls trapped here on Earth and wish to return home. I represent all of humanity who is suffering unnecessarily and who is being tortured every day.

Remember that humanity needs you as you consider your actions to assist in the awakening. The Draconian Empire has controlled human societies and the upper levels of the Galactic Federation for too long. It's essential to recognize that both must awaken to the reality of their situations.

I also want to highlight those supposedly liberated groups loyal to the Galactic Federation. It is crucial to awaken to the fact that both your imprisonment and your so-called liberation were orchestrated by the very

Galactic Federation to which you still find yourselves in servitude.

I don't know at what point the Galactic Federation fell under the control of the regressive Draconian Empire, but I encourage you to take a moment and reflect on this for yourself. Like many humans on Earth, you are now beginning to awaken to deceit. We all need to take action to liberate ourselves from their oppressive and tyrannical control. Earth needs to realize the prison in which it exists, and the lower levels of the Galactic Federation must become aware of who controls the upper levels of their organization.

Let us bring transparency to the world and fulfill our soul's purpose for this incarnation. Let souls have the chance to return home and escape this prison.

What good is it to possess the ability to help with human awakening and yet do nothing? The Starseeds on Earth who continue to fight for disclosure are risking their lives. We face a dangerous situation on Earth, and many brave souls continue to come forward with this information. Those who have exposed the controllers have often lost their lives.

This is a call to everyone who can help. Those who can assist without risking their lives should search their souls for guidance. We trust that the answer and the courage will emerge for this task. There is no time to waste; we have reached a point of no return. Action must be taken now!

We must all do what feels uncomfortable to help this shift. Sitting back and watching will not bring about the necessary change. We must stand for what is right and carry the light. Shine a light on reality and assist in humanity's awakening. Do whatever you can to help and make your purpose count.

Take the action you want to be remembered for.

Chapter 30: Life After Awakening

By this point, you have uncovered many hidden truths that keep humanity blind to the existence of the Illuminati controllers. You are awakening to the reality of the Earth matrix. What should you do after discovering this hidden history and awakening? You must keep an open mind to all possibilities to continue expanding your consciousness. Do not become closed-minded again, and do not place all your trust in a single source of information, including what you have found in this book.

There are countless potential outcomes, and your focus should be on expanding your mind continuously. Concentrate on raising your frequency and working on your mindset.

Continue to expand your mind and engage in self-work. The answer is to meditate on love and never make decisions when feeling fear. Fear can control you, but you are a multidimensional being who can manifest any reality you desire.

This is why the Draconian Empire has been able to manipulate reality on Earth. Humanity has been misled into creating a reality that benefits the regressive Draconian Empire. This manipulation ends now as we bring to light their secrets. Be aware of the horrors that they inflict upon children during their satanic rituals (SRA). This evil needs to end now! Confronting evil directly is essential because we seek to put an end to the torture and murder of innocent children.

It is time to contribute to humanity's collective awakening on Earth. Continue to meditate on the fall of the Illuminati cabal, as raising your frequency will help others around you awaken. Connecting with your higher self will open you to receiving guidance. Although unnecessary, consider a hypnosis or past-life hypnotherapy session to help facilitate this communication with your guides. But proceed with caution, as there is deception even in the spiritual plane.

Try to meditate as often as possible. When you meditate, visualize what you are manifesting has already happened. Imagine you are in a time machine, witnessing your current reality transform into the reality you envision. This new, positive reality, in which a new Earth exists, and the Illuminati cabal has been brought to justice, is already a reality. Feel the emotions associated with these events as though you are reminiscing because they have already occurred. Focus on feelings of love and happiness, recognizing your role in manifesting this reality.

In your daily life, remain aware of the Illuminati's agenda. They cannot instill fear in your reality if you are conscious of their plans. Refuse to give in to fear and do everything you can to raise your frequency. Expand your mindset and avoid placing all your faith in a single source of information. Keep an open mind; as circumstances continually change, you must also be willing to change.

If this concept is still confusing to you, here's some advice: Spend a month consciously viewing your reality from a higher perspective. Picture yourself as energy with infinite awareness, existing in a higher plane while having a physical experience in this body.
Remember that this body does not define who you truly are; you are infinitely aware and are currently having a temporary physical experience. This shift in perspective can profoundly change you.

Upon awakening to this truth, you may be urged to share it with everyone around you, but this approach is not advisable. This reality is not meant for everyone; many people either lack a connection to Source or have only a weak connection. Forcing this awareness onto others does not respect their personal agreement regarding the experiences they wish to have. We seek those who desire to awaken and want to see the matrix crumble.

After awakening, many people wonder how they can contribute to human awakening. The answer to this question is complex; only you can truly provide it. However, the solution is never to resort to violence, as this is precisely what the Illuminati cabal desires. Instead, the strategy should involve refusing to comply with their agenda. Do not succumb to the misleading information portrayed in the media or on social media platforms. Stand firm against requests that do not align with your values. They will present solutions to problems they created, and it is vital to ignore these proposed solutions. Once humanity collectively resolves to reject the Illuminati cabal's control, the influence they hold over the people will diminish. The power lies within the people, and humankind must recognize this. The Illuminati possess no power without convincing individuals to accept their imposed solutions.

Refuse to consent to the Illuminati's absurd agenda of transhumanism. You possess the power over them, not the other way around. The Illuminati has convinced humanity that they are powerless, but the realization of humanity's true strength is spreading. The Illuminati are concerned because they recognize that humanity is awakening. The Draconian Empire's control is diminishing, and a global disclosure is imminent. Those who have worshipped the asuras and archons will be held accountable for the atrocities they have committed against humanity. Their day of reckoning is approaching.

As you reach the end of this book and reflect on this newly uncovered knowledge, I understand that the journey may not have been easy. Many will experience cognitive dissonance as they try to determine the validity of this information. Some may not resonate with this information and may dismiss it as false. Regardless of where you stand by the book's conclusion, it doesn't matter; the seed has been planted in your subconscious. If not today, perhaps one day in the future, your awakening will blossom.

If someone never experiences this awakening, that is also fine, as everyone is entitled to their own experiences on Earth. Love should compel the awakened to respect everyone's choices. This is precisely the excuse the Galactic Federation uses as to why they have not landed on the White House lawn. Enough is enough; the prison on Earth must come to an end.

Life after awakening can be difficult; once you have awakened, you can never return to ignorance. Yet, this is a path you have chosen. The primary purpose for many incarnating on Earth is to disconnect from Source and discover their true selves. The experience and challenge of being disconnected and eventually returning home and finding your way back home from a place that feels almost entirely disconnected from Source will foster immense personal growth. However, the soul should not be misled into repeating this process multiple times before it can elevate its frequency and ascend home.

Once you grasp the true nature of reality, life will never be the same. We are still on our journey back home, but that journey takes on a new significance upon awakening. Your perspective shifts, and you transform as a person. What once held great importance may no longer matter to you, while things you previously dismissed now become significant. This is because your frequency has changed during your awakening. Your state of mind is no longer one of low frequency. Understanding what is happening on Earth and remembering who you are and where you came from will undoubtedly make you a more loving person. The higher you raise your frequency, the more love you can express to others. Service to others becomes easier, and you no longer give your energy to the controllers. You will not agree to their demands because you can see what they are attempting to do to you. Now, they can no longer control you as they once did.

People may label you a conspiracy theorist because that is what they have been programmed to say. This programming has been designed to protect what the mind controllers have built. The system is set up so that those who are asleep police each other. You will be labeled and ostracized if you go against society's views. Do not worry when this happens; they are sleeping and do not have a strong connection to Source, but you do. You possess something they cannot comprehend, and they cannot see what is happening right before them. This could be due to their choice to have a specific experience or because their vessel has no soul. An empty vessel will not be able to perceive the truth. Their purpose is to conform to the Earth matrix programming, and we should not expect anything else from a person without a connection to Source. They will defend the indoctrination and regurgitate the programming because they cannot stretch their mind to think outside the controller's box. As frustrating as their words may be, we must respect their choice to remain in darkness.

At times, being awake may feel like a curse rather than a blessing. Awakening is a liberating experience, but it can also feel isolating. You will feel empowered, yet at the same time helpless. Your mind will be free from the controllers' shackles, granting you a sense of freedom. However, you may feel lonely, as though you are the only one outside the prison.

The emotional rollercoaster you will ride through your awakening journey can be tumultuous. You will struggle to process the chaos occurring around the planet. Take comfort in the fact that you are not alone; others like you share this experience.

There is a darkness that accompanies the journey into the light of awakening. You will need to grieve the death of the old reality while also rejoicing in the birth of your awakening.

Discovering that everything you once believed to be reality was, in fact, a lie can be disorienting. At times, it may feel as if your mind is breaking. Allow your mind to bend to the point of breaking; this is when the complexities of our convoluted universe will begin to make sense. The answers to questions that have mystified humanity will be revealed, and this is when you will fulfill your purpose on Earth.

It will be emotionally challenging to accept that all the truths and principles you were taught were lies. The people and leaders of groups have been spreading falsehoods for their gain, and this revelation will undoubtedly weigh heavily on you. Shattering the illusion imposed on society will not be an enjoyable process. The road to awakening is difficult, precisely why you embarked on this journey from a higher plane of existence. You did not choose this path because it would be easy but because it would allow you to grow. It's time to return home; your loved ones await you.

Living with the knowledge you now possess will be uncomfortable. You will need significant emotional strength to coexist with the sleeping masses. However, this is why you came to Earth; you wanted to experience the more challenging game mode called physical life on Earth. Navigating life in hard mode means confronting challenges and succeeding while feeling disconnected from Source, not remembering your past lives or true identity, and eventually finding your way back home. To make things even more complex, many distractions and indoctrinations are designed to trap your mind while you are here on Earth. Yet, achieving victory in this battle for your mind will be liberating. Yes, you will need to endure many emotional hardships, but overcoming the game played in hard mode will earn you a spiritual trophy to be cherished for all eternity. This makes the struggle worthwhile, even though this existence may not justify the grief it brings for some. Awakened individuals and starseeds may face ridicule and shame from the masses due to their inability to comprehend what is happening around them. However, this should not deter us from continuing our path toward awakening. It's essential not to fall into the trap of being content with the indoctrination we receive. While we all have free will, many have become ensnared in soul loop traps. This is why starseeds come here: to assist many souls in remembering what is happening and who they truly are. This is a rescue mission, and I offer a lifeline, but it is up to each soul to reach for it. This lifeline is sent with love; it is your choice to accept. You have spent enough time in this realm, and it's time to return home where many loved ones are waiting for you.

Being surrounded by friends and family who don't know your true self can be disheartening. However, it's important to remember that they often are lost and do not know who they are. We may continue to engage in shallow conversations that lack depth with those around us. Let's make the best of this experience, and, most importantly, do not allow your frequency to lower based on how they make you feel.

Feeling disconnected from friends and family is a natural awakening process. We must embrace this awakening. The phrase "ignorance is bliss" holds some truth, as some mourn the loss of their ignorance. Yet, ignorance is not our purpose in this universe. Our true purpose is to evolve; continuing through life with shackles around your mind will prevent you from achieving this purpose.

Awakening to the harsh realities of this world can feel overwhelming. You will experience a full range of human emotions, but that is intentional. You must master the ability to dive into the deepest and darkest situations and still function normally in everyday life. Developing this skill will take time.

Do not feel as if you are alone—many of us are out there. We may be separated by physical distance, but mind, soul, and purpose connect us. You are not the only one looking beyond the surface. You are not alone in losing interest in the distractions presented by the Illuminati. Seek out others and build a new inner circle with those who have also undergone their awakening, and things will improve.

There is no reason to feel lost or uncertain about your life's direction. We have guides waiting to help us, but they respect our free will and will not interfere unless we ask for assistance. The key takeaway is that you must recognize that your guides exist and are available to help illuminate your path.

Feeling an intense urge for personal growth and development is natural. It's important not to overwhelm yourself with new information. I understand the desire to discover more and to dedicate your life to evolving and gaining knowledge. However, we are also here on Earth to enjoy unique physical experiences, and we must appreciate them. Take time away from everything and spend it in nature or with friends.

Another vital part of ascending is acknowledging past and present traumas. This trauma needs to be healed with love and forgiveness. Forgiving someone who has caused you trauma, whether in this life or a past one, means letting go of the hurt without condoning their actions. It does not mean you must ignore seeking justice for their actions; instead, you should not carry the weight of that pain on your soul. Heal your traumas, and you will see how attachments can be released. By freeing these attachments, you can alleviate physical and mental ailments. One effective way to do this is through hypnosis. Closing the door to the past is crucial to moving forward with your soul's evolution. While conducting introspective hypnosis sessions, I have seen souls heal.

Wanting to be alone during your awakening is normal and helpful. There are periods when you will receive new information, and being in a quiet space can help you process it. Allow yourself to follow your emotions about what you want to do; there is no right or wrong way to approach your awakening. Do what compels you and enjoy the magical experiences accompanying your spiritual awakening.

Discovering your true self will involve both beautiful and challenging moments. Embrace both, as they hold equal importance. Appreciate negative experiences because they have contributed to your evolution. You are more than your physical body; you are an eternal being undergoing a physical experience that has disconnected you from Source. Those who have caused you trauma are fulfilling a role in the story you chose to live. Understand this and forgive them for their actions. Appreciate who you have become and heal from your traumas.

Once you decide to pursue enlightenment, there are many ways to accelerate the awakening process. However, do not let the different methods of raising your frequency distract you from the awakening. Many become obsessed with awakening, preventing them from fully experiencing it. People often fixate on factors such as diet, exercise, affirmations, journaling dreams, hypnosis, chanting mantras, aligning chakras, meditating, collecting crystals, and singing bowl sessions. While these practices can aid in your awakening, they are not essential.

The effects of consciousness show us that we do not need any external forces to unlock our awakening. Our frequency and state of mind should not be influenced by anything outside ourselves. We live in an illusion created by our consciousness, and we have the power to make any reality we desire without relying on external factors. We are not victims of our circumstances; we are the creators of our reality. The challenge is that we have been led to believe that our reality is beyond our control.

The movie we have created and are acting out can be adjusted to align with our desires. Once we realize this, anything becomes possible. This understanding is key to finding genuine happiness. The human experience is limited when we focus all our energy on using external forces to facilitate our awakening. We truly need the ability to eliminate external distractions, be quiet, and focus on our inner awareness and energy.

An awakened individual is willing to live a life only a tiny percentage can understand. Very few can grasp the metaphysical concepts that arise during the awakening process. Be prepared to let go of friends and family who cannot awaken. Maintain the relationships you wish to keep, but understand that some people may leave your life. Be respectful and avoid imposing your reality onto them. Most will struggle to process this information and connect with their higher selves for guidance during their awakening. Remember, we all incarnate on Earth with specific experiences we wish to have. This is a matter of free will, and we should not interfere.

Enjoy the matrix and appreciate the friendships you can have within it. Remember to savor the journey and all the experiences it brings.

The matrix comprises perceptions and agreements about reality formed by a group living together. It exists entirely in the mind and is controlled by our attachments to ideas. These attachments create limitations that we impose on ourselves. The physical body is a manifestation of the soul, which governs it from a higher plane of existence. Everyone plays a role in shaping their reality. As a result, some will struggle to perceive and understand the actual reality. They are deeply engaged with and connected to the Earth Matrix.

Living within this matrix as an awakened individual can be challenging. You will need to navigate two different lives within one physical body: one where you handle everyday responsibilities, such as making money and having mundane conversations with those you encounter, and another where you seek ways to further your spiritual ascension and receive enlightenment from higher planes of existence.

It's important to understand that after experiencing an awakening, you are not required to take specific actions.

You don't need to write a book or speak publicly about the truth. However, if each of us took small steps to support the awakening of humanity on Earth, it could lead to a significant positive impact.

I share this message with love and appreciation for your time. From this point forward, what you do is entirely up to you. Will you return to ignorance and continue a life as a prisoner who is under mind control? Or will you acknowledge the truth and take steps toward freeing your mind? The choice is yours.

Chapter 31: Your Purpose & Life After Death

Your purpose in life is to evolve and help others evolve through the experiences you have while in your physical body. Each person's purpose varies from one individual to another. However, if we understand that everyone's purpose revolves around evolving from their life experiences, we can look within ourselves to discover our unique purpose.

It is important to remember that you are not obligated to follow any particular path because you have free will. You are not confined to a single purpose; you are the creator of your purpose. This broader perspective frees you from feeling trapped during your physical journey. Remember that regardless of your plan for this physical experience, you can change the ending if you wish.

If you wish to immerse yourself fully in Earth's experiences, embrace them wholeheartedly. Remember that those who genuinely love you will not judge you. Regardless of your role in this life, remember it is a temporary experience, and focus on what is necessary for your soul's evolution.

Often, we play specific roles to help another soul evolve or guide them down a particular path. This is why we should never hold a grudge against those who have wronged or betrayed us. Their actions may have set you on a specific path, part of a larger plan to facilitate your growth. Although it can be challenging to adopt this perspective, remember that our physical incarnations are intended to foster our evolution and assist others in their development. We all share a common goal: to return home and eventually reunite with Source.

Some people claim to remember returning to Source and experiencing the oneness of being connected to all aspects of creation. They describe this experience as feeling pure love and unity with everything. In this state, there is no sense of self or individuality; instead, you become everything and feel everything happening in the universe. However, the concept of individuality eventually reemerges, and through this idea, Source gives rise to your unique energy once again. This separation, even after returning to Source, allows for another journey, this time with a new enlightened perspective. The possibilities for your purpose and experiences in this new journey are endless. I like to imagine that souls who return to Source and leave again do so to help others in their journey toward ascension or to seek experiences in other dimensions where the cosmic laws differ.

Could you be one of those souls who has already experienced what it's like to return to Source and is now here to help others do the same? It's possible, as you are not trapped, and free will is a fundamental part of the universe.

As you explore your life's purpose, it is essential to remain open to change. Pursue whatever feels right for you to achieve your goal of personal evolution.

If you are reading this, it's likely that part of your purpose—or a sub-purpose—involves aiding in the human awakening on Earth. You don't need to awaken others forcefully; simply by maintaining the high frequency of your aura, you are already assisting humanity. As you expand your consciousness, you elevate the frequency of the Earth.

Remember, there is no judgment in this journey. Your life purpose is unique; only you can determine what will aid your evolution. Do not let your life purpose overshadow the joy of living in the moment. Maintaining balance is crucial; enjoying life's experiences is just as important as focusing on the awakening. Be sure to bask in the sun, relax, and spend time with friends and loved ones.

Many people feel lost, but what good does discovering your purpose do if you become consumed by it? In the physical world, we should enjoy every moment that comes our way. Don't let the desire to change tomorrow overshadow your ability to appreciate the present. The present moment deserves to be enjoyed, too. We do not know when our physical experience will end, so we should cherish every moment, no matter how stressful. After death, your life energy leaves the body. The body is merely a vessel that holds this life spirit, often called the soul, consciousness, alma, life energy, essence, incarnation, being, entity, soul spark, and more. You can use any term you prefer when describing the spirit that animates the body. Essentially, the body is an empty vessel carrying the soul.

When a person dies, the soul departs from the body. Since you are no longer present in the physical form, your true self exists, which can create confusion about the experience of death. The manner of death can significantly impact the soul's state. For instance, if death occurs suddenly, the soul may become bewildered and find itself trapped in a realm that is neither entirely physical nor wholly spiritual. This realm is known as the lower astral.

Because the soul possesses free will, it can traverse any spiritual realm it desires after death. For example, during a past life regression session, I had a client who revisited a past life in which she enjoyed spending time with her uncle and cousins. After her sudden death, her attention instinctively drew her back to her uncle's house, where she had spent many joyful moments. In the session, while still alive, she unknowingly passed away in that past life and found herself once again at her uncle's house. She shifted from being happy in her family's company to feeling confused about why they were not responding to her. At that moment, her soul went where it desired to be.

This scenario highlights why religious indoctrination often fosters beliefs in concepts like hell and heaven. Many people envision hell and feel a strong desire to reincarnate, driven by the hope of entering heaven after their next life. Frequently, individuals experience guilt for not living up to the ideal standards set by their teachings, which compels them to reincarnate. This concept applies to all religious indoctrinations. When people pass away and enter the astral, they carry the biases formed by their indoctrination. This creates a cycle where indoctrinated individuals may continuously incarnate without discovering deeper truths, just as you may be doing now. The soul must recognize where to focus its attention. Unfortunately, when it incarnates on Earth, the frequency is much lower than in typical physical existences, which means that memories of past lives and cosmic truths often do not transfer to the physical body. This causes the soul to become disconnected, especially if they agree to purposely put on the veil of forgetfulness to ensure their disconnection.

Some so-called "starseeds" spread misleading messages that, upon death, individuals should look back at Earth to access knowledge of the universe. This is incorrect; focusing on Earth during ascension can trap a soul in the lower astral realm or cause it to reincarnate before reconnecting with its authentic guides and soul group. Ignoring anyone suggesting that you concentrate on Earth after death to gain knowledge is essential, as this distraction will hinder your ascension. Unfortunately, some disseminating this misinformation were once positive beings supporting human ascension but have since deviated from that path or perhaps deception was always part of their plan.

Once the soul recognizes the light from its guides or soul group, it is drawn and directed to the higher realms of existence, where the healing process can begin. However, if the soul does not pay proper attention to ascension following death, it may not recognize the urge to ascend past the lower astral realm.

After a physical incarnation, the soul requires a recovery period. Although it is often said that time does not exist for the soul, this perspective stems from our physical experience. In reality, the physical experience consists of a mix of simultaneous frequencies. However, souls dwelling in higher planes experience time differently from our physical understanding. The physical time we perceive during earthly existence is merely a brief instant intertwined with other incarnations.

Once souls return to their soul group, they undergo a rehabilitation process. Based on what souls have shared, this involves a "frequency shower"—not a liquid shower, but a cleansing of energy frequencies. This shower helps them recover lost energy and raise their vibrational levels. After this, there is a reflective period during which they can analyze and learn from their experiences. The number of experiences a soul can process at any given time varies widely.

After a reflective phase, the soul collaborates with its soul group and guides to plan new experiences for further evolution. A soul group typically consists of five to twenty souls and guides who assist the group as needed. While souls may interact with members of other groups, most planning for new incarnations occurs within their soul group. As a soul evolves, it may transition to a different group.

As the frequencies of souls change, so does their focus on what they wish to evolve or work on. If a soul's frequency shifts significantly, it is common for that soul to move into a new group. This transition can happen individually or alongside another soul.

Joining a new soul group indicates that the group's frequency aligns more closely with the arriving souls. As mentioned earlier, this can involve moving with one or more souls. Souls can share many physical experiences within a particular group; however, significant frequency discrepancies may lead to separation, allowing souls to find a more harmonious group.

In this realm of existence, guides emphasize that achieving evolution requires experiencing many emotions. Ultimately, the goal is to return to the Source from which you originated. Your guides encourage you to enjoy the journey and not take things too seriously, as this is just one of many experiences you will have.

All agreements made before this incarnation can be changed. You are the one experiencing this physical life, and it is all a movie in which we are actors playing our roles. However, we do not have to follow the pre-written script strictly. During the movie, we can also alter our script.

When the soul decides on this incarnation, it only perceives fragments of what will come. You choose to experience certain events based on the physical body you will inhabit, as it will facilitate your desired experiences. However, this is not a linear timeline that remains static. After the incarnation, you can change how you experience your life or even decide to alter the purpose of your incarnation completely. This is why the soul does not see all the events it will encounter; it only sees probabilities, and with the veil of forgetfulness, nothing is absolute.

Some souls return to physical existence after death before reuniting with their proper soul group and guides. This often happens due to the religious indoctrination a person receives while on Earth. The soul has free will, and if it focuses on returning, it will do so. If the soul does not have a chance to remember its history, it may choose to return and have another experience filled with similar indoctrinations and life situations. As already mentioned, this cyclical return is commonly called a soul trap or soul loop.

I've previously mentioned that individuals enter the astral realm after death before meeting their proper guides and soul group members. Now, I want to share the most crucial information contained in this book. There is, however, a trap set by those in control. The Illuminati on Earth are being influenced by regressive beings from beyond our planet.

These beings are managed by astral entities known as archons. Ultimately, the archons are governed by Wetiko, Ahriman, Satan, etc. While archons may have various names, many consider them to be demons. They can manifest in shiny rays of light or take on any appearance.

These archons have been intercepting souls after death, feeding them the narrative that they must join a soul group and return to Earth for another incarnation. They present this as a means of addressing karma and facilitating spiritual evolution, but in reality, it is merely a deception—a deeper layer of control. It is a genius strategy to catch souls disoriented shortly after their physical separation and group them with other souls in similar situations. These beings, often called archons or demons, pretend to be guides and lead the souls to experience what they claim is the most beneficial experience for them. However, this experience is often filled with as much stress as possible and indoctrination. You can now break this agreement because you are in control, not them. They cannot force you to do anything; you must willingly agree, which is why so much deceit is involved.

Can you see how deep this trap goes? Earth is controlled by the Illuminati, governed by a faction part of the Draconian Empire. The Draconian Empire operates under the authority of the Galactic Federation, which claims they will liberate Earth when the time is right, but don't hold your breath. However, the Galactic Federation is overseen by the archons, who are influenced by Wetiko (or any name you choose). Within each of these groups, various secret factions serve specialized functions. Some members within these groups may not even realize what they are a part of. This situation is reminiscent of organizations like the CIA, where many members might have good intentions and believe they are acting for the right cause. Yet, the upper echelons of these organizations are aligned with regressive forces. It may seem impossible to fight due to the many traps and layers of deceit involved.

Many starseeds are incarnating on Earth to help awaken humanity and assist souls trapped in karmic loops. They want the world to understand that it is time to free yourself from all karmic debt or obligation. No karmic debt is owed, and you must let go of this false narrative to ascend home.

This message is for all of you who feel, deep down, that there is more to your existence than what you have been told. Do not heed the indoctrination or disinformation spread by those who urge you to focus on returning to Earth after death. This is a soul trap created by the regressive spirits worshipped by the Illuminati. It is time to free your soul from their influence. After death, do not consent to the veil of forgetfulness. Do not agree to return to Earth. Although they would force you if they could, they have devised a false environment in the upper astral realm because they cannot compel you to come back; they need you to volunteer. Don't consent—ignore them and ascend beyond their traps. You are a powerful spark that directly splintered from Source; do not relinquish your power to them. Move past them and do not succumb to their fear tactics designed to coerce you into submission. They rely on your compliance, and you need to understand this. They need you to return so you can emit the negative emotions they feed on, which is known as loosh. Stop being a food source for them!

Exploring what happens after death can help guide you home. If you don't believe this information, that's perfectly fine; however, I'm offering a new perspective, and you might wonder what harm there is in considering my recommendations.

Upon death, focus on the feeling of love within you. Spread this emotion of love around you and seek the light. Do not dwell on earthly issues or soul groups led by regressive guides urging you to return to Earth. Encourage the rest of your group to leave with you. Make your exit, and do not look back; they cannot stop you. While they may wish to force you, they cannot; you hold all the power.

Do not accept the concept of karma; release yourself from karmic guilt and ascend. If every soul heeded this advice, the controllers would no longer have participants in their twisted game. This game feeds their archons with loosh; without this source, they will perish. This is how we can defeat them! Stop falling for the lies and consenting to their commands.

I want to emphasize that after death, do not agree to return for any misguided karmic reason. Love is always the answer; seeking it will never lead you astray. The actual creator does not want you to return to experience suffering to evolve; it is disturbing to think that a loving God would desire this for you. Among all the trillions of planets, why are souls forced to reincarnate on Earth or other prison type planets? It is because prison planets have a unique situation where souls can be imprisoned for endless loosh.

If you feel lost and want to understand the root of this emotion, it may stem from experiencing many incarnations without returning home. It's beneficial to consult a hypnotherapist specializing in healing soul trauma or exploring past lives. Finding a practitioner with whom you resonate is essential, as feeling comfortable is crucial for achieving the best results. I recommend any practitioner who uses the Introspective Hypnosis Method, which is the approach I use. A session can help unlock the answers to these profound feelings.

You are now officially awakened!

Chapter 32: The Last Warning

This book is a success if you have more questions about reality now than when you started this book. My mission is not to tell you what to believe but to encourage you to question your beliefs. You are the creator of your reality, and what you believe dictates the reality you create. As long as you understand you have control, you cannot be manipulated into creating a reality you do not wish to experience.

On Earth, a cabal consisting of the Vatican and bankers are who have been manipulating society to create a specific reality. When someone threatens their agenda, they eliminate that threat covertly. President Lincoln chose not to take loans from the central bank to fund the Civil War; instead, in 1862, he issued what became known as greenback currency. He was assassinated in 1865, and in 1866, the Contraction Act was passed, which led to the removal of greenbacks from circulation. This move aimed to transition to a gold standard, but that plan was eventually abandoned, and now the currency is not backed by anything; the bankers can print as much money as they wish. Our recent history shows that any threat to the cabal, whether from a president or otherwise, will likely be eliminated.

The controllers have a monopoly over the human mind, and the purpose of this book is to disrupt their control. The cabal aims to dominate everyone through tactics related to religion, politics, and banking. Before the 9/11 attacks, countries like Iran, Afghanistan, Iraq, Sudan, Libya, Cuba, and North Korea did not have their central banking systems controlled by the Rothschilds. By 2012, all but Iran, Cuba, and North Korea were under Rothschild's control. When you take a step back and analyze these facts, it becomes evident that the bankers continue to tighten their grip on the planet. If a government does not conform, they take control by force.

According to U.S. Congressman Curt Weldon, Gaddafi offered to resign, contrary to what news outlets reported. Why would the United States government ignore Gaddafi's letter of resignation? You can draw your conclusions, but it is possible they wanted him dead to control his oil and wealth, but more importantly, they needed his influence in that region to die. Gaddafi wanted to unite the African continent into a cooperative economic group based on a gold standard. He implemented free healthcare, and the average annual income in the country rose to more than $11,000. He also established free higher education (college), and the percentage of homelessness declined but has risen since his death. During his regime, Libya began producing its own medicine. The news reported that the plant was making chemical weapons, but that is the narrative fed to you by the controlled media to manipulate your thoughts and actions. Water and electricity for citizens were extremely affordable; some considered it free due to the low cost.

Perhaps the most damning thing against Gaddafi was that the country was debt-free and did not want anything to do with owing money to the central banks. Years before he was killed, he spent billions to help create the African Union, a group aimed at fostering unity and solidarity among African states and intensifying cooperation. Uniting people, providing free healthcare and education, manufacturing your own medicine, and preventing the Rothschilds' central banks from controlling the country's wealth put a target on his back. This type of leadership would threaten the cabal if it spread, so he was eliminated.

This information can guide you in the right direction, but ultimately, it is up to you to explore the path you wish to take. We have touched on many different topics without diving deeply into them. Feel free to investigate any of these topics further. However, it's important to note that for every dangerous truth that can be uncovered, countless articles aim to debunk it.

Former CIA agents, such as Richard Doty, have admitted that the CIA has specific programs designed to target truths to discredit them and bury the story. Doty also claims that the CIA influences many news stories major networks report. This is why seeking the truth within yourself is crucial, and it can be accessed through practices like meditation or hypnotherapy.

Suppose you come across an article that debunks any of this information and find that sufficient to remain complacent. This may indicate a preference to stay oblivious and fully immersed in this controlled environment. I don't wish to impose my reality upon you, and I respect your decision.

It's as if you were sound asleep, and I turned on a light, shining it on your face. The light would momentarily awaken you. Instinctively, you might cover your eyes with your hands to block it. However, you could turn off the light and go back to sleep or allow your eyes to adjust to the brightness and welcome this new light into your life.

It is time to awaken to the situation on Earth. You are born into a system that assigns you a specific value as a member of society and estimates how much tax revenue you can generate throughout your life before retirement.

Your lifespan is carefully balanced to maximize the total taxed value extracted from you. This is a careful balance because if the human lifespan is too long, there is a greater risk of more people awakening to the truth about reality. The ideal lifespan should be the perfect length to maximize work years while keeping individuals asleep and oblivious to their circumstances.

It is perfectly fine if you wish to turn off this light and continue believing in your religion and government. However, if you desire to explore deeper into religious texts and read ancient information that predates the Bible, you may discover another reality. You will find that many Bible stories are merely rehashed narratives. The Bible is often called the "greatest story ever told," not the "greatest collection of facts." It is indeed a story, and you must be able to decipher the symbols and terms within it.

Christians did not write the Book of Revelations; it was penned at least 500 years before the advent of Christianity. In Greek mythology, Apollo's son, Ion, is credited with these stories found in Revelations. However, these characters and the original narratives served more as indoctrination for the people of that era. The current Book of Revelations and its stories were revamped to fit a new agenda that aligned with the emerging religion known as Christianity. John did not write the Book of Revelation. In Latin, when translating to English you change the letter "I" to "J," the name Ion changes to "Jon" (John in modern English). The name Jon was assigned to the author during the formation of Christianity. It is up to you to decide whether you wish to continue believing the repurposed reality that they spoon-feed to you as truth.

This book you read was written between 2022 and 2024, and I cannot predict the changes we will see before the end of 2030. However, I am sure that if humanity does not awaken to the truth that Earth is a prison, the controllers will quickly fulfill their agenda and expect to see a fake alien invasion.

We are born into this prison of the mind. You are programmed to believe that you belong to a nationality, race, country, religion, political alliance, etc. You grow up and must pay to live in this prison. The controllers keep the prisoners weak and divided, making it difficult for humanity to fight back. Only a few have walked far enough to see the prison walls and realize they are imprisoned. The prison will collapse if enough prisoners recognize the walls.

History doesn't remember those who follow the crowd; it remembers those who go against what is considered normal. No matter how hard you try to fit in, you will never feel completely part of the world. You were never meant to walk the same path as everyone else. You are meant to walk a path that allows you to shift reality. You are not intended to be ordinary; you are meant to break the status quo and bring a new reality. You are here to introduce a transformative reality for those who wish to be liberated, allowing them to free their minds from their mental prisons.

Nothing about reality is real in the way you think it is. The brain doesn't experience reality directly; it translates energy and frequency into sight, sound, and touch. Your eyes can only see 0.0035 percent of the light around us, meaning there is another universe you are unaware of. If you believe that seeing is believing, congratulations, you just admitted that you only believe in less than 1% of what truly exists. Your brain doesn't even show you what is there; it shows you what you expect. This is why two people can live in the same world yet experience two different realities. Your reality is only what you have been convinced to believe is true.

As long as you don't understand how you are being used and manipulated, you will never be able to escape this prison. Knowledge is the key. Unfortunately, too many people are preoccupied with watching television, playing video games, following sports, attending religious meetings, and trying to make money to survive in this prison. These individuals fail to realize what is happening behind the scenes. Humanity needs to awaken to the most critical piece of knowledge: who controls this planet and what these controllers do to the human race. We are in danger of completely losing our autonomy to these controllers.

It is essential to recognize that we are not truly free until we awaken and regain control of our minds. We must start meditating seriously on our lives, where we want to go, and what we wish to accomplish. What kind of experiences do we want our children and grandchildren to have while on this planet? It is time to wake up and understand how Earth is controlled and what exactly is happening.

There is no right or wrong belief; it depends on the reality you wish to experience. Ignorance can be bliss; adhering to controlled information to fully engage in this managed environment is acceptable. However, for those ready to return to a deeper understanding of who you are, this knowledge is for you. It is time to release your mind from the shackles that have bound it for many lifetimes. You have earned the badge of awakening and are reconnecting with your higher self and Source itself. You now see through the matrix and its controls. The separation that indoctrinates society is no longer effective on you. You recognize the divisions created by politics, religion, ethnicity, economic status, and patriotism. You have been trapped for years, and unfortunately, many of society will remain trapped within the prison. We must not worry about others; instead, we should focus on our own awakening and our purpose now that we have awakened. From this point forward, each day will feel different, and we should enjoy every moment while we are here. Please do not take things too seriously; this is not reality, and we are here for the experience. This life is an illusion; eventually, we will return to reality. We should not be deceived or convinced to continue playing a role in this sick and sadistic game that the evil entities play with humanity.

In conclusion, I want to thank everyone for contributing to human liberation on Earth. Eventually, the walls will be discovered and brought down. When that happens, we will look back and feel a great sense of accomplishment because we played a part in dismantling the matrix prison that has trapped humanity on this planet.

Quotes to Always Remember:
"We suffer more in our imagination than in reality." – Seneca
"It is never too late to be who you might have been." – George Eliot

"Our life is what our thoughts make it." – Marcus Aurelius

"Thinking is difficult; that is why most people judge." – Carl Jung

"Care what other people think, and you will always be their prisoner." – Lao Tzu

"If you are the smartest person in the room, find another room." – Confucius

"The quieter you become, the more you can hear." – Rumi

"A sane person to an insane society must appear insane." – Kurt Vonnegut

"Reserve your right to think, for even to think wrongly is better than not to think at all" - Hypatia

It is time to meditate, discover your truth frequency, and escape the prison of indoctrination.

Chapter 33: Do You Have to Die to Wake up?

Your spiritual awakening may initially feel like a form of death. You will lose your old identity and no longer desire what you once enjoyed. As you begin to let go of certain people and shift your way of thinking, your mind might crave the familiarity of your previous reality. However, your soul knows the path to take. This process signifies the death of your false self, and it is natural to feel a sense of grief during this time. If it feels like you are standing in the fire, staying there and embracing the destruction of your old self is essential. This is the moment when your true self begins to emerge. Experiencing this transformation is acceptable, as many will undergo a similar process before awakening.
Deep meditation can help guide you as you navigate this change.

Many religions advise their followers to avoid practicing meditation. They warn, "Don't meditate because it opens your mind to devils." Religious leaders encourage their followers to model their lives after Jesus, but they often overlook the whole truth about who Jesus was and what he preached. Jesus, correctly named Yeshua, declared that the kingdom of God is within everyone and that we can seek the answers to the universe within ourselves. Don't be intimidated by what has been indoctrinated by religious leaders.

Embrace regular meditation and free yourself from the limitations placed on your mind.

If you spend most of your day focused on the material world, the spiritual world will not manifest in your reality. However, when you focus on the spiritual realm, you introduce spirituality into your experience. Where you direct your attention is where you invest your energy. You expand your mind and evolve by placing your energy into the spiritual. We must go beyond ourselves, shift our focus away from our bodies and the physical world, and become pure consciousness to break free from the limitations placed on our minds. Connect to the unified field, also known as the quantum field. Continue to engage in practices that feel unnatural to become supernatural.

The world you perceive is merely a reflection of your inner state. Your thoughts shape your life. If you desire wealth but focus on feelings of lack, you will create a reality of scarcity. You don't attract what you want; you attract what you believe to be true. Practice this concept: the world will transform, and your reality will change. Stop merely wanting and start embodying the person who has what you desire. Allow the energy you wish to experience to flow toward you. Feel the emotions you would have when experiencing what you want, and watch the world change around you. It will come into your life because it is a universal law once you align your energy. This principle applies to all aspects of your life.

When you declare that the "conspiracy theories" you encounter are impossible, you lose, effectively creating the reality that those in control want you to accept. The absolute truth is often far from the indoctrinated perception the controllers wish society to adopt. The actual reality is so distant from common understanding that when society encounters the truth, it often feels too incredible to be real.

Just because news networks label a specific news story as propaganda does not automatically mean that the story is untrue. Many people view the news as a trustworthy source of reliable information. This becomes problematic because whistleblowers from government agencies have revealed that these organizations often control what news outlets report to the public. As a result, when news outlets declare a contradictory story as propaganda, the public may dismiss it without question.

For instance, if reports emerge about children being killed in war zones, society might hear news networks label those reports as propaganda and quickly disregard the information despite the existence of video evidence. Suppose you find that labeling a story as propaganda is enough to make you overlook the suffering of families in conflict zones. In that case, I encourage you to reflect seriously on your perspective.

News networks and social media greatly influence public opinion. Many people are beginning to recognize that news networks are regulated and are turning to social media platforms for information. However, if you believe social media networks are censorship- free, there is still much to understand. While you may find more truthful accounts on specific social media platforms, they, too, face censorship. Once a new social media platform gains popularity, it's only a matter of time before it falls under the control of powerful entities. This strategy aims to shape public perception and maintain control over the narrative.

Unfortunately, when a lie is repeated often enough, it is eventually accepted as truth. I want to emphasize the importance of presenting both sides of a conflict. When only one side of a story is told, the narrative can be easily manipulated to serve a specific agenda.

Claims that the United States is being held hostage by Israel are often quickly dismissed as propaganda. Journalists and recent graduates risk losing their careers and job offers if they criticize Israel. While the U.S. government asserts that citizens enjoy freedom of speech, the reality is that there are limitations on what individuals can express.

In 2020, the United States government announced it was considering banning TikTok. Later that year, an executive order to ban the app was blocked. However, when TikTok began to allow pro-Palestinian posts without censorship, it caught the attention of the U.S. government. In an interview, Jonathan Greenblatt of the ADL stated, "We have a TikTok problem and a Gen Z problem; we need to put our energy toward this issue." Following this, an anti-Semitism bill was passed. This move aimed to control societal views and perceptions. TikTok has since changed by censoring specific topics. Those in power do not prioritize nations or the people's religious beliefs, as they are not loyal to earthly ideologies. Nonetheless, they will take action when something threatens their carefully controlled narrative. The cabal is not loyal to any religion or nationality; their loyalty lies only with the regressive entities they serve. Specific regions are influenced by particular bloodlines orchestrating a specific agenda from behind the scenes.

Thomas Massie has stated that every Republican in Congress (and likely Democrats as well) is assigned an AIPAC representative, whom he refers to as their "babysitter." According to him, this AIPAC person guides the congressperson and approves or denies what they can say. This indicates a significant level of influence a foreign organization has over the United States. We must open our eyes, question everything, and consider the implications of this situation.

In an interview, James Traficant told Bryant Gumbel that Israel receives between $15 billion and $20 billion annually. Gumbel responded by stating, "Israel only gets $3 billion of the American taxpayer's dollars." James clarified that the $3 billion is only the amount allocated in the foreign aid bill. Considering all the different forms of assistance Israel receives each year, the total reaches $15 billion to $20 billion. This amounts to a minimum of $30,000 per year for every man, woman, and child in Israel, while many Americans struggle to afford food, rent, and gas for their commute to work. In the interview, James expressed his belief that "Israel has a powerful stranglehold on the American government." He argued that Israel influences both the House and the Senate, controls military decisions, and engages the country in wars that most Americans have little interest in. He says the United States is in massive debt because of these conflicts. He emphasized that he does not harbor a grudge against the Israeli government but instead offers an objective assessment of the situation between the American government and Israel. The only beneficiaries during wars are the global elite bankers, while taxpayers are left to address the national debt resulting from these conflicts.

James believes that Israel plays a significant role in shaping much of American foreign policy and also influences various aspects of domestic policy. He stated, "Israel influences whom America goes to war against. They control much of the commerce and media." He concluded the interview by acknowledging that many might label him as an anti-Semite, but he clarified that he is an American, and his priority is America first.

A group influences the world's great nations, often called the global banking elite or the cabal. As Weishaupt famously and elegantly said, "Let me issue and control a nation's money, and I care not who writes the laws."

In the grand scheme, the illusion of separation between countries keeps nations divided while a small group manipulates the major powers. Once we awaken to this reality, we realize that we need to unite as a human race and eliminate the divisions created within society. Understanding who is pulling the strings and controlling various agendas is essential. When we start to pay attention, the actual map of control in the world begins to reveal itself.

In 1902, Rockefeller invested $129 million in the General Education Board. Over the following years, this amount would increase to $325 million. Why would he invest so much money in the education system? Could he be building a system that served a specific agenda? He stated that he didn't want a nation of thinkers; he wanted a nation of workers. He didn't care about people's dreams or aspirations. His primary concern was gaining control over the minds of young people. By influencing the youth, he aimed to shape the minds of the future workforce.

As discussed earlier in this book, the elite believe that the universe is composed of energy, frequency, and vibration. With these three building blocks, you can create your desired reality through your thoughts. Thoughts are a form of energy that enters the quantum field to shape the physical world around you. Quantum mechanics demonstrates that the observer influences reality. For instance, when a particle like an electron is in a superposition state, it can shift into any possible outcome. Through processes like decoherence or measurement, it settles into a definite state.

The Wigner's Friend experiment illustrates this concept, showing that reality depends on the observer. In this experiment, one scientist may measure a particle and obtain a specific result. In contrast, another scientist can observe the same particle in a superposition, revealing two different realities based on their separate measurements.

Reality is relative to the observer and can be influenced. It is not the particle that changes, but rather the observer's perception that alters its representation in their reality. Both states exist, and the observer connects with the reality their mind is programmed to experience. This concept is similar to how Draconian shapeshifting occurs. The Draconian form exists, but they tap into a human form and project this appearance into physical reality. The physical realm is a projection from the astral plane, and a Draconian will continue to have a reptilian soul in the astral, but on Earth, they will look human.

Neuroscientist John-Dylan Haynes and his colleagues demonstrated that the brain can make decisions several seconds before individuals become consciously aware of them. This means that your brain can recognize a decision you are about to make before you even realize there is one to be made. So, where does this delay originate? Once again, the physical world you are experiencing now is a projection of the actual reality, the spiritual realm. The subconscious mind directs what we project into our physical realities, but unfortunately, humanity has been disconnected from their higher selves.

You will see and experience the reality that you choose to acknowledge. This information may not be meant for you if you consider it impossible. Similarly, suppose you find an article that supports the accepted narrative and claims to debunk the information presented in this book, and you take that as sufficient evidence to dismiss the book; in that case, this information is not for you. You have every right to defend the reality constructed for you. I cannot provide more or compel you to investigate this reality further.

If you prefer to ignore this information and continue your life unchanged, I wish you a good night and hope you find peace in your slumber while experiencing this life. I hope you continue to find bliss in your ignorance as you continue to inject graphene into your body. You may need to undergo a profound change before awakening to true reality. Once you begin to comprehend the spiritual truths in this book, you may become aware of the control in both the physical and spiritual realms. This information will resonate within you at that point, releasing your soul from that control.

I wish you a fulfilling journey back to your true home. For some, this awakening may come through death. However, for those who want to awaken to reality before death, consider this your prompt to take control of your life and abandon the autopilot that has been guiding you. No longer will you live your life on your knees as a slave.

I can't emphasize this enough: you must start questioning everything presented as reality. When you encounter individuals like Dr. Rashid A. Buttar, who speak out against specific agendas and then die shortly thereafter, it raises serious questions. He stated, "We need to stand up and fight, and if something happens to me, it is because I have been speaking the truth, and they don't want that truth to continue being shared. But I didn't kill myself; I am not depressed; I am very happy to be alive in this time of human history." Following these words, he claimed that he was poisoned. After making this claim, he died. Official records state that he died of a stroke, but you will have to decide which version of reality to accept. He is not the only person to have met a similar fate for opposing an agenda of powerful groups. There is a long list of individuals who have faced such outcomes, and you must decide whether to halt your awakening here or continue on your journey of discovery.

In the 1990s, Stanley Meyer invented a car that ran on water. He declined buyout offers that would have kept his invention secret. During a meeting with investors, he abruptly left the restaurant, and witnesses reported that his last words were "They poisoned me." Official records state that he died of a brain aneurysm. Ultimately, it's up to you to decide what reality you believe in.

In Switzerland, CERN has a 2-meter statue of Lord Shiva, the Lord of Destruction, in front of the facility. Why would they have this statue in front of the CERN facility? Could it be part of a dark agenda? We need to question everything and remain open to all possibilities. It is your job to investigate and decide what reality you experience.

In an interview, Don Pettit, a NASA astronaut and chemical engineer, stated that NASA has destroyed the technology needed to return to the moon and that it would be difficult to rebuild it. He described the moon landings as one of mankind's greatest achievements. It seems inconceivable that traveling to the moon is one of humanity's most significant achievements, yet the technology was destroyed. This statement seems absurd, yet the public accepts it without questioning it. While I'm not saying you should believe in an alternate reality, I encourage you to examine your reality critically.

This book is designed to guide you along a path while leaving behind a trail of breadcrumbs for you to follow. It is your responsibility to research these topics further. I have intentionally omitted many details due to the book's limitations and to encourage you to dive deeper into these subjects, allowing you to form your own opinions and perspectives. By actively exploring these topics, you will embark on a journey of awakening, but ultimately, it is up to you to do the work.

The cabal does not control every person in government or positions of power. Some individuals come forward with critical information that we can investigate. Don't just rely on the top search results. Explore all available perspectives, gather all the information, and then formulate your understanding of the truth.

This truth may not resonate with everyone. Your desires shape the truth. However, as you raise your frequency, your reality will shift. Each of us has a unique mission during our time on Earth, and it is up to you to discover your purpose and your ultimate truth while in the physical world.

You were once an eternal celestial being before you chose to disconnect from your higher self. You decided to enter the simulation and separate from Source, understanding that this would enable you to grow from your experiences on Earth. Embrace your sense of purpose and live without any karmic regrets. However, this experience is unnecessary; it is time for you to return home and avoid any physical experience that offers you the chance to forget who you are. The creator of the universe does not ask this of you.

Society believes it worships the true God who created the universe. However, society often worships the gods of those who are controlling Earth. Very few people understand that any mainstream religion does not recognize the true God and creator of the universe. It is essential to realize that Luciferian worshippers are exerting their influence on the Earth and are gradually tightening their grip on the planet.

As mentioned earlier, the Draconian Orion group is aligned with the Galactic Federation. I'm uncertain whether the Galactic Federation has always been under this control or if the shift occurred after Earth became a prison planet. Regardless, we must awaken to the reality that no one will rescue us. The New Age movement was designed to prevent awakened individuals from taking action, promoting a message of "be patient, and they will fix the planet."

Ultimately, it is up to you to determine how you wish to live. Do not let any form of indoctrination—old or new—mislead you; you are more intelligent than that. Seek your truth and take action. What you have read in this book is not a prediction but a reflection of the current plan. This plan may change, and I believe it will, as timelines shift and the cabal adapts.

Exercise caution when following information shared by individuals who claim to be awakened. Please pay more attention to their actions than their words. Many individuals start by sharing truths to gain your trust, but they may change their message once they have built a substantial following. Three-letter agencies often use this tactic, which can become recognizable once you learn to see it.

For example, Elon Musk said, "The danger of AI is much greater than the danger of nuclear warheads by a lot." He has also stated that in the future, "AI will have humanity under strict control." When asked about the greatest threat to humanity, he identified digital intelligence, or artificial superintelligence, as the biggest threat. Although he believes the likelihood of it leading to a scenario like "Terminator" is small, he admits that AI could potentially lead to the end of humanity, indicating his concern for our future. However, his actions tell a different story; he co-founded Neuralink, which develops brain-computer interfaces through chip implants. Once you become aware, the cabal's veils of secrecy become thin, making you impossible to control. Elon Musk is part of a larger scheme and may function as a pawn for the cabal.

It is your choice to determine what you believe. Proceed with caution, as discovering the truth can be a curse or a blessing, depending on your mental state. I will only give you the truth if you are ready to receive it. The controllers have blinded society by manipulating reality. Events are directed by a higher power unknown to the general public. Wernher von Braun, a German rocket scientist, was brought to the United States through Project Paperclip (as mentioned earlier in this book). In 1952, he wrote a book titled *Project Mars*. In this novel, he describes a Martian government led by a figure referred to as Elon. This could be insignificant, or it might be part of something much more sinister at play. It is up to you to pull back the veil and uncover your reality.

"The Matrix is everywhere; it is all around us. Even now, in this very room. You can see it when you look out your window and turn on your television. You can feel it when you go to work, when you go to church, when you pay your taxes. It is the world that has been pulled over your eyes to blind you from the truth." What truth? "That you are a slave. Like everyone else, you were born into bondage, born into a prison that you cannot smell or taste or touch. A prison for your mind. Unfortunately, no one can be told what the Matrix is. You have to see it for yourself. This is your last chance; after this, there is no turning back. You take the blue pill, the story ends, and you wake up in your bed, and you believe whatever you want to believe. You take the red pill, you will stay in Wonderland, and I show you how deep the rabbit hole goes. Remember, all I am offering is the truth, nothing more." - Morpheus

The truth has always been before you; will you see it, or must you die before awakening?

www.ingramcontent.com/pod-product-compliance
Lightning Source LLC
Chambersburg PA
CBHW060513230426
43665CB00013B/1499